FIGURE OF EIGHT

By the same author

The Years of *The Week*

FIGURE OF EIGHT

Patricia Cockburn

CHATTO & WINDUS
THE HOGARTH PRESS
LONDON

Published in 1985 by
Chatto & Windus · The Hogarth Press
40 William IV Street
London WC2N 4DF

British Library Cataloguing in Publication Data

Cockburn, Patricia
Figure of eight.
1. Cockburn, Patricia
I. Title
070'.92'4 PN5123.C4/

ISBN 0-7011-2897-6

Photoset in Linotron Sabon by
Rowland Phototypesetting Ltd,
Bury St Edmunds, Suffolk
Printed in Great Britain by
Redwood Burn Ltd
Trowbridge, Wiltshire

Contents

List of illustrations

between pages 88–89

CHAPTER 1

My Birth and Background

I was born on 17 March 1914, in Derry House, Rosscarbery, at the western end of County Cork in Ireland, the youngest of the six children of Major John Bernard Arbuthnot and his wife, Olive Blake. The family, with a couple of exceptions, were delighted to greet me; my mother in particular, as after a sequence of four boys she had wanted another girl. The exceptions consisted of my sister, the eldest of the children, and my youngest brother; the former because she liked being the only girl in the family and the latter because – being two and a half years old at the time – he had been the centre of attention as The Baby. Both were bitterly jealous of the interloper. Joan mostly nursed her resentment in silence, but 'Teeny' was made of sterner stuff and later, when he was three, made two determined attempts to kill me. But he was not cut out by nature for the role of murderer, and was detected and restrained – though he did succeed in overturning my pram, sending me rolling down a gravel slope.

The Arbuthnots were an Anglo-Irish family who had settled in Ireland some time in the late eighteenth century. They were Scottish by origin and had come, via the border country in England, from Aberdeenshire. My mother's family, the Blakes, one of the 'Twelve Tribes of Galway', were native Irish. The progenitor of the tribe, one Raymond le Noir, had come over with Strongbow, Earl of Pembroke, in the year 1169 but he, like most of the Norman or, more correctly, Welsh–Norman invasion, was one of the many grandsons of Queen Nesta of Wales and was three-quarters Celtic. 'Le Noir' got translated into English as Black and then mutated into Blake and Burke. Some stayed as Black, though there are very few of them around Ireland. But racial origins mean little, as a study of the surnames in any Irish village will tell you. It is mostly inherited culture which counts, and in culture the Arbuthnots were unquestionably Anglo-Irish – a culture which draws its assumptions and values from both Celtic-Catholic Ireland

and pre-industrial England, while differing in many respects from both.

My family, however, differed from the characters depicted by many writers, from 'Somerville and Ross', through Maria Edgeworth to Trollope and beyond, in two respects: thanks to the business acumen of various ancestors they were comparatively rich, being majority shareholders in the banking firm of Arbuthnot-Lathum. Most of the Irish landowner families whose fortunes had always been based on rents from land had been finally ruined by the Land Acts of 1891 and 1903, whereby the government enabled the tenant farmers to buy out their farms, while most of the landowners either gradually spent the compensation money or invested it badly – hence the cliché of the decaying Georgian mansion, about which so much has been written. Thanks to my grandmother, the formidable Edith, Lady Blake, we had strong Nationalist connections, she having been a great friend of Anna Parnell, sister of Charles Stewart Parnell, and an executive member of the Ladies' Land League.

In October 1881 the entire leadership of the Land League had been jailed, and with all the male leaders out of circulation its organisation and management were assumed by Parnell's sister Anna, who formed the Ladies' Land League. This, so far as I know, was the first instance of women taking anything but a supportive role in politics in Ireland, at any rate since the quasi-mythical days of Queen Maeve or Eileen O'Malley, 'Queen of the Sea'.

The Ladies proved to be efficient and honest, but considerably more revolutionary than Charles Stewart Parnell, who was a reformist. The amount of violence in the country increased. From his cell Parnell pointed out that if he were taken out of circulation, 'Captain Moonlight' would take over, and as this was evidently the case negotiations for his release commenced immediately, resulting after six months with his signing the 'Kilmainham Treaty', regarded by many as a supreme sell-out.

His first act upon release was to suppress the Ladies' Land League and drive the female Nationalists out of politics.

My parents however, were not Irish Nationalists. They were quite ignorant of all politics and of the conditions and feelings of the people among whom they lived. And in April 1914 they were much too busy organising the party to celebrate my arrival to notice either social conditions or the imminence of World War I.

In our culture at that time christenings were conducted somewhat like mini-weddings. Friends and neighbours (landowning ones, that is) were issued with printed invitation cards and the servants – we had thirteen – and the more lowly neighbours invited by word of mouth. Large quantities of food and drink – in our case champagne and Guinness – were ordered, an elaborately iced Christening Cake constructed and the church (Protestant) liberally decorated with flowers. Finally the good Bishop Heard, a friend of the family, was asked to come down from his palace in Cork City, by that train immortalised by Percy French in his song 'Are you right, Michael, are you right', to perform the ceremony.

When all was ready, the family dressed in their best clothes and I was stuffed, I am told, into a rather too small Limerick-lace christening robe. Everyone assembled in the church and the ceremony began. The bishop asked the god-parents what he should name the child. 'Kawara Finnbaragh Evangeline,' they chanted – whereupon he promptly suspended operations and went on strike.

'I couldn't,' he said afterwards, 'inflict such terrible names on that unfortunate baby. It would have been on my conscience forever.' My mother was responsible for the imbroglio. She had a penchant for romantic, or what she regarded as romantic, names. She had more or less held it in restraint with her other five children – Irene Joan Grace, David George, Terence John, Bernard Kieran Charles. With her youngest boy she had become confused, registering him as Richard Henry and having him christened Myles Henry with the result that for years we did not know what his real legal name was and later, when he joined the army in World War II, everyone assumed he was two people and he was constantly asked where his twin brother was. We knew him by his nickname, Teeny.

But with me, possibly her last child, she had let her fancy rip. Where she got Kawara from was a mystery, but Finnbaragh was an invented feminisation of Finnbar, one of the patron saints of that part of west Cork, -agh in Ireland being pronounced -a as in Sheelagh/Sheila or Oonagh/Una. Evangeline was chosen because she liked Longfellow's poem about Evangeline and the deep dark woods.

The congregation waited in fascination while the argument raged on in whispers. My mother pleaded. The bishop stood firm and threatened to return to Cork City at once. He held the high cards and so naturally won his demand that he should name the child. He called me Patricia as I was born on St Patrick's Day, Evangeline as a sop to my defeated mother, and Anne after a great-aunt. And I have always been satisfied with the names he gave me and bless the memory of that great and good man.

I had convulsions after the christening, perhaps brought on by the constriction of the tight lace. The convulsions continued from time to time so it was decided that I was allergic to cow's milk. There was no suitable dried milk formula in those days and since ladies did not feed their own children the alternatives were either a wet nurse, which was out of the question because of the enormous prevalence of T.B. in the local population, or goat's milk or mare's milk. I have always been surprised that goat's milk was not chosen, since there were certainly plenty of goats around in West Cork, but in fact a small donkey with foal was purchased. After that my health improved, for what reason is not known, so perhaps the local doctor was right about the milk. I do know that I had to put up with a great deal of teasing from my younger brothers about being half a donkey from then on.

In August Armageddon began, though contemporaries did not see it that way, when the Germans invaded Belgium and my father went off to join his regiment, the Scots Guards, in which he was a reserve. He was a most unusual man, certainly not cut out to be a soldier, though he did become Brigade Major to the Brigade of Guards, quite a distinguished position. He was a very good amateur painter-sculptor and, with a puckish wit, an excellent story-teller. He had been the original Beachcomber columnist on the *Daily Express*. Why he took that job I cannot imagine. It cannot have been for the money, so it must have been for the fun of the thing. He used to tell the story of how he would scribble his column in Fleet Street and then rush to Waterloo station to catch the special train he had ordered to take him to Windsor Castle where he was on guard.

He had been brought up largely in England as his father had a house, Norton Court, in Gloucestershire, and also another in Cumberland, and was educated in England at some public school, I can't remember which, though it was probably Eton, as all my four brothers were sent there without question. After that he joined the Scots Guards and presumably went to some Officers' Training establishment.

Anyway he regarded himself as English, ignoring his Scottish and Anglo-Irish blood, and once wrote a book called *Arms and the Irishman* which caused deep offence among rich and poor alike in Ireland – the rich because he depicted them in an accurate but derisive way with highly recognisable characters, and the poor because they came out as ignorant peasants of the Pat and Mick variety. He did not have much impact on my young life, being a shadowy figure who came and went like the family ghost. Needless to say, he disliked my grandmother whom I loved, and was always misquoting Oscar Wilde, saying 'Lady Blake has a great deal of taste, all of it bad.'

After he left and went to war, Derry House in Rosscarbery was given up. It had only been leased, and the whole tribe, six children, my mother and the thirteen servants removed to another rented house. We shifted from one decaying mansion to another, never buying one as my parents knew that one day my mother would inherit Myrtle Grove, a charming and mysterious place. It was a manor house built in 1461, for the warden of the Ecclesiastical College of St Mary's and was the home of Sir Walter Raleigh when he was Governor of Ireland in 1588. They quite reasonably felt that they did not want to be lumbered with two large houses.

Then came 1916 and the siege of the Post Office in Dublin, and the Irish War of Independence followed. This is no place to describe the long history of misgovernment, misery and misfortune to which Ireland had been subjected during the last few centuries and the complex web of oppression, insurrection and lack of sensible political and economic administration which finally culminated in the Treaty of 1922 and the inevitable and tragic Civil War which followed – though of course the effect on my life was indeed profound.

In 1916 my grandfather, Sir Henry Blake, died and we all moved to Myrtle Grove to be with my grandmother. From then on it became my home, with various forays to rented houses on the west of Ireland for holidays and also to England. I can't honestly say that I really remember those early days: just isolated incidents with a background of gunfire and explosions – and the gloom of the grown-ups when the news came that one more of the great houses of family friends and relations had gone up in flames, and the excitement when Danny the second gardener, a pro I.R.A. man, was seen marching Tudgy, the head gardener, who had been in the British Navy, across the pond-garden at gun point with his hands in the air.

Very few of the Anglo-Irish got shot, though a great deal of property was destroyed. A minor contributory factor to this latter fact may have been the silly story that was going around at the time among the Anglo-Irish, in which the head gardener of a Great House was supposed to have written to the absentee owner saying, 'We had a battle here last week but fortunately no one was hurt, and both sides greatly admired the antirrhinums.' This of course leaked out, and the infuriated local populous, agonising amid the horrors of the war, were inclined to rush out and burn the nearest big house and shoot the nearest head gardener.

Another story, true this time, is of a large house near us where the I.R.A. turned up one night and announced that they were going to burn the place to the ground in two hours. The servants were alone in the house, the owner having fled, and they were given that amount of time to take out anything they wanted to save from the flames. They consulted together about what they should rescue, and the butler said, 'Himself, when he is at home, spends most of his time in the billiard room, so perhaps we should save the billiard table.' This they proceeded to try and do, but as it was too large to be got out by the door or windows they started to take it to pieces. One leg had been laboriously unscrewed and placed on the front lawn when the I.R.A. came back. Time was up, and dozens of priceless pictures and wonderful pieces of eighteenth-century furniture were incinerated.

Most of the Anglo-Irish of that time, and indeed today, lived like white settlers in a colonial country. They had very little political education and did not realise at all what was going on in the minds and hearts of the mass of the people, or at least important sections of them. This can be seen very clearly in the works of 'Somerville and Ross', who wrote *Memoirs of an Irish R.M.* and other books about Ireland. The characters in their books are like photographs – accurate so far as they go, but utterly one-dimensional. This kind of political myopia had tragic results in 1936 when Admiral Boyle Somerville, brother of the same authoress Edith Somerville, received letters warning that, if he continued to recommend Irish boys for the Royal Navy, he would be killed. I sent urgent messages that this was serious, that the letters meant what they said, and that 'Uncle Boyle' was in great danger and should be careful. I was thoroughly snubbed for my pains and told that it was all nonsense, since Boyle was 'immensely popular with the Irish', and that it was all just talk. In March 1936 he opened his front door and was shot and killed on the doorstep. In contrast, many landowners and some of the more recent English immigrants – particularly those with military connections – had the sense to leave the country during the War of Independence and the Civil War.

When World War I was over, my mother and the rest of the family had rejoined my father in London where we had a large house, No. 42 Grosvenor Place, overlooking the gardens of Buckingham Palace. I had been taken with them to start with, but I was unhappy and unwell, and finally in 1918 the Victory celebrations put an end to the experiment.

As a very special treat I was told that I was to be allowed to go to Hyde Park, late at night, to watch the firework display. When I arrived there in the company of my nurse, and clutching my teddy-bear, who had been brought to watch the show, I found the enormous crowds, the darkness, the flashing lights and above all the tremendous bangs of the rockets so terrifying that I had a sort of fit, and screamed for hours after I got home, until I became semi-conscious. Thereafter I seem to have become more and more difficult, crying at night, refusing to eat, and ceaselessly demanding to be taken 'home'. So it was very sensibly decided to send me back to my grandmother. This was done and in the company of a Swiss nursery governess called Liza I went back to Myrtle Grove, and so began many happy years there.

Edith Blake, my grandmother, had been born in 1845, the elder of the two daughters of Bernal Osborne and his wife Catherine Isabella. He was a Member of Parliament for Waterford and had begun life as Ralph Bernal, but on marrying Catherine Isabella Osborne, who was a great heiress, owning vast numbers of acres, he had changed his name to hers and became Bernal Osborne. Edith and her younger sister Grace were born and brought up at their beautiful Georgian house Newtown Anner near Clonmel in County Tipperary – largely by their mother, as the Osbornes proved an ill-matched pair and he spent most of his time in London. It is reported that on his periodic visits home to Newtown Anner his wife would greet Bernal Osborne with the words 'I trust you are well, Mr Osborne, and how did you leave your mistresses?'

My grandmother, who believed conversation was one of the best forms of education, told me many stories about my ancestors, including one about the last King of Munster. It seems that the first Osborne to come to Ireland was called John. He was an officer in some invading English army at the time of the Tudors, possibly the army of the Earl of Essex or Sir Walter Raleigh, and was granted large tracts of land in County Tipperary, that had been in the possession of The McGrath, King of Munster. John, deciding to stay permanently in Ireland, seems either to have had a certain sense of justice or, more likely, a desire for a quiet life. He wrote to the King of Munster saying that though he, John, could be reasonably assumed to be the king's enemy, matters could be resolved between them. He understood that the king had no son, only three daughters and if he, John, could marry one of them, the lands would ultimately revert to The McGrath's descendants. This was, of course, a misconception, as primogeniture was unknown in Ireland at that time and, in theory at least, the five provincial kings were elected by their extended families, and the current king, not the individual, held the lands. However, the king agreed and said that he would ask which of his daughters would marry the invader. The eldest refused, on patriotic and nationalistic grounds. The second said she planned to take the veil. The youngest agreed, but stipulated that as she was a princess she could or would not live in any army camp or 'Norman keep' but must have a palace, like her father's at Cashel, with a 'feather-lined' bower. The palace took seven years to construct, after which they married and had a son who was my eighth great-grandfather. My brother Bernard knew where the ruins of that palace were – somewhere on the Knockmealdown Mountains – and always promised to take me there but unfortunately he died before he could do so. It was from Grandmama that I first heard of the attempted abduction of my father's great-great-aunt Elinor Arbuthnot which was widely and delightedly reported in the London *Times* of the 1850s, who took it as further proof, if that were needed, of the absurdity and barbarity of the Irish people of all classes. It was motivated, not by money but by love.

Elinor Arbuthnot's parents were dead and so she lived with her elder sister, who was married to Lord Gough, in County Tipperary. The 'Lord Lieutenant' of that county at that time was named Cardon. He was an extensive landowner and apparently an unusually bad one as his tenants were always trying to shoot him. In fact they tried so often and failed so often, that they had nicknamed him 'the woodcock' – that bird being, because if its swift and zig-zag flight, notoriously difficult to hit. Instead of being annoyed by this, he took it as a great compliment and changed his name by deed-poll to become Woodcock Cardon.

When not quite in his first youth, he conceived the entirely erroneous idea that Elinor, for whom he had developed a passion, was also in love with him and that it was only the inexplicable opposition of the wicked Lord and Lady Gough which prevented their marriage. So he decided to kidnap her.

He laid his plans carefully and bought a large yacht which he had moored in Galway Bay and hired a crew and captain, also an impecunious clergyman to perform the marriage ceremony. Relays of fresh horses were put along the road from Tipperary to Galway. He bought lots of charming little gifts to ingratiate himself with Elinor, but he also brought a bottle of chloroform in case she proved recalcitrant. So he may not have been as convinced of her willingness to be abducted as he claimed at his trial.

His plan was to abduct her one Sunday as she and the other ladies of the Gough household were returning from church. During the service, according to *The Times*, he was seen in the churchyard 'idly examining a tombstone'. What happened next proved disastrous for him.

It began to rain.

The ladies had arrived at the church in an open carriage, from which anyone could easily be plucked out, but when Lord Gough heard the rain pattering on the church roof, he sent it home to be replaced by a closed carriage, whose only exit was a narrow door at the back. When church was over, the ladies got into this carriage and started home. Lord Gough and other gentlemen were to follow later on horseback.

Woodcock Cardon mounted and rode after the carriage. At a pre-arranged point in the road, where his men were waiting with another light vehicle in which to put his victim, he spurred his horse forward, cut the traces of the Gough carriage and shouting 'Elinor,

Elinor, it's you I want', tried to pull her out of the narrow door at the back.

The carriage contained Lady Gough, who was pregnant at the time, Elinor, an elderly aunt, a teenage Gough daughter and her governess. These women put up such a fight that he couldn't extract Elinor. The governess broke his nose with her umbrella.

Some passers-by, seeing the battle, rushed back to tell Lord Gough and his men that they had better hurry up. When the Gough party arrived at a gallop, Woodcock, as 'Lord Lieutenant' of the county, ordered his men, who were all armed, to fire on them. This they very sensibly refused to do as if they had killed anyone and been caught, they would most certainly have been hanged.

Realising the game was up, Woodcock Cardon jumped on his horse and made off towards Galway with all the others in pursuit. He galloped until his horse died under him and he was captured.

At his trial in Clonmel, the opinion of his tenants, who had for so long and so earnestly tried to kill him, suddenly turned in his favour and there were riots, with people shouting 'Release Cardon, what could Elinor want better than a fine Irish gentleman.' He got two years hard labour. He does not seem to have regretted his mad action while he was breaking stones; though he had written from jail to Lord Gough apologising for his behaviour, the very first thing he did on his release was to rush to Greece where the Goughs had taken Elinor so that she would be out of the way when he came out, and tried to bribe a bandit chief to kidnap her for him. The bandit took the bribe and then betrayed him to Lord Gough, whom he estimated correctly to have more money.

Woodcock Cardon pursued the Goughs about for some years and then returned home and turned his house into the first Turkish Bath in Ireland.

Elinor Arbuthnot never married.

Grandmama had many stories of the distant past, but was silent on her own fairly turbulent history, which later I was to piece together from family papers and oral tradition, which was in plentiful supply. Memories are long in isolated communities.

She grew up as the destined heiress to great estates and wealth, a highly intelligent and forceful personality with a passionate interest in all things around her, both in nature and the community. Though I can't trace that we have any Spanish blood, she was tall and dark and very Spanish-looking, as can be seen from her portrait, painted when she was young and which now hangs in the drawing room at Myrtle Grove.

As I remember her, she was large but stooped and very crippled with rheumatism. She always supported herself with an ebony walking stick which had an elaborately worked silver handle and she always dressed in black. Her magnificent hair, long and thick as when she was a girl, was as white as fresh fallen snow; her eyebrows, however, had remained black, so, looking back down the years, I am slightly reminded of a panda, though she certainly didn't have that animal's cuddly expression. In her youth she must have been in direct contrast to her sister Grace who was fair and pretty and feminine.

Grandmother's great passion was botany and lepidoptery, for which she later became famous, and she had a long correspondence with Joseph Paxton, the great landscape designer who seems to have stayed at Newtown Anner, and helped design the gardens. She was also fascinated by archaeology and was an extremely good linguist. When I knew her she could speak nine languages: Irish, English, Spanish, French, German, Portuguese, Italian, Russian and Chinese, which later she learned to both read and write. Her paintings of flowers and plants are exquisite, an essential ability for botanists in the days before colour photography.

She was also highly political and was a keen Nationalist of the romantic variety prevalent in the nineteenth century. I used to wonder at her evident dislike and contempt for Charles Stewart Parnell who has, in modern Ireland, more streets and squares and places named after him than almost any other national hero – in contrast to her affectionate nostalgia for Anna, and to a lesser extent, Fanny, his sister. It couldn't be, I thought, because of his affair with Kitty O'Shea, since outrage at that was not at all in line with my grandmother's largely eighteenth-century culture. It was only when I later read Irish history that I understood her bitter memories of the Ladies' Land League and the fate of Anna, as well as their fundamental clash of policies and objectives.

Some time in the late 1860s or early 1870s she did the 'Grand Tour' of Europe, finishing up at Constantinople, as it then was, and wrote a book about it called *Twelve Months in Southern Europe*, which was published in 1872. It seems that her only companion, except a lady's-maid, was a cousin, a young clergyman. This seems odd in the context of what we understand to be Victorian conventions, as is the description of her walking down a street in Constantinople in her dressing-gown to go to the Public Baths.

The explanation, I believe, lies in the fact that there had been no Industrial Revolution in Ireland and hence no middle-class bourgeois ethic such as succeeded the 'Age of Enlightenment' in England. The big landowning families, at least, went on thinking and behaving very much as they had done in the eighteenth century. There was, of course, a small middle class composed of the clergy, solicitors, land-agents and entrepreneurs who, to quote from James Downey's excellent book *Them and Us*, 'had made their way up the social scale by way of crafts and petty trade or making money from land, or smuggling – the latter a large industry because of the trade restrictions then in force'. But by and large there were only two classes – wealthy landowners and the rack-rented peasant farmers, plus landless labourers.

An eighteenth-century custom which had survived among the 'great' families was the 'arranged marriage', echoes of which still existed in my own day.

Just such a marriage was being negotiated for my grandmother when, to the fury of my great-grandparents, she eloped down a ladder from her bedroom window with Captain Henry Blake, head of the Clonmel police, the R.I.C. Bernal Osborne came dashing over from London to support his wife. The shame, the humiliation and the disappointment almost brought that warring couple together. From their letters, I gather that almost the only thing that the Osbornes ever agreed upon was to disinherit Edith utterly and never to allow her name to be mentioned in their house again. They maintained that they now had only one daughter, Grace, who was subsequently successfully married, as his second wife, to the Duke of St Albans. They even added a clause to their will to say that no descendant of Mrs Blake could ever inherit any of their property.

Where my grandmother had run to was actually not very far away – Marfield House, a few miles the other side of town, the home of another Anglo-Irish family called Bagwell, who had liberal tendencies and a fondness for my grandmother. Instead of sending her straight back home as the Osbornes thought they should have done, the Bagwells harboured her for three weeks to enable the banns to be read in church, and then escorted her to her wedding with Captain Blake.

As a result the Osbornes never spoke to the Bagwells again. There is a story that once the wheels of the carriages of the two ladies locked when passing under the narrow arch in Clonmel's main street, and that as neither of them would allow her coachman to back her carriage, they each sat there looking straight ahead for four hours while the wheels were taken off, disentangled and replaced.

It is not hard to understand why my grandmother made that spectacular elopement. I do not remember my grandfather, but his portrait looked down at me from the oak-panelled walls of Myrtle Grove for many years. He was tall and immensely good-looking with the traditional Irish colouring of very dark hair and bright blue eyes. Like most Blakes he came from Galway where his family laid claim to be descended from Lord Walscort. Whether this was true or not the family certainly was poor and he helped to support his widowed mother and his twelve brothers and sisters on his pay from the R.I.C.

One of the many things that was held against him at the time of this elopement was that he was a widower, having been married to yet another heiress, from the north of Ireland this time, who had also been disinherited for running away with him. By his first marriage he had a son, a mysterious figure who later emigrated to Australia where he committed suicide by the unusual method of blowing up himself and his horse with gunpowder. Many years later when I was in Galway, I traced some of my Blake cousins and found them charming and most welcoming and all Roman Catholics. Like most of the 'Old English', who had arrived many years before the Reformation, they still maintained the old Faith.

My grandfather was Church of Ireland, i.e., Protestant, but when he or his family changed over, I don't know. This may seem to be of little significance to anyone not living in Ireland, but at that time it was of immense social, political and economic importance. Though in the Republic today the division of the two cultures is not apparent or a matter of any great dissatisfaction to any but a few, in the North its full horrors are still with us.

After their wedding the Henry Blakes contrived to be moved to the north of Ireland and my mother was born in Belfast, the eldest of their children. Henry was promoted in the police, but the young couple had little money and I understand had quite a hard time of it. Then suddenly he was offered a knighthood and made Governor of Newfoundland. This abrupt turn of events can only be explained, I feel, by the influence of my great-aunt Grace, by now Duchess of St Albans. Though my grandfather certainly had great charm and ability, I doubt if he could have done it on his own.

Grace had always loved her sister and felt guilty that she had everything while, in a worldly sense, Edith had nothing. Duchesses in those days had access to people in high places in government and thus wielded some influence. In any case the fact remained that the job was offered, and off they went to Government House in St John's, Newfoundland. Henry Blake had begun a career which lasted the rest of his life. He was in turn governor of Newfoundland, the Bahamas, Jamaica (twice), Hong Kong and Ceylon.

As a postscript to the story of my grandparents' elopement, showing how gossip can persist in country places and in closed communities for well over a hundred years, I will add a conversation I had with an old lady in 1982. We had been discussing my grandparents when she said 'You know my mother used to say that the particular shock and anger of Mrs Osborne at the elopement was not only due to Blake's inferior social and financial position but to the fact that he used to visit Newtown Anner where she herself and he used to play duets on the piano together and you know what *that* means.'

My mother, like my grandmother, was a strong character, but she was, despite being intelligent, adventurous and interested in people and things around her, highly conventional. She never questioned most of the tenets of the Victorian and Edwardian age and believed absolutely that the British Empire was God's gift to the unhappy and backward races that made up the majority of the world's population. Any suggestion that it had any shortcomings at all annoyed her, and she always played down her mother's connection with the Irish Nationalist cause.

She also had enormous charm and must have been beautiful when young, having inherited her father's dark good looks and bright blue eyes. As she was thirty-seven when I was born, I only remember her as a middle-aged woman, but she was still handsome. In her youth she had been a good and keen horsewoman, though she was never really interested in or knowledgeable about horses and had given up riding before I was born. Like many ladies of that era, she was tough and efficient and ran her large family and household smoothly and without apparent effort.

Of her adventurous side I had many instances. It seems that after my father had been chosen from her many suitors, and the grand, almost royal, wedding in Hong Kong had been organised, the question of where the newly wedded couple should go came up for discussion. My father, who liked his creature comforts, voted for some luxury hotel not too far away. But she was adamant that what she really wanted was to go to an ancient and remote Buddhist monastery in Japan that she had read about. When they got there they found they had to sleep on a hard wooden floor which was covered only with a straw mat, while rats, of which there were thousands, ran over them. She said, still laughing at the memory, 'You know, Daddy didn't like it a bit. He had to stay awake all night shooting at them with his revolver, but really the monastery was a most interesting and beautiful place, well worth a visit.'

As I grew up I both loved and trusted her, but we disagreed on very many subjects. Nobody had heard of teenage rebellion in those days. She couldn't understand how her previously charming and well-mannered daughter had become so wilful and difficult.

As she had been brought up entirely in Government Houses in the British colonies, my mother told, when I was little, many exciting stories of tropical islands, of the adventures she had had, and accounts of the exotic pets she had kept. These included a puma, who was obedient only to her and who had once escaped and walked into the banqueting hall at Government House while an official dinner was taking place, the guests including minor royalty. She had had to be got out of bed and brought down in her nightdress to remove the beast as the guards had taken fright and locked themselves in the guard room.

She had few memories of Newfoundland, where my grandfather had first served as Governor and which she does not seem to have liked very much, though I have a photograph of her taken at an early age sitting in a little sleigh drawn by a large black Newfoundland dog against a background of great mounds of snow. Both she and the dog look delighted with themselves, so she must have been happy for some of the time.

Most of her stories were of Jamaica, where she spent her youth from the age of nine to nineteen, when her father was Governor. There were also tales of Hong Kong, very different from the overcrowded city it is today, and of her trips into the interior of China accompanied only by her brother, and riding side-saddle on a Chinese pony. It was in Hong Kong that she met and married my father, who had been seconded by his regiment, the Scots Guards, to serve as A.D.C. to my grandfather the Governor. Government Houses as presided over by my grandparents must have been unusual ones, considering my mother's pets, for as well as the puma my mother had a monkey who lived uncaged and who used to go round the bedrooms putting any small object he could find, including watches and clocks, into the water jugs which stood in every room. She also kept a mongoose, a cotimundi and an alligator.

Grandmama was bored with the English expatriates who lived and worked in the British colonies and with the visiting dignitaries. Pleading ill health (she was as strong as an ox) she refused to entertain them and confined herself to painting and collecting the wild flora, while fraternising with the educated native population. Typically enough, my grandmother's first act on arriving in Hong Kong was to engage a Chinese tutor to teach both herself and her daughter Cantonese, but my mother never really mastered it or learned how to read and write Chinese. Grandmama of course did.

CHAPTER 2

A Privileged Child

While the rooks cawed in the recently charred ruins of the mansions around us and the Civil War tore the newly independent country apart, I settled down quietly with my widowed grandmother at Myrtle Grove. My grandfather had acquired the place from Sir John Pope-Hennessey, another colonial governor who was a friend of his, with very much the same background as Grandpapa. I say 'acquired', because there are two stories about how he got it. One is that he bought it, and the other is that he won it at cards.

In any case one of the 'conditions of sale' was that two aunts of Pope-Hennessey, who were then in occupation, should remain undisturbed during their lifetime. As they were well on in their eighties, nobody bothered much about this but they lived on and on and the time for my grandfather's retirement got ominously near. At last they both died and my grandparents were able to start the extensive repairs, restorations and alterations they had set their hearts on. These included building a two-storey servants' wing at right angles to the original house, converting the old stables into a separate and charming 'guest or nursery' house, and building new stables and a large stable yard at the far end of the property. They also took hundreds of tons of earth from the back of the old house, as it originally came up to the first floor, thus making the ground floor damp. A vast old brewery which stood in the part of the gardens at the far side of the town walls was partially demolished. Out of the remains of that brewery they constructed romantic ruins in the 'Victorian Gothic' style, plus a large conservatory where sky-blue plumbago and beautiful but poisonous white datura covered the walls.

It was a delightful place to grow up in, with its secret gardens and ruins and summer houses. When Sir Walter Raleigh acquired it he must have thought that he was going to spend a great deal more time in Ireland than he actually did because he made extensive alterations and repairs himself, installing the beautiful oak panelling on the first floor and the elaborately carved mantlepieces. He was in some ways a civilised man and he preferred the airiness and brightness of the large windows of Myrtle Grove – which being inside the walls of the Town of Youghal, had no need of defence – to the darkness of the arrow-slits of Lismore Castle, eighteen miles away, which he also owned.

It was to Myrtle Grove that Sir Walter's friend Edmund Spenser came running when he got burned out of Kilcoleman and it is reputed that he wrote some stanzas of the *Faerie Queen* there. The large and beautiful room which he occupied has now been rather spoilt by being divided in half with Victorian panelling to make a passage. In Elizabethan times the rooms opened into one another.

In the large garden, but close to the house, stand four enormous yew trees. They have been dated by some dendrologists from America as being about 900 years old; one can well believe it as the trunks are well corded and the large branches have grown into one another, so that in a sense all four trees are now one. They are growing in an exact square so that the chances of their being self-sown are remote – which in turn means that there was a house with a garden there nearly a thousand years ago. This is backed up by the finding, in a flower-bed, of a coin from the states of eastern Europe of the tenth century, dropped no doubt, by some returned Irish missionary.

Grandmother's household at Myrtle Grove was small compared to what I had been used to. There was Anny the cook and Anny the housemaid; my grandmother's lady's-maid, a ferocious and eccentric German called Trion; my nursery-governess, the Swiss Liza, who was meant to teach me French but who soon learned English, which she spoke with a thick Irish brogue; and a couple of 'girls' whose function I don't remember.

Outside there was the gatekeeper and his daughter, the Walshes. Mike Walsh spent all day raking the front gravel, a never-ending job; like Sisyphus, as soon as he had got to the end, near the ancient yews, the beginning by the front gates needed attention and he started all over again. His daughter Kate saw to the front gates, opening them for verifiable visitors and tradesmen, and driving away sightseers who tried to view the historic buildings with fierce Irish imprecations. 'My soul do be blistered with them damned 'oleshers!' she used to say.

There were various gardeners, including Tudgy the head gardener and Danny, who had both survived the War of Independence and now were on good terms again. Tudgy lived in a pretty but insanitary cottage on the far side of the croquet lawn with his mother who was nearly a hundred years old and so must have survived the Great Famine of the 1850s. She looked as old as the ancient yew trees but was full of energy and volubility.

I was not allowed to go into their cottage but constantly did so. There she taught me how to dance a jig, accompanied by Tudgy on the fiddle, and how to make little men out of soda bread with currant eyes and waistcoat buttons. I remember once when my father came over for a visit, having shaved off his 'guardsman's' moustache. She looked at him in horror and wailed 'In the name of God, Major, what compelled ye to tear out your whiskers?' She always infuriated my eldest brother David when he came back for the school holidays. He was on the plump side and sensitive about it, so when she paid him the traditional Irish compliment – 'Welcome home, Master David, you're fine and gross' – he would scowl and back away and she would cackle with derisive laughter and her eyes would glint. Danny died in 1983 after being in the employment of my family for seventy years. He was a tiny little man, a wonderful piper who later formed the Youghal pipe and drum band. He was very nice to children, of whom he had twelve of his own. As a child I loved him dearly.

There was also a groom who looked after my three ponies – Ariel, Puck and Star. They were New Forest ponies, about thirteen hands high, who had been imported from England for the eldest of my brothers and my sister, David and Terry and Joan. They had been bought unbroken, had never been properly schooled, and were consequently undisciplined. By the time I inherited them, they were too old for retraining to have much effect. Anyway, at that age I was incapable of any form of sophisticated riding and was quite content just to be able to stay in the saddle, but like many little girls I had a passion for horses and spent a great deal of my time hanging about the stables.

The ponies were not only my pride and joy but also my only means of transport. My grandmother had no car nor did she keep a carriage. She had no need of one, for after my grandfather's death she had gone into total retirement, never leaving the house except in unusually fine weather, when she would sit in the pond garden. I can never remember her leaving the property for any reason whatever and she saw very few people, as she had in her colonial days, pleading ill-health as a reason for not receiving them.

Like Genghis Khan's Mongols, I had to ride if I wanted to go anywhere – but there were not many Anglo-Irish children within easy reach. Later, when I was older, and a much more experienced rider, if I was invited to a party I had to get there on horseback. I remember riding over the Knockmealdown Mountains to Clonmel forty miles away for just such an occasion. On the morning of the festivities, having posted my party dress on two days in advance, I would set out on my horse. After spending the night with my hosts, I posted my dress back again, remounted and rode home. It says a lot for the postal system of those days that never once did my dress fail to arrive on time for the party.

Because of the distances involved, it was some years before I could do this, and as a child I simply had no friends of my own age and background except for one Anglo-Irish family who lived four miles away. They were the Holroyd-Smyths. The original Smyth had come over in the train of Sir Walter Raleigh, who had given him the lands that had previously belonged to the Abbey of St Molana. For this reason there was said to be a curse on the family, and certainly since my time they have been subject to a remarkable series of misfortunes. The beautiful house, though spared in the Troubles, is in partial ruins and the lands have gone to maternal cousins not descended from the original Smyth. Though there were five Smyth children, those near my age were boys who were away at school most of the time.

Grandmother's nationalism being untouched by ideas of social equality, I was not supposed to meet anyone who was not a Protestant of my own class. It was rather like the Caste System in India. I was not even allowed to go into the kitchen at home and talk to the maids, though of course I did, and was constantly ticked off for it. 'My dear, while passing, I heard a loud laugh from the kitchen, a very vulgar laugh, and to my horror I realised that that voice was yours.' Grandmama never punished me but the force of her personality was such that I dreaded her disapproval. She was locally reported to have the power of the 'evil eye', and I remember once seeing Danny crawling on his hands and knees on the gravel under the library window. I said, 'Danny, what on earth are you doing?' 'Her Ladyship is in there looking out the window and I am afeared of meeting her eye.'

The existence of rules never stopped a determined child from doing anything if she wanted to enough and I spent a good deal of time sneaking out the back gates and visiting the cottages on Cork Hill where some of the poorest of the citizens of Youghal lived – and that was very poor indeed.

The beautiful old town of Youghal – or in Irish *Eochille*, which means Place of the Yews or Yew Forest – is situated on the mouth of the Blackwater, the second largest river in Ireland. It had probably been founded by the Phoenicians who came there to trade for skins and for the local pottery clay which was considered to be of a high quality. The wide, gently sloping sandy beach was eminently suitable for drawing up their boats, and later on the Vikings and Danes invaded and settled there.

I have been lucky enough to see the remains of part of the original yew forest though there are no ancient yews left in Youghal itself, except the four at Myrtle Grove.

The sea has encroached greatly on the land during the last two thousand years or so, and part of the yew forest evidently grew on what is now the bed of Youghal Bay. When a south-easterly gale combines with a spring tide, the sand gets temporarily drawn out to sea and from under it appears the boles of those ancient trees, with their roots spread out and disappearing into the turf, which is also still there unchanged. With the next high tide it will be covered up with sand again. This is a rare occurrence and I have only seen it three times in my life.

Youghal became one of the most important ports of the south coast of Ireland, if not the most important, and a garrison town with high walls from which cannon could command the mouth of Blackwater, which is navigable for about twenty miles. Trade and communications with England took place via its quays. Sir Walter Raleigh always went that way except when he was in a particular hurry, when he would gallop to Wexford, sail to Bristol and ride post-horses to London. He seems to have done it, surprisingly enough, in very little more time than it takes to get there by train and boat today.

There is a tradition that Shakespeare visited Youghal when he was with a touring company based on Bristol, and that Shylock in the *Merchant of Venice* is based on a Jewish Lord Mayor of Youghal. True or not, I don't know, but there was a Jewish mayor of Youghal and certainly the dates coincide.

The population of Ireland has fluctuated very considerably in historical times. In 1603, after a series of rebellions and minor famines, it is estimated to have fallen to half a million. Just before the Great Famine, in 1845, it had risen to 8,500,000, and after the Famine, due to death and emigration, it had fallen by about 2,000,000. The survivors flocked to towns like Youghal where there was the possibility of work, and their descendants had stayed there. The British garrison had engendered jobs of a service variety, but after it had left in 1922 there was practically nothing for the people of Youghal to do. The port had silted up, and the eighty ships once based there had moved to other harbours. There was no industry.

As a result, when I was a child in Youghal it was in a position of Oriental or African poverty. Ragged, shoeless children ran about the streets; sallow hopeless men leaned against the houses all day. A local joke was that the leaning men were the only things that were keeping the houses from falling down. Tuberculosis was rampant, encouraged by very bad housing and malnutrition, though food was cheap, round steak being only *6d.* a pound and chickens 1*s.* 6*d.* a pair. Most of the people out of work lived on potatoes, with salted pigs' cheek or 'crubeens' (pigs' trotters) on Sunday. There was no proper drainage system in the town and the disease rate was terrible. I remember one charming family of thirteen children who died one after another until the two old parents were left alone.

Looking back I can see, of course, that the strict prohibition against my going into cabins and cottages and hob-nobbing with the natives was not only made for class reasons but was also an effort to prevent me catching T.B., the germs of which were everywhere. In fact I seem to have built up an immunity to the germs around me. When many years later my husband Claud was discovered to have raging T.B. in both lungs, the doctors were surprised that I had not caught it, but X-rays and blood tests showed that I was completely free of the disease.

I have always believed that the insanitary conditions I lived amongst in my childhood – the milk must have been lethal, and I was always eating little goodies scraped up off Tudgy's filthy kitchen table – stood me in good stead later in my travels to primitive places. Only once was I seriously poisoned, and small cuts and scratches never turned septic. Children who have been brought up in aseptic conditions, eating only food 'untouched by human hand' usually seem to fall victim much more easily to any strange bug that they may meet when they grow up.

Despite her seeming isolation, Grandmama must have had contacts and kept more in touch with events than was apparent, because one day she sent for me and told me that my ponies would be needed. In fact only Star disappeared in the night and we did get him back; he was returned mysteriously to his stable six months later, in very poor condition with his back coat turned yellow, but unharmed. He lived to be forty-five years old, a great age for a horse. I am not sure just when this took place but it must have been during the War of Independence or possibly the Civil War. Nor do I know whether Grandmama supported the Republicans or the Free Staters in the Civil War, as she never talked of contemporary politics to me, only of past struggles for Irish Independence.

As soon as things had quieted down a bit, the rest of the family came flooding back for the school holidays, plus most of the thirteen servants. These consisted of a butler and three footmen, the cook, kitchen maid and scullery maid, the head housemaid and two under-housemaids, my mother's lady's-maid, and the boy who cleaned the knives and boots. The resident Myrtle Grove staff were of course there as well, quarrelling with them. All except the lady's-maid, the butler and the cook and, of course, Liza, came from Youghal, mostly from Cork Hill, and they were delighted to get home again and see their families.

Their salaries were miserably small. The butler got the most, £90 per annum – and from this peak the rates sank down to the scullery maid, who got £18 p.a., and the boot boy, who just got his keep. Despite this there was great competition to get a job in the Big House. The work was easy and the food good, and there were many other perks as well. One tiny example was that every morning, when the whole tribe was in residence, a donkey cart, piled to the very top with loaves of bread, used to arrive at the gates and slowly wind its way across the gravel to the back yard.

I asked my mother how the household, numerous as we were, could possibly eat all those dozens of loaves in one day. She said, 'Of course they are not eaten, but every evening the servants are allowed to take the bread, including the loaves that have not been cut, to their families in the town and we start each morning with fresh bread.'

Of course, it wasn't only bread that found its way to Cork Hill, but petty pilfering was considered part of life and it was considered ill-bred to make a fuss about it. Only when something really valuable disappeared was there an outcry and the culprit unmasked and sacked.

In the T.V. series *Upstairs Downstairs* I noticed that all the servants, from the butler down to the kitchen maid, ate in the kitchen. In my experience this would be out of the question. There was an absolutely unbridgeable caste line between the 'upper' and the 'lower' servants. The 'upper' servants, consisting of the butler, the head housemaid, the cook and the two lady's-maids would have thrown up their jobs instantly at whatever cost and walked out if they had been asked to eat with the lower servants in the servants' hall. Nobody ate in the actual kitchen. Upper servants ate in the 'steward's room', while Liza, as a nursery governess, ate in the schoolroom with me and my two younger brothers.

I did not eat in the dining room till I was thirteen and then only for lunch, though before that age Grandmama, during term time, would sometimes invite me to join her, though never in the evening. Perhaps she considered that civilised conversation at meals would improve my manners, or perhaps she was just lonely. Anyway, I considered it a great honour and was almost too overawed to eat.

The servants also had absolutely unbreakable demarcation rules about their work and were always quarrelling about it. I remember a blazing row that went on for weeks, almost driving my mother to distraction, about 'who should turn down the cook's bed'. The cook said the third housemaid should do it. The head housemaid said the kitchen maid should do it. No one would give way. Finally the matter was resolved by the hiring of a 'tweeny' who owed allegiance to neither the cook nor the head housemaid. It was stipulated that she should also clean the backstairs, another bone of contention.

During one summer holiday a largish number of White Russian aristocrats came to stay. They were distant cousins, due to the fact that some generations ago a Volkov had married an Irish woman, one of our many great-great-great-aunts. Almost totally penniless, they had escaped from the Russian Revolution of 1917 via Odessa, and slowly wended their way across Turkey and Europe. The landowning classes in Russia being as familiar with their family trees as we were, they decided, on reaching Europe's western fringes, to pay us a visit. My family was delighted to see them and anxious to be of help in any way that they could. They were 'kin' and the extended family means a lot in Ireland, as it did in Russia.

They fitted into our household like a foot into an old shoe. They said it was like coming home again. All being highly educated and excellent linguists, there was no language barrier except for the youngest, Vladimir, nicknamed 'Dima'. He only spoke bad French and of course Russian. He was a strong rather peasant-looking boy, big for his age, and when I was told that I was to entertain him, I was delighted. The reason for this was that at that time I was deeply concerned to find the Silver Bells and Church Treasure of St Mary's Collegiate Church, which tradition said were hurriedly buried in the grounds of Myrtle Grove just before Oliver Cromwell arrived at Youghal with his ferocious troops. I had made several ineffective efforts to find them, making little holes in likely places and poking around the sentry boxes in the old town walls. But now, with this great big strong Russian boy who could obviously dig, we were certain to find the treasure.

Poor Dima dug and dug – he didn't know why. This horrible little Irish girl just handed him a spade and pointed to the ground. We found several sixteenth- and seventeenth-century broken wine bottles with the beautiful rainbow sheen that old glass acquires, and a couple of pieces of ancient military scaling ladders, but no treasure. Finally Dima dug a hole so deep that the sides caved in, almost burying him alive, and I flew screaming to the grown-ups for help. After that, further treasure hunting was strictly forbidden and Dima was told in Russian that though he must be nice to his little cousin, that did not mean obeying her every whim.

The matriarch of the group had managed to conceal a large diamond brooch in her corsets which she had also preserved during their wanderings across Europe. My father helped her to sell it at Christie's or Sotheby's, and with the proceeds she bought a big dilapidated house in

Earl's Court, which she turned into a rooming house and eventually ended up quite well-off again.

All this time my parents, and my father in particular, had been worrying about me. He felt that a country in a state of war was not the ideal place to bring up a child. True, Myrtle Grove had never been raided by either side and I had actually seen nothing of the fighting, but it was felt that I was becoming isolated from the rest of the family and he, for one, mistrusted the influence of his mother-in-law, Lady Blake. He, of course, never called her anything else, at the time, and to have done so would have been unthinkable.

I was now eight years old and totally illiterate. Liza had proved a failure. Grandmama had tried to educate me by reading the first of the twelve volumes of Gibbon's *Decline and Fall of the Roman Empire* and also Plutarch's *Lives*, believing that one should always start with the classics. But this was not considered to make up for a total lack of the three r's, so it was decided that I was to return with the family to London and go to an English school – a little day school at first and then, following in my sister's footsteps, to Heathfield, which in 1922 was considered the most 'élite' boarding school for girls in England. My brothers in their turn all went to Eton.

From the first day I hated my school and hated all the other little girls in it. Due to my lack of education, I couldn't understand the lessons. Anti-Irish feeling was at its height and as I spoke with an Irish brogue at that time, of which my mother was desperately trying to cure me, the other children immediately guessed my national origin and were as nasty and hostile as they could be. I in turn became rude and violent. Then, halfway through my first term, on 22 June, I was walking down Eaton Square when I saw an old gentleman in a black coat standing on the steps of one of the great pillared doorways of the houses there, when another man standing below him on the pavement pulled out a gun and shot him. The old gentleman half turned round and then slowly collapsed. I wasn't at all frightened, just supremely interested, and stood there watching while the man with the gun and a companion quietly walked away. When I got home I was, of course, full of the incident and anxious to tell everyone about it, to their extreme annoyance.

I was told 'Patricia, you really must not tell such lies,' and my father said 'There, I told you so, the child's mind is full of murder and bloodshed and now she imagines that she sees horrors wherever she goes, even in Eaton Square. It all comes of leaving her so long in Ireland.' Then the newspapers arrived with the headline: 'Field Marshal Sir Henry Wilson murdered on own doorstep in Eaton Square.' After that there was uproar at 42 Grosvenor Place. Sir Henry Wilson, lately Chief of the Imperial General Staff and now the Member of Parliament for Longford in Ireland, had long been a particular target for Sinn Fein, and no one had any doubt as to who had shot him.

The long account in the newspaper which was printed under the headlines bore little resemblance to the scene I had stood watching. For one thing, the assassins were supposed to have been chased by a heroic, unarmed milkman who threw milk bottles at them. I saw no milkman, nor anybody running. The two men just walked quietly away. There were various other wrong details which I pointed out to my by now deeply interested parents, who were terribly upset.

My father said, 'She is possibly the only witness and is therefore in grave danger. Now Patricia, you must *never never never* tell anybody about what you have seen. Not anybody, or the most terrible things will happen to you.' As I went upstairs I heard him say to my mother, 'Now we can never send her back to Ireland, you can't trust a child to keep her mouth shut, and even if she didn't see the faces of the men who shot Wilson, as she says, it would be only too easy to silence her, just in case.' Never be able to go home, I thought, how awful. I'd rather be dead. I must think of some way to make them change their minds.

My father was wrong when he thought that I was the only witness to that murder. There was at least one other genuine one, as I only discovered sixty years later. I was talking to my friend Mrs Veronica Anderson from Waterford, the mother of Perry Anderson, the writer and editor, whom I have known for many years, when Claud, my husband, remarked that it was ironic that I should have been dragged to London to get me out of a war zone and there, in Eaton Square of all places, been witness to a murder. She said, 'Good Heavens, you were there too?' It transpired that she was walking down Eaton Square in the opposite direction to go to classes in Eaton Place when Wilson was shot. When we compared notes I was interested to find that both our memories coincided. We both had a very clear picture as to what had happened, and our pictures were the same.

But to go back to 1922, there I was, brooding miserably on how to get away from that terrible school in this horrible country. I considered various projects including, of course, running away, but discarded them all as totally impractical. In the end I decided on a hunger strike. I would drink only water and I would *not* go to school.

The idea of a hunger strike almost certainly came to me because it was not so long since Terence McSwiney, Lord Mayor of Cork, had died as a result of a hunger strike lasting an incredible seventy-four days and I had secretly gone to a Mass for the repose of his soul.

I don't remember how long I fasted, but unlike the unfortunate Lord Mayor, I won my point. My parents, and the doctor who had been called on, were sufficiently worried to agree that at the beginning of the autumn term I should go back to Youghal, accompanied by an English governess. I in my turn was to promise that I would do what the governess told me and work hard at my lessons for not less than five hours a day.

My parents' panic about the possible elimination of one small witness had obviously evaporated after the conviction of those allegedly responsible for Wilson's death. The carrying out of their part of the bargain, however, proved more difficult than they had imagined. Ireland was still in a state of civil war, and no teacher who could possibly get a job elsewhere felt inclined to go to so dangerous a country. Finally one was found, a Miss Warwick, who was brave or poor enough to accept the post and the good salary offered, so we set off together after the summer holidays.

These holidays the family had spent in Brittany, near St Malo, in a rented villa large enough to hold all eight of us as well as a couple of cousins and half the servants. It was my first visit to Europe and I can still recall with pleasure the excitement of finding new kinds of sea shells, and also the wonderful sights and smells of the cobbled streets of St Brieuc. It certainly abetted my already budding desire to travel the world.

When we returned from France there was another upset in the family, and for once I was not the cause of it. My second oldest brother, Terry, announced that he wanted to join the Royal Air Force which had been recently formed out of the old Army Air Corps, and make it his career. This would involve leaving Eton early and going to Cranwell Training College to learn how to fly. He met with strong opposition. In those days the Air Force was not only considered dangerous but an unsuitable career for a gentleman. Only the Navy or Brigade of Guards or a very few other regiments such as the Black Watch were considered appropriate.

I missed the full excitement of this great row as I and Miss Warwick were packed off to Youghal as promised. Terry, by stubborn determination, won his point, joined up, survived and had a successful and interesting life.

It may seem odd but I have no very clear memory of my elder brothers and my sister when we were growing up. My sister Joan was ten years older than myself. She quite obviously didn't like little girls and we had no interests in common. I only saw the rest of the family during the school holidays, and then everyone was busy with their own friends and hobbies. Later on, in London, the house was so large that it was quite possible to go two or three days without meeting any of them, even on the stairs, as there were two staircases and a passenger lift to choose from.

All the boys were tall and good-looking and Joan was very beautiful, with an absolutely classical profile. She was more interested in theoretical subjects than I was and most of her friends seem to have been Austrians or White Russians. She absolutely hated horses, which were then my great preoccupation, and appeared to despise my country friends. It was only in our later lives that we really became friends and came to understand each other.

David, my eldest brother, was a very talented pianist, and was usually to be found practising in the music room at the back of the house. His friends were mostly musical and all were so much older than me that they did not impinge at all on my life. The exception was Sir Malcolm Sargent, the conductor – whom I remember as always charming, and who made a point of appearing interested in subjects that must have bored him to distraction. While I was abroad David married Elizabeth, the daughter of Lord and Lady Wharton, and they emigrated to South Africa, where he still lives.

Terry and Bernard I hardly knew at that time. They were always away – Bernard in the Navy, and Terry in the Air Force. After my mother's death Bernard inherited Myrtle Grove. We became next door neighbours and for the first time really got to know each other, and became very devoted. He took a large part in the life of the community in Youghal and founded the 'Youghal Fishermens' Co-operative' which runs to this day.

Only 'Teeny', the youngest, and I were always very close. He was only two and a half years older than I and when we were apart we corresponded regularly – and he was a great influence on my life. He was incredibly charming, intelligent and understanding.

He understood everyone in the family, with the possible exception of himself. He never really found his 'métier' in life until the Second War, when he volunteered at the outbreak as a private and rose in the two years before his death to being a Major in the Signals. After his death, his wife, Helen gave me back many of my letters to him, which he had kept, and it is from these that I have been reminded of the days of my youth.

So, to go back to that distant time, I went back to Myrtle Grove, where I kept my side of the bargain and slowly learned to read and write. My lessons, which took place in the schoolroom in the 'nursery house' from 9 a.m. to 1 p.m. were always interrupted at eleven o'clock, when I would run across the gravel to the library to drink a glass of port and eat a slice of Madeira cake with my grandmother. Miss Warwick was scandalised – 'Giving the child alcohol at her age. The very idea of it.' Grandmama was adamant. She said I looked anaemic and port wine would build me up – an eighteenth-century conception. As usual, no one dared contradict her.

Once I could read everything changed. There were no modern books in the library, which was largely composed of eighteenth- and early nineteenth-century volumes, leather-bound and with almost indecipherable print. I finished the twelve volumes of *Decline and Fall of the Roman Empire* by the light of a candle, there being no electricity in the house until years later. Despite the dire predictions of Miss Warwick, it did my eyes no harm, though it was a first edition with faint eighteenth-century print. I also read many of the Greek and Roman classical writers in translation, my Greek and Latin being the despair of all who tried to teach me. Once lessons and lunch were over I would make a dash for the stables. I had developed a passion for riding and horses occupied a great deal of my thoughts. Many parents have seen the same phenomenon in their young daughters, to the detriment of their nerves and bank balances.

Though I loved them dearly, I was getting increasingly dissatisfied with my three ageing ponies. I wanted a 'proper' horse, and I wanted to be allowed to go hunting. Every letter to my parents at that period harped on these two subjects. Finally a steady, elderly, chestnut mare named Isabella, about fifteen hands high, was purchased for me, not at all what I had had in mind. I was told I could go out with hounds as soon as I was twelve, accompanied by the groom.

It is curious how rich people who spend money like water on some things, nearly always have some pet economy about which they are incredibly mean. With my great-uncle Charles Arbuthnot, who was a millionaire and a Governor of the Bank of England, it was medicine bottles. He was a bachelor who lived with his spinster sister at 69 Eaton Square, a large gloomy house which always smelt of barley water. When in London, I used to be sent to lunch with him once a week, and after lunch I was handed a small bag of empty medicine bottles and told to take them back to the chemist on my way home and ask for a half-penny for each bottle. These halfpennies I was to return to great-uncle Charles the following week. My parents' pet economy was horses. Isabella cost very little. It was a policy which they were to regret later.

At last my much longed-for twelfth St Patrick's Day arrived and as I watched the town band parading round the town of Youghal, with Danny blowing the pipes and Tudgy beating the big drum, I thought only of the November to come when, like Surtees's Jorrocks, I would cry 'Hurrah, hurrah, the dahlias are dead' and ride out to the opening meet of the West Waterford Foxhounds.

1926, however, proved a sad year, for my grandmother died.

I missed her very much indeed and after her death the routine of my life changed. The rest of the family spent much more time at Myrtle Grove, of which my mother became the owner. Her two brothers, neither of whom had any children, had in their turn been disinherited as had the son of my mother's half-brother, Arthur Blake, who suddenly turned up from Australia, clearly envious of the luxury he saw around him. My mother tried to explain to him that the money came from the Arbuthnots, not the Blakes, but I think he remained unconvinced.

Now that my mother owned Myrtle Grove, the practice of renting large houses in the West of Ireland for the summer holidays was discontinued and we often went abroad for holidays. One summer holiday, when I was fourteen, we went to Calvi on the north coast of Corsica where my mother's youngest brother, my uncle Maurice, lived at that time. He had a lovely house, very old, as were all the houses on the 'Citadel' of Calvi. I remember with pleasure its large rooms which were cool and bare with amber-washed walls and octagonal red tiled floors.

Uncle Maurice was a wild and unusual character who had led an interesting life. He had been educated in England and had read for the bar, but he didn't stay long as a barrister. On one of his early cases he earned £4000 as junior counsel, a huge sum in those days – whereupon he quit the bar, took the money and went off to look for diamonds in Brazil. I don't think he found many, but since that time he had never settled down but had travelled all over the world doing strange and adventurous jobs. Though very clever in other ways, he was hopeless about money, and I think my grandfather was always having to bail him out of some trouble or other. Uncle Maurice's most spectacular mistake concerned Montego Bay. When Sir Henry Blake was Governor of Jamaica he seems to have done a good bit of land speculation. For a Governor to do this would be unheard of today and was very ill-looked on even in the 1890s, but Henry Blake had not made his way up from poverty to retire to a humble cottage at the end of his life. He had acquired about 2,000 acres on the north coast of Jamaica, which included Montego Bay. This Grandpapa gave to his youngest son, Maurice. My uncle promptly sold the whole property for £200, thus denying himself the opportunity of becoming a multi-millionaire.

It was for these reasons and also, I imagine, because Maurice had married an actress that he was cut out of my grandparents' will which, ignoring their eldest son, left everything to my mother.

Calvi was quite beautiful when I knew it, unchanged since Napoleon's day. The citadel was built on a high steep rocky island, connected to the mainland. The pine trees came down to the long arc of sandy beach below, the ground beneath them sprinkled with wild flowers. There was not a villa or hotel to be seen anywhere. The ancient citadel itself was a triumph of military architecture. Though several times besieged, it has never been taken – one reason for which is that it had no road into it, only high-walled twisting steps which wind around it to the top where my uncle's house was situated. The climb to the summit was long and steep and very exhausting.

One day I was returning home after a solitary bathe when I saw a very old peasant woman draped in black and carrying a heavy axe. She was struggling up the steps and she looked on the point of collapse, dripping with sweat and puffing and blowing. Being on the whole a well-mannered child I asked in my halting French if I could help her. She seemed to understand and gave me the axe. Carrying it over my shoulder and supporting her with my other arm, we slowly wended our way upwards. At the top I gave her back her axe. She thanked me profusely, calling on the Holy Virgin to protect me always.

Next day my uncle's maid arrived in a great state of pleasure and excitement. She said there had been a '*crime passionnel*' in the citadel the night before and on our very street. It seemed that an eighty-three-year-old man who lived in the town below had eloped with a seventy-nine-year-old widow, abandoning his eighty-four-year-old wife. The guilty pair had run to the top of the citadel where the widow had a house, evidently considering themselves safer, being up so high. But the injured wife had followed them and hit her husband on the head with an axe and killed him. What nobody could understand was how she had managed to carry that heavy axe up all those steps, as she was always thought to be rather feeble.

I had avoided catching the eyes of any of my family whom I had told about the episode with the old woman and, unlike the time in Eaton Square when Sir Henry Wilson was shot, they knew they didn't have to tell me to keep my mouth shut.

As well as passionate Corsican octogenarians, the citadel housed a lot of White Russian refugees – mostly Cossacks, who had some horses and took me riding with them. They were being well supported by Prince Felix Yussoupov, the man who killed Rasputin. He was immensely rich, some said richer than the Romanovs; because of the murder he had been obliged to leave Russia before the Revolution and seemed to have done so with his fortune intact. We saw a lot of him that summer. Like many Russian aristocrats, he was charming to meet and he liked young people. We used to play silly games on the beach together. After dinner he would sing sad Russian songs, accompanying himself on a balalaika. At a certain point he would stop and tell his audience, in detail, the story of the night of the murder and of how Rasputin simply would not die, although he had been given enough poison to kill a regiment, as well as being shot. He had obviously never got over the trauma of that terrible night and it was on his mind constantly. I felt that in his heart he really did believe that the 'mad monk' had supernatural powers and that he, Felix, could never escape him.

Of the houses we used to take in Ireland before my grandmother's death, one was called Glenbarrahane, in Castletownsend in West Cork, which we took for several successive summers. The Anglo-Irish in Castletownsend, of which there were many, were composed entirely of three families, all related – an extended family on a grand scale. They were the Somervilles, the Coghills and the Townsends.

The most distinguished inhabitant of Castletownsend was Miss Edith Oenone Somerville, the authoress, half of that 'Somerville and Ross' team who wrote the *Memoirs of an Irish R.M.* and many other books. She wasn't really a half, as there was no Ross. Violet Martin, the original Ross, had died prematurely after the first book they wrote together, but Miss Somerville – or Dr Somerville, as she preferred to be called after Trinity College, Dublin had made her an honorary Doctor of Literature – was a keen spiritualist and believed that the ghost of Violet Martin was directing her pen.

My chief memories of Castletownsend are of Dr Somerville herself, and of rats. Like almost every other Irish mansion that I have known, Glenbarrahane was infested with rats.

Rats and spiritualism are two subjects which have generally been neglected in the many books that have been written about our class and nation. Horses have been exhaustively dealt with but rats, no. Practically everybody had rats. Some houseowners fought back and spent endless hours discussing different methods of exterminating them, but most simply regarded them as an Act of God and gave up the struggle.

I had, and have, a particular horror of the creatures and all my youth would never go to bed without my enormous black cat, Nero, the terror of the local dogs. If possible, I took him with me wherever I went.

It would be tedious to expatiate on the psychological or historic reasons for the amount of table-turning that went on, but nearly everyone did it. After dinner, the lights would be turned low and the ouija board would be got out. Mediums or people reported to have psychic powers were in hot demand as house-guests. Despite her dislike of visitors, even my grandmother, that product of the Age of Reason, used to invite a Miss Barlow to stay. She did 'automatic-writing' and could therefore put Grandmama in touch with the late adored Sir Henry. He used to send little messages of a not very enlightening kind to me, which were duly delivered the next morning.

All this did not entirely apply to the hard-riding and hunting set who mostly just got drunk in the evenings, but attempted contact with another world was very widespread indeed.

Dr Edith Somerville paid a good deal of flattering attention to me as a child. She was a tiny little woman, always dressed in grey hand-woven tweeds, with a high, starched collar on her shirt and a man's tie. She looked to me immensely old. She had been a keen horsewoman in her day and had hunted her own pack of fox hounds, side-saddle of course. As well as being a very good and successful writer, she painted very well, her works being mostly water-colours of landscapes or horses.

She was obviously a lesbian but I agree with Mr Collis, who wrote her biography, that she was not a practising one, in fact I doubt if she knew such a choice existed. I think she was interested in me because of my painting and my love of riding, though she warned me against the horses. 'Concentrate on becoming an artist,' she would say. 'Let the hunting go by, painting will last you all your life.'

Altogether she was a curious mixture of qualities, a highly intelligent writer but at the same time naive and credulous, even sometimes just plain silly. She once called me into her study and said solemnly, 'Now I am going to show you something of great importance.' She went to a safe built into the wall, opened it and from it produced a box which contained a small object wrapped in tissue paper. 'This,' she said, 'is a genuine fairy shoe. It was found by a shepherd early one morning on a barren hill-top as he counted his sheep. Look, you can see how the sole and heel are worn down from walking on it.' She then produced from the tissue paper a three-inch-long doll's shoe, with a sole and heel as shiny as patent leather. I nodded respectfully and she re-wrapped the shoe and reverently put it back in the safe.

All the Somerville kinsfolk lived in the reflected glory of the authoress, and they all thought they knew a great deal more about the Irish people than they really did. Hence the tragic death, already referred to, of poor old Admiral Boyle Somerville, who used to sing those Percy French songs with such verve, without ever realising how offensive they were to any of the native Irish within hearing.

CHAPTER 3

The Sporting Life

At last the summer of 1926 ended, the dahlias blackened with the first light frost and, accompanied by Willy Brown, our groom, and riding Isabella, I trotted out to attend the opening meet of the West Waterford Foxhounds.

Willy had been acquired on the recommendation of the Holroyd-Smyths, the exceedingly horsey family who lived up river from us at Ballinatrae. He owned a ramshackle farm on a mountain above their place where he kept a varied collection of nags, including an illegal stallion. He was brilliant about horses, knowing more about them than anyone I have known. He was also what in Ireland is known as a 'desperate chancer', meaning he was up to every dirty trick of the horse-coping trade. But he was very good to me, looking after me like a mother-hen and teaching me most of what I know about horses and hunting.

Going out with the hounds opened up a whole new world to me, introducing me to a set of people I had hardly ever met before as my grandmother despised them so much.

Many of them were the descendants of, to quote Jim Downey in *Them and Us* 'the wine-swilling, hard-riding, heiress-abducting, Sir Condy Rackrents of Maria Edgeworth's novels'. Some were more recent immigrants from England and there were many farmers of native Irish origin as well as members of the small middle class from the towns who had taken up hunting to begin with as a means of social advancement, and then became hooked. But together they formed a culture all of their own, and a pretty strange one at that. Horses, hunting and, to a lesser extent, racing were like a drug addiction to them. They worshipped them with religious intensity.

They talked of little else, and parents would turn against their children if they disliked hunting or were bad horsemen.

Now that I have given up riding, friends often say to me 'Don't you miss the hunting?' To which I quite honestly reply 'No, I had the best of it.'

Nobody who has not the memory of what it was like to gallop on a good horse over those grassy fields in a straight line towards those high, but sound, stone-faced banks, can know what the chase in Ireland was really like in the past. There was practically no barbed-wire. Most farmers were poor, labour was plentiful and cheap or even free, and with many farms being worked with the help of unmarried and penniless relatives, it was much more sensible to laboriously construct those magnificent banks by hand rather than spend good money on wire.

Little corn was grown in our part of Ireland so there were few ploughed fields to slow you up and tire your horse. Irish hunting has always been a dangerous sport, owing to the size and solidity of the jumps, often with wide drainage ditches on either side of them, and the rough uneven character of the heather-covered mountains. Accidents were fairly frequent.

Once a friend of mine went to the aid of a woman whose horse had fallen.

'Are you all right?'

'No, I've broken my leg.'

'Oh dear, does it hurt much?'

'No, not much.'

'Well, perhaps it isn't broken.'

The woman looked up angrily. 'How many bones have you broken?'

'None, thank God, so far.'

'Well, this is my sixteenth, it's broken all right.'

I hunted two days a week, even in term time: one day with the West Waterford Foxhounds, and one with the Mount Uniacke Harriers.

The term harriers is confusing, as in fact harriers don't hunt hares in Ireland but foxes, like the recognised official foxhounds. Hunting hares is illegal. They are preserved for that far more cruel 'sport' of coursing, efforts to ban which have so far failed.

I had no horse-box nor car to pull it with, and so had to ride to meets on one of the three ponies, with Willy on his own horse leading Isabella so that she should be as fresh as possible for the hunt. We would often go as far as thirteen miles to a meet which meant, of course, that before going to bed that night I had ridden twenty-six miles as well as taken part in a four- to five-hour hunt. Naturally my lessons suffered next day and there were bitter complaints from my governess. To minimise these long rides we became adept at leaving the roads and cutting across country, Willy knowing every path and gate as well as the farmers whose lands we crossed.

Until the 1850s there were very few roads in Ireland and what there were were very bad – almost impassable, in fact, for wheeled traffic. The thousands of miles of winding by-roads that exist today are mostly 'Famine Roads'. During the Great Famine of the late 1840s, the Victorian ethic decreed that neither food nor money should be given to people just because they were starving and destitute. They must somehow work for them – and the work they were given was mostly making these roads and the dry-stone walls that run along each side of them.

Before that time, and even after it, the rivers were the major highways. All the way up to Cappoquin, twenty miles from its mouth, the steep banks of the Blackwater River were dotted with castles. The Normans built them first and then they were adapted and improved for defence by later generations, until finally they were rebuilt as Georgian and Early Victorian mansions. When I was young, these houses and castles were already in varying stages of decay and were far too big for even the large families that inhabited them. In the eighteenth and early nineteenth centuries owning large tracts of land in Ireland was immensely profitable and the landlords of that time were only comparable to the Texan millionaires of today. The tenant farmers grew potatoes which they lived on, and wheat, barley and oats, which they sold for export to England to pay the rents, which were high. They had no rights and could be evicted at the whim of the landowner, with no compensation for any improvement they had made over the years. So if they could possibly avoid it, they were never behind with the rent.

These landlords, consequently, grew immensely rich and they built ever bigger and grander mansions, employing architects from abroad who trained local craftsmen. The 'great house' was their major status symbol.

Then came the Repeal of the Corn Laws in 1846. The price of corn fell as cheap imports came flooding in from further abroad; this was immediately followed by the Great Famine when the entire potato crop was blighted and hundreds of thousands starved, more died of disease or emigrated, and the population sank by one quarter of its previous level of 8,500,000. The final blow to the landlords came just as times were improving for them. The British Government passed a series of 'Land Acts' enabling tenants to buy their farm, which they did as a result of the extreme agitation of the Irish people, aided by those same emigrants who had fled the famine to the U.S.A. Many of the original landowning families who had built these beautiful and magnificent 'white elephants' stayed on in them, loving them but quite unable to keep them up in their former glory.

In these mansions lived a lot of my new friends and I soon learned their families' histories. The original Smyth of Ballinatrae, for instance, had come over as a young officer in the train of Sir Walter Raleigh. Further up river was an enormous and beautiful house called Dromana, the home of the Villiers-Stuarts, descendants of the great Earls of Desmond, who had raised so many rebellions against the English from the fourteenth century onwards. Many other houses and castles were still in the hands of the descendants of the original builders.

In one of them, a great Victorian-Gothic pile called Strancally Castle, lived an old widower and his two ill-favoured spinster daughters. It was said that once, having been turned down by every suitable girl in the county and desperate for a second wife, he had been driven to advertise in the *Cork Examiner*: 'Healthy middle-aged gentleman (Church of Ireland) of good lineage and extensive property would like to hear from attractive young lady with a view to matrimony. No dowry required.' He signed it with a box number. There were only two replies, each from his own two daughters. So there they lived on, in their great gloomy castle on the edge of the river with the dark, damp woods closing in on them, rejected and hating each other.

I believe they all drank heavily. In most of these big houses, however, lived people with families a lot younger and jollier than the inhabitants of Strancally Castle and with them and my new hunting friends – who were indeed often the same people – I was soon leading a fairly full social life.

I was beginning to get very fed up with hunting Isabella. She was a sound steady jumper who never gave me a fall but she was slow and she also 'roosted' on top of banks, stopping and looking carefully for the safest way to jump off them, she had no looks or breeding to speak of and was altogether a very unglamorous mount.

I implored my parents to buy me something a bit more dashing but without results, so I turned to Willy Brown for comfort and consolation, complaining that I was being treated as a child, though I was nearly fifteen.

'You want to ride something with a bit of class to it? That's right and proper for a fine young lady like yourself and a great rider too. Don't you worry, leave it to me and I'll fix it.' And fix it he did. At that time almost every small farmer kept a mare or two, mostly of the Irish Draught breed, which he would use around the farm and in the early spring send to a thoroughbred stallion, the resulting half-bred progeny being sold when three years old as hunters.

Naturally, if these young horses were well trained and had had some experience in the hunting field, you got a better price for them. If the colts were big and up to carrying a heavy man, there was no difficulty for the farmer himself or one of his sons would take them out with the hounds. But if a young horse grew only to about 15.3 hands and was a bit light, the only way to get any reasonable price for it was to sell it as a 'lady's hunter', which was made much easier if the horse had been seen out hunting with a lady on board.

In the 1920s not very many of the farmers' daughters could ride, so the farmer had problems. Willy, who knew every farmer and every horse in the neighbourhood, easily arranged (for I assume, a small cut in the hoped-for selling price of the horse) that I should hunt it. We would set off on a crisp winter morning as usual, with me hacking along on Isabella, but when we got to the meet there was some farmer waiting and holding his three-year-old by the bridle. Saddles were changed and off I went.

Of course these horses were totally inexperienced and though I hunted some very good ones, I rode some very dangerous ones as well. However, 'the devil looks after his own' as the saying goes – or maybe it was due to my Guardian Angel – so for a long time nothing disastrous happened.

There was one little grey mare that I was particularly fond of. She was light, small and supple, very fast and with the spring of a kangaroo.

The only trouble was that I could seldom get her to change feet – to pause for a split second on top of a bank to get the impetus to clear a possible ditch on the far side. She just flew right over them, a very dangerous habit – so much so that a Mrs O'Brien, after watching me for a few days, took the step of writing to my mother, asking if she knew that her young daughter was taking appalling risks, and that if she continued riding that grey mare she would probably break her neck.

My mother sent for me.

'Patricia, I have received a letter which somewhat disturbs me. An unknown woman has written to me to say that you are taking absurd risks out hunting and that the horse you are riding is positively dangerous. Is there any truth to this?'

'Absolutely not,' I lied. 'I am always careful and cautious, and in any case Willy takes good care of me.'

'I am so glad to hear it. For a moment this letter worried me.' And that was that.

I continued hunting the grey mare without mishap until some dealer, recognising her potential, bought her, and Willy had to look around for a replacement.

He found it in the shape of a truly magnificent bay gelding. Why the owner wanted me to hunt him, I shall never know. Possibly it was the result of some Byzantine deal with Willy. The young horse was big and strong, about 16.2 hands, well up to a man's weight, and was beautiful. Obviously three-quarters thoroughbred, he was full of spirit but entirely gentle. He had a perfect mouth, was easy to control and was almost a natural jumper. He was named Cuchullain, after the mythical Irish hero. Falling in love with him at once, I begged my parents to buy him for me, but with no result.

'We can't afford it,' they said. 'Next year you will be seventeen and will be coming out in London, which will cost a lot of money. We have your brothers and sister to think of too. Don't be greedy.'

Among my special friends at that time was Elspeth Villiers-Stuart, wife of Ion Villiers-Stuart, owner of the beautiful and enormous house Dromana and Master of the West Waterford Foxhounds. A good deal older than myself but still young and beautiful, and full of fun, she made a great pet of me, taking me around with her to parties.

My mother did not altogether approve of the friendship, feeling that I was too young and that I was getting into a 'fast set'. However she did nothing about it and in the winter of 1929 went abroad, leaving a friend, Stella Annesley to 'chaperone' me, the last of my governesses having left in despair.

Among the letters that I wrote to my brother Teeny around this time I have found a very long one giving an account of a visit to Elspeth and Ion Villiers-Stuart at Dromena and also of the 'Great Bore Competition' which had kept us amused in the winter of 1929.

The idea was born because of an argument between Elspeth and myself as to who was the most boring person of our set in the neighbourhood. We could not agree – and so to settle the question once and for all we hit on the idea of running a competition.

The organisation was simple. Fifteen of our brighter friends were asked to form themselves into three teams. Each team member had to select a candidate for the title 'Supreme Bore of the Neighbourhood' and invite him or her to dinner along with the other four members of the team. After these five dinner parties had taken place the team convened and decided by majority vote which of the members' candidates was to be their champion bore.

The instant the vote was taken the team leader had to rush the name of their champion to Ion Villiers-Stuart, who had agreed to be Master of Ceremonies. Speed was essential, as it was likely that a well known bore would be chosen by more than one team. This rule proved essential as in the first instance all three teams tried to register the same person.

Finding that that individual had already been booked the two slower teams had to go back and think again.

It must have been a wonderful experience for the unwitting champions. Never had they been in such social demand. Their telephones seldom stopped ringing. Hitherto aloof hostesses almost burst into tears when they were told 'I'm sorry I can't come that night, I've just accepted another invitation. What about next week?'

When the innocent candidates got to the parties people crowded round them urging them to talk and to '*please* tell once again that marvellous story of your Great-Uncle Toby's taste in food.' They couldn't even sit on a chair without two people kneeling down on either side of them and listening with rapt attention to their conversation.

Eventually all three teams settled on their champions. Team A chose Mrs Y., a childless widow, who owned a medium-sized Victorian castle. She had fluffy hair and owned a very small dog that she doted on, which was locally known as 'Maisie's rat'. She also had complete confidence in the universal appeal of her domestic problems. Although she herself did not ride she moved with the hunting set and was to be seen at every meet, offering dry nasty sandwiches to the riders. She knew they were nasty, and said so as she offered them, blaming, in her whining voice, her cook. Mrs Y. always alluded to the native Irish as 'Them', and seemed to occupy most of her time in a war of attrition with her servants whom she changed constantly. Every skirmish and encounter of this never-ending battle she would recount in detail.

Team B's champion was Colonel M., a tall stooping man with pale blue eyes, a kindly disposition and total recall of all his fishing exploits, which were protracted and innumerable.

Sir W.A. represented Team C. He was bald, arrogant and rotund and formerly in the administration of a very small island dependency of the British Empire, the knowledge of which, he considered, permitted him to lecture all within range about international affairs. His only source of information was the *Cork Examiner*, a local paper not noted for its coverage of foreign news. Despite this, Sir W.A. had only to overhear some remark about foreign politics and he would snort with contempt, and in a lecturing voice state what the situation *really* was and what the Government should do about it. He went on for hours, illustrating his talk with reminiscences of his tiny island.

Those invited to the final dinner held at Dromana were the three teams, their champions and five judges who had been summoned from far away.

Also present were a number of punters who had laid heavy bets on who would be declared Supreme Bore.

Dinner was good, and the wine flowed but despite this the atmosphere was hardly convivial. It tingled with suppressed tension. Under the indifferent eyes of the Villiers-Stuart ancestors whose portraits ringed the dining-room walls, the guests sat rigid with nerves and anticipation. The butler who had overheard us planning the tournament had plunged heavily on Mrs Y. with the result that his shaking hand spilled wine on her and the linen tablecloth.

Only the bores, ignorant of their role in the proceedings, ploughed remorselessly on with their monologues. The fifteen team members paid no attention whatever to their dinner partners, but tried to listen to their champions across the table and muttered encouragement under their breaths.

Colonel M. was saying 'You know that clump of reeds just below Ballyduff, not the ones near the beech trees, the ones lower down by the blackthorn bushes, no, I am telling a lie, it wasn't those reeds at all, but the ones about a hundred yards downstream on the left. I saw this fish was heading for them, so I reeled in a bit, not too much, just a bit, and then he made a run for those rocks near the ruined cottage, the cottage that used to belong to old Twomey – no, not Twomey, O'Brien and then I . . .'

At the other end of the room Mrs Y.'s piercing voice could be heard squeaking with indignation. 'I told her, I know there was more than half that joint of beef left after Sunday, and now look at it! There is not even enough on the plate for my darling little doggie's dinner. You've been eating it in the kitchen.'

The judges had a terrible time making up their minds. They were dead locked between Colonel M., who had risen to the occasion by telling all three judges the same immense and detailed saga of the salmon he had failed to land, and Mrs Y., who had excelled herself with an impassioned speech on the impossibility of getting honest, properly trained servants these days.

Finally the judges had to be locked into a reputedly haunted room, refused all drink, and told they would be released only after a unanimous decision.

In the end Mrs Y. was the winner, and she was declared Supreme Bore.

The social success of the unknowing competitors did not end with the finals. The bores continued to be asked out so that they could display their prowess, and people continued to hang on their words, so that later, in private, they could discuss endlessly whether the judges had been right or whether, shameful thought, they had been nobbled.

St Patrick's Day 1930 drew near and with it my sixteenth birthday.

The 17th of March is traditionally the last day of the hunting season, though there are usually a few 'bye' days after it, and I had been invited to stay at Dromana for a hunt and for a party that Elspeth was giving for me afterwards.

On 15 March I set off happily on Cuchullain to ride the eighteen miles up river to Dromana. No shade of apprehension crossed my mind: I was looking forward to a wonderful time. On St Patrick's Day the sun shone for my birthday. Being a public holiday, there was the usual large crowd at the village where the meet was held. The fiddlers played in the street, the pubs were filled to bursting point with country people.

At noon the hounds moved to the first cover, a steep rocky glen. St Stephen's Day and St Patrick's Day, both being bank holidays, were usually very bad days from a purely hunting point of view. There were simply too many people out – people on anything with four legs, from a donkey to a carthorse, and hundreds of foot-followers, heading the fox and getting in the way of the huntsman and the hounds. But on this day we were not impeded. Hounds found at once, went streaming over the top of the glen towards a lovely stretch to country and we flew after them, Cuchullain covering the short grass with his long strides and jumping superbly. I was totally exhilarated, so much so that I completely lost my sense of judgement. I was riding a good horse but he was barely three years old, and young horses haven't the stamina of more mature ones.

I felt Cuchullain beginning to tire and instead of easing him off, I urged him on. Finally we headed for a high narrow stone bank at top speed; he just didn't rise enough to it, but hit the bank just above his knees, turned a complete somersault in the air and landed on the far side on his back, with me underneath him.

And that was the end of the way of life that I had enjoyed up to then.

CHAPTER 4

Among the Arabs

My injuries were far worse than they at first appeared – in fact, I got to my feet and asked a friend to catch my horse, Cuchullain having risen and galloped after the hunt. Then I collapsed and was carried on a gate by some farmers back to Dromana, where the local doctor was sent for. He said that there was nothing much to worry about. He thought that I had broken my collar-bone and possibly a few ribs and torn some muscles. He advised bed-rest and quiet, then he went away. I just lay there dazed and unable to move. I continued to lie there on my back, looking up at the ceiling which was painted bright mauve. I could move my legs so I knew my back was not broken, but any other movement was agony.

Stella Annesley came racing up from Myrtle Grove, took one look at me and sent a cable to my mother who was visiting South America, telling her of the accident and urging her to come home immediately. And so, as I could not be moved, I stayed on, lying on my back, in that vast bedroom at Dromana. I was the original 'Man who came to Dinner': I had been invited for a weekend, and now the Villiers-Stuarts were landed with me.

They were extremely nice about it. Elspeth came constantly and sat by my bed, chatting to me, and Ion used to come up after hunting, in his muddy pink coat, and give me a round-by-round account of the day's sport.

One evening Elspeth came up and said, rather tactlessly, 'My poor child, I can't bear to think of you, lying up here by yourself – when we are all having such fun downstairs.'

'That's all right,' I replied and petulantly added, 'I do get tired of looking at that ceiling all day. If only it wasn't bright mauve.'

Next day several workmen invaded my room. They covered me and my bed entirely with a large sheet and then made a great many bumping and dragging noises as they brought in ladders and planks.

When they removed the sheet the mauve on the ceiling had been replaced by a particularly gloomy mustardy gold. After that I learned to keep my complaints to myself.

Dromana was a magical place, set high on a cliff over the river Blackwater and surrounded by beautiful ancient woods. It was enormous, almost as big as Buckingham Palace. It had a circular ballroom where once I went to a party attended by 300 guests, which was considered a flop because, as the host put it, 'they looked like a few flies in Waterloo station'.

The original castle, built by the Fitzgeralds in the thirteenth century, formed the base, and was built into the side of the cliff. When that was destroyed after being besieged by English troops in the first Desmond Rebellion, and the Great Earl of Desmond executed, it remained a ruin. Later the family built a large and charming manor house on the terrace formed by the truncated top of the castle and the rising ground. Not content with that in the eighteenth century, at the height of the land boom, the enormous Georgian wings were added round a small courtyard dwarfing and hiding the original seventeenth-century building. Now time has almost run full circle. Dry rot, that principal enemy of Irish country houses, set in and the eighteenth-century part of the house has had to be pulled down. The walls of that beautiful round ballroom form part of the terrace in front of the carved stone entrance of the manor house, imprisoned for so long in its dark courtyard, and the room that I lay in, with its mustard-gold ceiling, is no more.

The whole place, with its history of bloodshed and massacre, had a great reputation for being haunted and I have met many who declared that they had seen apparitions there – particularly an eighteenth-century Lord Barrymore, ancestor of another local family, who shot himself in the card-room at dawn, after gambling all night and losing his entire fortune and estates. However, his fellow gambler must not have claimed his winnings, as the descendants of Lord Barrymore still lived at their old home when I was young.

I personally never saw or heard anything supernatural but I must admit that, despite its beauty, the whole place did have a rather sinister atmosphere. I used to wonder what I would do if a ghost walked into my room but as it was obvious that I could do nothing, being immobile,

I used to comfort myself with the thought that at least it would be a very interesting experience.

After what seemed a long time – there being, of course, no transatlantic airplanes in those days – my mother came home.

She immediately sent for an ambulance and I was taken to a convent hospital in Cork. There I was at last X-rayed and it was discovered that almost the only bone I had not broken was my collar-bone. As all the other bones had now begun to set in the wrong position, I had to have an operation where they were re-broken and re-set and a small portion of my shoulder joint replaced with silver.

I was strapped into an iron frame and left to the care of the good Bon Secours nuns. My mother nobly drove herself in her ancient Ford the sixty-two miles to Cork and back every day to read to me, as in my position I could not read to myself. She read the entire works of Anthony Trollope. I am sure she felt guilty that she had paid so little attention to Mrs O'Brien's timely warning.

I spent the rest of the time talking to the nuns. There seemed to be plenty of them, so they could often come in for a chat with me. Most of them were perfectly happy in their vocation, but one little nun, who had taken her vows at seventeen, was like a linnet in a cage. She was forever asking me about life in the world outside. Coming from a small farm inland, she had rarely seen the sea and was fascinated by it and all the creatures that live in it, particularly the molluscs. So I got my mother to give some books on marine biology to the hospital library with the hope that the little nun would get the chance to look at them. I can still see in my mind's eye her eager face as she leaned over me, discussing clams and winkles. If she is still alive she must be a very old woman, and I hope so much that in the end her life turned out to be a full and happy one.

The situation of Sister Philomena, as the little nun was called, was not unusual in the 1920s and 1930s. There was a large surplus of women due to the mass emigration of young men. There were few restrictions on going to America, as the 'Irish quota' was so large and many of the boys went there, as well as to England. America had the advantage that so many Irishmen had emigrated there in earlier days that nearly every family had a relative already established in the U.S.A. and ready to help the new immigrant.

As a result, many devout young girls, particularly from small remote farms, were easily persuaded that they had a vocation when in reality they had not. Having little prospect of marriage they shut themselves away from the world before they had seen anything of it. Once having taken their vows, it was in those days almost impossible to leave the convent and, in any case, where could they go? Their families were unlikely to be willing to take them back, and there was little hope of employment for untrained ex-nuns.

When I got back home to Youghal I was very weak and depressed. I didn't want to go to London with the rest of the family and I looked forward gloomily to the coming wet, dark winter with no hunting and no transport, as I had been forbidden to ride by the hospital doctors. I should seldom see my friends and when I did, I should feel thoroughly out of it. Worst of all, I felt the accident had been entirely my own fault.

Then my parents made a rather odd decision. They thought I needed a holiday in the sun, so they decided to send me to Biskra, in southern Algeria, accompanied only by a young lady's-maid called Sheelagh, who had never been out of Ireland before. I was to stay at a hotel and rest, taking only a little 'walking exercise'. They had been to Biskra the year before and knew that the climate was good and the hotel comfortable. I was excited by the prospect but apprehensive, and Sheelagh was frankly terrified.

Wondering if we should ever get there, we set off by boat and train to London, then by train and boat to Algeria. Despite my abominable French, we somehow managed to avoid getting ourselves lost and arrived at the oasis after four days. For the first time I felt I was really 'abroad'. Biskra is situated on the edge of the Sahara desert. Behind it rise the Atlas Mountains, once the bread basket of the Roman Empire but now stark and barren. To reach Biskra we had come through the gorge of El Kantara, known as the 'Gateway to the Desert', and I found it all wildly exciting.

At that time, mass tourism had not yet arrived. There *were* a few tourists around, hence the existence of my comfortable hotel, but not enough to spoil the view, and certainly not enough to affect the economy of the place. The things for sale in the bazaar reflected the tastes of the local Arab population and the life that one saw in the narrow mud-walled streets had remained unchanged for generations, or at any rate since the French conquest of Algeria.

There was practically no wheeled traffic, as Biskra is nearly surrounded by that area of the Sahara which is composed of sand dunes only passable by vehicles with caterpillar tracks – few of which were available, all owned by the French army. Most goods were transported by camels or, around the oasis, in panniers carried on the backs of donkeys.

Altogether I was enchanted with the place, and my depression soon lifted. In the evenings I used to go up onto the flat roof of the hotel and look at the stars which were so much brighter than in Ireland as there was no moisture in the atmosphere to dim them, and listen to the mullah calling from the local mosque. I remember I used to recite Fitzgerald's *Rubaiyat of Omar Khayyám* to myself, a delightful occupation for a romantic and unsophisticated sixteen-year-old.

As my strength began to return, I got bored and longed for some companions of my own age. The other guests at the hotel were mostly middle-aged women from England and America who had come to Biskra to avoid the cold northern winter and because they had seen Rudolph Valentino in *The Sheik* or read *The Garden of Allah*, a current best-seller.

Sheelagh was no use to me. She had practically no conversation, and in any case she had quite got over her fear of foreign lands and got off with an Arab guide, so I saw little of her.

There was nothing to do, except wander about in the Arab village among the crowds of busy workmen and veiled women, or sit in a deck chair in the hotel courtyard and read.

I had only brought two books with me – Herodotus' *Travels* and a book of crossword puzzles. I loved and still love Herodotus, but I had read it before and the crossword puzzles proved too easy and I had soon solved them all.

One morning I got up and decided that I simply could not spend the whole winter doing nothing and so I decided to break one of the three instructions that had been drummed into me before I left home, *viz*.

That I must not spend the money I had been given all at once, but must make it last till the end of March.

That I must not speak to strange men.

That I must not get on a horse.

It was the last of these that was going to be ignored. It wasn't difficult to do so. Most Arabs in Biskra were extremely poor, and practically everything in the oasis was for sale or hire.

I asked Sheelagh's guide to find me a steed and next day he arrived with one, complete with a red leather Arab saddle and bridle. He had bought a black stallion, rather thin, but looking in better condition than any of the horses I had so far seen around Biskra. The animal had rather a nasty look in his eye and his ears back, but I didn't mind that – I had ridden lots of difficult horses before, so up I got. The horse stood straight up on his hind legs and then took off like a shooting star. I couldn't even begin to stop him. The savage Eastern curb bit had no chain behind the horse's jaw. I learned later that the guide had borrowed the stallion from his brother who was a groom in an Arab chief's racing stable – who had lent the beast without the knowledge of its owner.

On we flew, scattering the local population and knocking things over, into the military parade ground where a regiment of Spahis was drawn up for inspection. We went through them like a bullet, and out of the village into the date-palm groves. Biskra is a large oasis, about four miles across, but we were soon nearing its south-eastern edge. Luckily the horse wasn't very fit, and he began to tire. Gradually I got control, and I managed to stop him in front of the gates of a beautiful little house that I had not seen before.

I got off and leaned against a palm tree, almost fainting with exhaustion, and then sat on the ground.

An Arab came out of the house, said something I couldn't understand, and then led my horse away. He was followed by two Europeans, a girl about my own age and an older woman. They helped me into their house and started asking me questions.

By an extraordinary piece of luck, my whirlwind ride had ended at Bab-el-M'Cid, the home of Clare Sheridan. When she learned who I was and why I had landed up in her front garden in such a state of collapse, she was most sympathetic.

It turned out that she knew my family and was surprised that they had not warned her of my arrival. Later, when I learned more about her and her present set-up, I could guess why they had not done so.

Clare and her daughter Margaret chided me about the stupidity of climbing onto an unknown horse when I was still only convalescent, but quite understood the frustration that had led me to do so.

'Of course, you must leave the company of those dreary 'blue-hairs' at once and come and stay here. I will tell Ali to go to the hotel, have them pack up your things and bring them here. It's all settled.'

Thanking them very much for their kindness, I protested that there was the problem of Sheelagh. I was already a bit worried about her and her guide, fearing dire consequences for which I, in some way, would be blamed. Could I leave her alone at the hotel?

Clare dismissed the objection, waved her hands and said she would deal with everything. And so I moved into Bab-el-M'Cid.

Clare Sheridan was a very remarkable woman. She wrote her autobiography at least a couple of times and her cousin, Anita Leslie, has written her biography. What she told me of her past certainly did not appear in *Nuda Veritas*, her first autobiography, except perhaps by implication. She was half-American, her mother being one of the three beautiful Jerome sisters – the other two being Jenny, Lady Randolph Churchill, mother of Winston Churchill, and Leone, Lady Leslie, mother of Shane Leslie. So she was brought up in the company of the rich and famous.

Clare married Wilfred Sheridan, a descendant of Richard Brinsley Sheridan, the Irish eighteenth-century playwright, just before the First World War. He was killed in that slaughter, and she was left with three children and practically no money to bring them up with. As well as being extremely beautiful, she was enterprising and determined, and decided to earn her own living. In the class and circles in which she lived this was practically unheard of at the time and no girl was educated with any sort of career in view. They were laboriously trained for marriage and how to behave in high society and the intricacies of managing their households and servants. These lessons did not include the art of cooking.

Clare was very artistic. She was brilliant at interior decorating, painted well, and was an exceptionally good sculptor. She decided to make her way in portrait sculpting – not, unless you reach the very top, a lucrative profession.

Right at the start she had a lucky break – though perhaps lucky is the wrong word – thanks to her own unconventionality and enterprise. She was invited to Russia, just after the Revolution, to sculpt the heads of the new Soviet leaders, including Lenin. To the horror of her friends and relations, she accepted the commission.

While in Russia she had an affair with Trotsky, who loaded her with wonderful Russian sables and other gifts, to the extreme annoyance of the then Mrs Trotsky who, Clare told me, once publicly slapped her face. The portrait busts finished, she returned triumphantly to London, only disgusted by the fact that the Russian frontier guards confiscated all Trotsky's gifts, including the sable coat which she was wearing. So she arrived home shivering, to discover that she was completely ostracised. The horrors of the Russian Revolution, mostly committed against their own class, were still fresh in these people's minds. None of her former circle would have anything to do with her. She had been consorting with the Devil. No rich and influential friends meant no commissions. What was she to do?

What she did was to go to the U.S.A., where she began her most profitable career. She became what I can only describe, for want of a better word, as possibly the last of the eighteenth- and nineteenth-century courtesans. She once gave me an almost complete list of her lovers, but I have long forgotten both their names and their sequence, remembering only that they included Barney Baruch and Charlie Chaplin, and that they were all either multi-millionaires or politically powerful. She did not confine her activities to the U.S.A. but at various times lived in different European countries.

Quite soon she seems to have become a status symbol in her own right. To be seen with her proved that you had finally reached the top.

One of her advantages to the powerful men she consorted with must have been the fact she was totally unpolitical, and therefore most unlikely to indulge in intrigues on her own account. In some ways she was very innocent, as was shown by her surprise at her reception in London after her return from Russia. I often asked her about the historical figures she had known and the situation in the countries where she had lived, usually at the centres of power. Her answers were always benign and unenlightening. It may have been discretion, but I don't think so. She wasn't discreet about anything else.

Once, after reading a life of Kemal Ataturk, the ruthless creator of modern Turkey, known as the Grey Wolf, and remembering that she had lived in a palace on the Bosporus with one of his principal ministers, I asked her, 'Did you ever meet Mustapha Kemal?'

'Oh yes, I knew him quite well.'

'What was he really like?'

A smile of remembrance lighted up her face. 'You know, Patricia, he was such a dear.'

I never asked if she had known Stalin when she was in Russia. If she had, I wondered if she would have found him equally endearing.

When I first knew her she was still beautiful but getting stout. She must have weighed about thirteen stone, but that was no disadvantage as her current 'friend' was the Aga Ali Ben Gana, regent and brother of the Bash Aga, who in theory ruled that part of Southern Algeria under the French, and Arabs are well known to dislike thin women. She was very tall and so carried her weight well. With her warm smile and lively conversation, she was a delight to be with.

She had two children, Margaret, the eldest of the family, two years older than myself, and Dick, who was away in England being educated. Her second daughter, Elizabeth, had died in early childhood.

Margaret and I hit it off instantly and soon became devoted friends. She was very different from her mother, both in looks and character, and they were often at loggerheads. This was partly due to Margaret's jealousy of her brother Dick, who was obviously very much his mother's favourite, and partly due to the usual teenage rebellion against the previous generation's values. In Margaret's case this took the form of being much more conventional than Clare, despite her unconventional upbringing, and her inquiring and analytical mind. Like myself, she had had little formal education, but unlike myself she had a natural talent for languages and spoke perfect French and fluent Arabic.

The household at Bab-el-M'Cid consisted of Ali-the-Gardener and Ali-the-Cook. They ran the house assisted by an army of small boys, most apparently also called Ali, who came and went and whom I never did succeed in getting sorted out. We lived entirely on Arab food which, when well cooked, can be delicious, and Ali was a very good cook.

Of course there were no Arab women about. They were still strictly enclosed and did no work. One saw plenty of them in the streets, totally enveloped in a *hiak*, a large white sheet which they wound round themselves and over their heads, leaving only one eye visible. All looked like a Victorian illustration of a ghost. This humiliating and ridiculous disguise did have some advantages, since nobody could recognise you and know what you were doing. Margaret and I would sometimes put on *hiaks* when we did not want anyone in the village to know where we were going, though I could never really manage mine and tripped over it as I walked or couldn't see properly and bumped into things.

A constant visitor to the house was, of course, the regent, Ali Ben Gana and his many male friends, who were also his relations. The Islamic inheritance laws as interpreted in Algeria at that time were not unfavourable to women, in that a daughter had a right to her share of her family's fortune. This law had a disastrous result. As all marriages were arranged between parents – the bride never seeing her husband until after the ceremony – the only way to keep an extended family's fortune intact was for everybody to marry their first cousins. After a few generations the propertied class became as interbred as rabbits or the European royal families. Hereditary insanity was common. Those afflicted were locked away but well treated, as Moslems regarded them as being 'touched by God'.

I never saw an Arab in European clothes while I was in Biskra. Ali-the-Regent was magnificent in his traditional robes. He was taller than most of his relations, who tended to be small. He always wore a scarlet burnous embroidered with gold thread, a loose white cotton shirt, baggy trousers tucked into red leather riding boots, and an enormous white turban, which I never saw him remove. A burnous is a long, finely woven, woollen cloak with a hood hanging down at the back. The scarlet and gold ones were the prerogative of the Ben Gana extended family, and though there was no law forbidding its being worn by anyone not related, it would have been an unthinkable and highly dangerous thing to do so.

With his white skin, jet black beard and rather hawk-like features, he looked like an illustration from the *Arabian Nights*, and the middle-aged ladies at the hotel must have nearly fainted in ecstasy when they saw him passing by. Most of the senior men of the Ben Gana family, including the regent, had been educated in France and, like the nobility in Russia before the Revolution, seemed to talk French among themselves. None of their women, though, could speak anything but Arabic.

Ali-the-Regent had acquired some progressive ideas from his French education, one of which was the desirability of unveiling Arab women. He said he felt that the community would never prosper until then, but he also felt that it could not be done without more general approval among the people. I was surprised to hear that much of the strongest opposition came not just from the mullahs, but from the women themselves. Ali suggested that Margaret and I should visit the harems of his family and try and persuade their wives, mothers and sisters to discard the veil and to be seen to be doing so. Fashion and the desire for upward social mobility being as strong among Arabs as it is among other races, he felt that once the relatives of the Aga were seen walking about freely, it might be the thin edge of the wedge of the women's liberation.

Margaret and I had already visited the regent's home several times. It was a large rectangular building without windows standing just outside the town. The walls were whitewashed and it looked like an enormous, very skilfully made iced Christmas cake, with the elaborate decorations which topped the three-foot wall surrounding its flat roof resembling frosting. It was built on the side of a small hill or mound, and wide steps led up to the great wooden entrance gates. On these steps were always sitting or lying about forty guards. They were ferocious-looking men, wrapped in raggedy brown burnouses and carrying very long antique rifles. From a distance they looked like a collection of rubbish sacks with sticks poking out of them, which someone had thoughtlessly scattered around.

Inside the palace there was a series of courtyards, deeply colonnaded. The first was the public court where petitioners came to see the ruler about their troubles. It was undecorated and unfurnished and was always crowded with elderly men, some harassed-looking, but many quietly sleeping, bundled up on the floor. I often saw the same people there day after day and wondered if they had decided to live in this comparatively cool, comfortable and sociable place.

Through a small door at its far end one entered the second court, that of the numerous servants and attendants; and beyond that, through a gate guarded by a sentry who was usually asleep, was the court where

Ali lived, with some unmarried male members of his family. The back walls of this court were completely covered with beautiful blue and green tiles, as was the floor under the colonnades. The centre, open to the sky was, like all the other courts, of beaten earth which had dried hard like cement.

Round the walls were saddlebags, some covered with carpets, some with hand-woven material patterned with gold and silver thread, and many low, round tables. Round the walls, doorways opened into rooms which were very dark, as there were no windows – the only light came through the doorways under the colonnades. At the back of these rooms, little stairways led up onto the flat roof.

The women's court was designed and furnished in the same way and only differed because it was larger and also because at some point someone had tried to make a flowerbed in the middle and planted some orange and pomegranate trees; but as nobody bothered to water them, they were nearly all dead or dying.

There never seemed to be anyone in the regent's court except an occasional servant flitting through and the guard on the gate to the women's apartments, who was a very old man with a long white beard, dressed in what looked like a white nightgown reaching to the ground. He was very grave and gentle looking and he always bowed every time we went in or out.

In contrast to Ali's court, the harem was a hive of activity. Women servitors – in reality slaves, though nobody called them that – and small boys were everywhere and seemed to be in constant motion. Ali had two wives – Miza his chief wife, who in the Ottoman Empire would have been called the Sultana, and Ziada, both of them good-tempered and seeming to live in perfect amity. Miza looked quite middle-aged though she was probably in her thirties, and was immensely fat. Ziada was young, about the same age as Margaret and myself, and also rather plump. She was naturally dark but had dyed her hair a brassy yellow with peroxide. She was always giggling and seemed to get a good deal of fun out of life.

They were at all times carefully and beautifully dressed in traditional Arab costume, which would make even the plainest woman look magnificent. This consisted of an underdress of gauze, heavily embroidered in bright coloured silk with an 'all over' pattern. This underdress had very full, long sleeves caught at the wrist with band of silk. Over it they wore a sleeveless dress of silk damask, woven with a pattern of gold or silver thread. It was trimmed at the neck and arm-holes with gold braid. Both wore a great deal of jewellery – several necklaces of gold filigree and ropes of semi-precious stones, at least five bracelets on each arm and several rings on their fingers. They had anklets on their legs which jangled when they walked.

Their heads were covered with a small turban of fine silk around which was fastened a linked gold crown with little ornaments dangling from the edge. These crowns were the prerogative of the wives of the ruler and the regent and no other women were allowed to wear them. Being gold, they were heavy and uncomfortable, and Miza and Ziada were constantly taking them off and putting them on again.

They were both heavily made up in a formalistic way. The eyebrows were darkened with kohl and joined across the bridge of their noses by a thick dark line. They used white powder all over their faces and necks and had three black dots on their foreheads and sometimes a little cross. The palms of their hands and the soles of their feet were stained with henna. I never saw them wear any shoes or slippers.

All day long they sat side by side on their saddlebags, drinking mint tea and nibbling little sweet cakes. In the evening they would go up onto the roof and walk about a little.

I soon discovered what all the women and small boys were so busy about. Miza maintained an intelligence system that would have done credit to the C.I.A. Not a thing happened in Biskra that her spies did not report instantly to her. The women in their *hiaks* and the small boys went everywhere, and no detail was too small to escape their attention.

My escapade with the black stallion had been prime news, and Miza and Ziada were probably discussing it at the same time that I was explaining myself to Clare and Margaret. Miza told me where the stallion had come from and what the owner had said to the groom when he discovered what had become of his horse.

Both Miza and Ziada were illiterate. If they had been able to read, I am sure that they would have been avid readers of gossip columns and the more sensational women's magazines.

Our mission to liberate the women of Biskra got exactly nowhere.

'You know, there is absolutely nothing in the Koran which says that women should be veiled in public.'

This remark was greeted in silence.

'Wouldn't you like to go about freely as we do?'

'No, why should we?'

'You could go to the bazaar and choose what you wanted to buy.'

'If we want anything, we just send word to the merchant to send his goods here. We can then sit in comfort and have them brought here before us.'

'You could go to the edge of the oasis and look across the Great Desert.'

'Why should we want to do that, there is absolutely nothing in the Desert.'

As a last desperate throw, Margaret said, 'You could visit your friends and relations.'

There was a slightly awkward pause and then they both said in unison, 'No.'

Actually, there was nothing to prevent them, suitably veiled, from visiting any of the women's courts in Biskra, but they never did. The reason was that being a guest in someone else's home was regarded as putting oneself in a 'down one' position, and neither of them could stand that.

So they never left their home, except very occasionally to visit the women's court of some bridegroom's house on the occasion of a grand wedding.

There they had lived, year after year, encompassed by four walls and only seeing the wide sky during their little evening strolls on the roof, and they seemed quite content with their lot. I found it incredible. There was no use going on about it; their minds were obviously made up and nothing would persuade them to change.

It turned out that Ali Ben Gana's liberal ideas about his wives were ambiguous to say the least.

Once, we thought it would be amusing for Margaret and I to dress up in Arab clothes. Ziada volunteered to have one of her dresses taken in to fit me and to get out some of her best jewels. Next day we arrived, bringing cameras, and hours were spent braiding our hair, making up our faces and dressing us up. Then we went up onto the roof to take photographs.

We were having a great deal of fun in a schoolgirlish sort of way when suddenly the regent stormed in. He was very angry and started to abuse us violently in Arabic – an excellent language for cursing in. It seems that someone had come running to him to say that the ladies of his house were cavorting on his roof, unveiled and entirely visible from the ground below. He had said that it was probably only the European girls. 'No,' said his informant, 'they were in Arab dress and the sun could be seen shining on their gold crowns.' He had come back at once to see what was going on.

His tirade was directed at the other three. I got off with a scowl, as I was the youngest and therefore deemed irresponsible, and also because he knew I couldn't understand Arabic.

Margaret only translated his final words – that we were to get back into our own clothes immediately, leave his house, and not return. This we did, not even being allowed to say goodbye to a tearful Miza and Ziada. The ban was lifted, however, as soon as Ali recovered his temper.

Of course, this acquiescent attitude to the purdah was not reflected in the minds of many of the younger and poorer women in the community, though a great many had been persuaded that it was the will of Allah, and as good Moslems they must accept their lot.

The full horror of their situation was brought home to me when we visited Sheriffa, wife of Ali-the-Gardener. Here there were no airy courtyards, but three hot, dark, box-like rooms, the noise from the narrow, mud-walled street echoing through them. Sheriffa sat all day, fanning away the millions of flies that were trying to settle on her baby's face. She could not go out in her *hiak* as there was no one to leave the baby with. A small boy did her marketing and fetched water for her. She had Turkish blood and unlike the grand ladies, could read and write. She very occasionally got letters from distant female relatives in Turkey telling her of the emancipated life they led. This always reduced her to floods of tears.

One of the worst effects of this Moslem culture was the total lack of medical services for these women. If the family was rich, a female French doctor could be engaged and brought from Algiers, but there was none resident in Biskra and many women suffered and died, particularly in childbirth. Thank God these conditions, at least in Algeria, are a thing of the past, or so I am told. But in many Moslem countries they still exist, and in an even worse form. At least the women I knew in Algeria did not have to do all the work, including building the mud houses, as for instance, they would be forced to do in Afghanistan. In a refugee camp in Pakistan, the other day, an Afghan man said to an American woman journalist, who protested at the heavy work his wife was doing, 'I paid a lot for her and I'm going to get my money's worth.'

So the winter came and went, as did my seventeenth birthday. I had a close-up view of small-town Algerian Moslem life. I had made a great friend in Margaret. My mind had been broadened by conversations with Clare, and I had fully recovered my health. Now it was time to go back to my family to be 'presented at court', and 'come out' as a debutante in London.

CHAPTER 5

Grown up and Brought out

I have read several books of memoirs by ex-debutantes about the London Season in the early thirties. Few of them seem to have enjoyed their 'coming out' as it was called, and the ones that did look back in an almost reverentially uncritical way, regretting only how times have changed. I personally had a very good time and found all the ramifications of the labyrinthine etiquette interesting and amusing. On the whole I was a successful 'deb' despite my unconventional upbringing, or perhaps because of it. Practically all the other girls had been to boarding schools in England and then to 'finishing schools' in Paris or Lausanne and consequently all knew each other, which put me at a disadvantage to begin with. But this was soon nullified as the 'Young Entry' met practically every day and I speedily got to know most of the brighter ones.

The season in London in the Thirties was the last flourish of the Social Life, centred round the court of Imperial Britain. Modern times and economic and political realities were creeping in round the edges; the rainstorm of the social revolution was on the horizon but so far only a few drops of water were falling.

As far as the young girls were concerned, the whole operation was a marriage market, and a very expensive one for their parents. Each debutante had to have a coming out ball given for her. This took place in the home of her parents. It was considered very inferior to hold it in one of the big hotels, like the Ritz or the Berkeley. As all the big houses in Belgrave Square, Eaton Square and the streets nearby were still in private hands and had not yet been divided into flats; and as all contained ballrooms, this presented no difficulty. Those families who did not own large London houses rented one for the Season.

As well as a coming out ball, each girl had to be presented to the king and queen at Buckingham Palace by a lady who, in her turn, had previously been presented to the sovereign. This ceremony was ringed around with tradition and elaborate etiquette. It was a wonderful sight which I am very glad not to have missed. The majority of girls were presented by their mothers, but by the early thirties the realities of life were already taking a hold on London Society. For instance, it was well known that some impoverished peeresses made a very good living by 'bringing out' the daughters of big, newly rich, commercial families and presenting them at Court. If it had been proved that they had taken money for this service, they would have been banned from doing so in the future and also excluded from the Royal Enclosure at Ascot, but it was very much an open secret that they made a profession of it. I believe that their charges were high and business was good.

For the actual presentation, the obligatory court dress for women was full evening dress and a long train hanging from the shoulders, about two feet of which dragged on the ground. On one's head one wore three ostrich feathers with about eighteen inches of gathered white tulle hanging from it at the back. It was also compulsory to wear long white kid gloves coming up above the elbow. The debutantes all wore white dresses and carried either a bouquet of flowers or a large ostrich feather fan, as I did. They did not wear jewellery other than one small pearl necklace, but their mothers, who could wear any coloured dress they liked, were ablaze with diamond tiaras, necklaces, bracelets and rings. The men – who could, if they wished, accompany their families – wore a uniform if they were entitled to it, and if not, white tie and tails and any decorations they might happen to have.

When these formal presentation ceremonies were abandoned after the Second World War as being undemocratic, it was a disaster for the ostrich farms in Africa. Half their custom was gone at the stroke of a pen.

As can be imagined, a great deal of preparation had to go into the job of presenting a debutante at court. First the designers for the dresses of mother and daughter had to be approved and the material chosen and then made up by the selected fashion house; they were never, never, bought 'ready made'. Then the girl had to be put through a rigorous course of training on how to walk five steps forward, make a deep curtsey to the king, two steps, a deep curtsey to the queen, another two steps and another curtsey to any other member of the royal family who happened to be there to view the Young Entry – and then walk out five steps backwards so as to avoid turning her back on the royals. This may sound easy, but it wasn't. To do this manoeuvre gracefully, wearing very high-heeled evening shoes and a ground-length dress, requires the suppleness and balancing ability of a circus performer. The trickiest bit was not falling over one's train or getting it wound round one's legs when walking out backwards. I practised it endlessly, using a large bathtowel as a train and managed all right when I was finally 'on stage', but I was very sorry for some of the more disorganised, less athletic girls who stumbled, got tangled up and turned bright pink with embarrassment while the nastier debutantes sitting in serried rows on either side of them giggled audibly.

One of the traditions of Presentation Day was that though the invitation card commanded that one should be at Buckingham Palace at 8 p.m., one had to arrive at 6 p.m. and park outside the gates. So from 6 to 8 a long line of black (it wasn't good form to have any other colour) chauffeur-driven limousines stretched from the palace right down the Mall to Admiralty Arch. One sat there for two hours keeping still and looking straight ahead in a dignified manner while large crowds milled along the sidewalk, peering in through the windows and making loud comments on the occupants. Outstandingly pretty girls or particularly magnificent jewels caused a crush and a traffic jam among the pedestrians on the pavement.

All this took place in 1931, at the height of the Great Depression. All these onlookers must have been suffering in some way. Many were certainly unemployed and were trying to keep their families on the miserably small unemployment dole of those days. The extraordinary thing was that they were such a good-humoured crowd. I didn't hear a single hostile comment on that conspicuous display of wealth. The diamonds, the orchids and the shiny Rolls-Royces and their indifferent-looking owners only seemed to evoke their admiration. The people were out to see a show, and enjoying it thoroughly.

Inside our car we were having a rather uncomfortable time. Both my parents were in a vile temper, my father because he was wearing the dress uniform of a major of the Scots Guards and he hadn't bought a new uniform since his retirement from the army, so the tunic was consequently extremely tight. It was also hot and stuffy in the car with the windows on the pavement side shut. My mother was annoyed because Daddy had announced earlier that as we should not get supper at Buckingham Palace until after the last debutante had been presented, he would get hungry – so he had brought sandwiches which, as he had nowhere else to put them, he had put in his bearskin helmet (never to be called a busby). Due to the heat, the lavish amount of butter in the sandwiches had melted, soaking his bearskin and was spreading everywhere. Mummy was terrified it would get on her, or my, dress. There she sat in her diamond tiara, trying to look calm and benign and muttering under her breath, 'Jack, Jack, how *could* you, I shall never forgive you.'

Then there was a major disturbance. A small open car drew up alongside us. At the wheel was my brother Bernard, who was a sub-lieutenant in the Navy, and with him were six of his shipmates. They all had long toasting-forks, on the end of which they had impaled buns. These they tried to thrust into the open window of our car. As we furiously wound the windows up I heard Bernard say, 'It seems they don't eat buns, let's try them with some peanuts and bananas.'

The crowd loved it. They cheered and whooped. So for the last half hour we sat there sweltering, as now all the windows were tight shut.

A debutante's life was a busy one. There were girls' lunches almost every day. These were organised by the debs themselves and took place in the restaurant of a big hotel – the smart one being the Berkeley, though one could go to the Ritz without loss of status. Usually it was a table for four. To be seen with only one other girl laid one open to the suspicion that one was plotting something. In the afternoon there were dress fittings and photographic sessions, for one was inundated with letters from photographers offering to take one's portrait free – the photographers hoped to sell the pictures to a magazine, or at any rate to one's family. Then there were interviews with gossip columnists. In those days it seemed every newspaper except *The Times* ran long gossip columns which were immensely popular, although there was a great deal of talk about 'the vulgarity of such publicity' and 'the intrusion into one's private life'. In actual fact, most people loved to see their names in print and I never knew a successful deb who did not secretly keep a little press-cutting book in which she lovingly pasted all photographs and comments relating to herself. The successful debs were those who had the most invitations, the most admirers, and the most publicity.

In the afternoon, it was considered good form to be seen at 'private views' at art galleries, and even those who positively disliked any form of art went to them. It was important to get one's lunch over fairly smartly so as to have time for these afternoon activities, as at 5 p.m. one had to go home to change one's clothes for the cocktail parties which usually began at 6 p.m. A successful debutante would visit between three and five of these cocktail parties each day.

Most nights there was a coming out dance for some girl. I seem to have gone to about three or four a week. These were organised by the girl's mother, who asked her friends, the mothers of other debs, to give dinner parties of about fifteen to twenty people before her dance. She supplied her list of the guests to be invited but the final list was only arrived at by consultation between the women. If you were not included in a dinner party, you got an invitation card inviting Lady Blank, Miss Jemima Blank and Partner – which meant that you could bring along your own young man. There always seemed to be a shortage of suitable single young men for these dances. Quite a few unfortunate debs were fat, shy, and bewildered and had no admirers of their own, and few suitable single men would go to a dance except with a partner of their own choice, as they found these dances boring and tiring and there was the likelihood of being stuck with a lemon, as all the most attractive girls would be taken up with their own partners.

One usually met young men, not at the dances, but at the cocktail parties held earlier. I was exceedingly popular with dowagers because I had four brothers, two of whom at a pinch, and the other two when they were on leave, I could force to accompany me to dinner parties and dances.

In 1931 chaperones had come back after the free-wheeling days of the 'bright young things' in the 1920s, but it was a matter of discretion and keeping up appearances, rather than a return to Victorian morals. In fact most of the more glamorous and publicised debutantes had lovers. Many had several, though in sequence and not all at the same time. Too much promiscuity would have caused the deb to be ostracised by all the other girls. Besides 'letting down the side', rumours would certainly have got about, which might have led to the curtailment of their own freedoms.

Never for one moment did I feel myself part of the London social roundabout. My Irish background and culture were too different. I always saw myself as an onlooker and therefore, able to enjoy uninhibitedly the spectacle and the fun more than the other participants, who were always worrying about something: above all the doubt that they would be able to make that 'good, even spectacular match' in the two years allowed them before they became ex-debs. Most were well aware that a suitable marriage was the real purpose of all the energy and thousands of pounds that were being expended on them, and they became very competitive about the task that they had been set.

The sad thing was that though the beautiful girls could get away with having no interest in anything except themselves, their clothes, and the gossip of their set, the plain ones, unless their parents were outstandingly rich, had nothing to offer and often retired after a couple of years into boring little jobs such as being salesgirls in dress-shops, not because they needed the money but because they had to have something to do. Even in those days, before there was any talk of women's liberation, I felt indignant at such human waste, and compared my friends in a vague sort of way to the Moslem women I had known in Algeria.

The London 'Season' ran from May 1st to July 27th or 28th so the first thing to do at the beginning of May was to decide on the date of the debutante's Coming Out dance and place an advertisement in *The Times* in the 'Arrangements' column, simply stating under the heading 'Dances' – 'Lady Blank for her daughter Letitia June 28th'. This had two advantages: it booked the date, so nobody else could have June 28th for their dance; and it officially entered Lady Blank's Letitia in the list of debs coming out that year. It had one disadvantage: it alerted 'gate-crashers', hungry young men who could borrow a white tie and tails, and now knew where there was free champagne and a delicious supper going on June 28th. As so many girls brought their own partners who would probably be unknown to their hostess, it was impossible to detect gate-crashers.

Looking back, it seems difficult to believe that all this took place at the height of the Great Depression in England. One certainly saw no sign that the financial and industrial world was in chaos. The upper classes still had money, or at any rate found it somewhere and spent it on their daughters.

My dance was held at our home, 42 Grosvenor Place, and there was plenty of caviar, salmon, lobster and various cold meat dishes for the 500 guests invited. Gallons of champagne were drunk. We had supper at 1 a.m. in the large dining room and in the even larger 'music room' at the back of the house. The survivors were fed again on bacon and eggs at 6 a.m. I noted at the time that though hundreds of people were dancing and a full band was playing in the ballroom on the first floor, not a sound could be heard on the ground floor below them. The explanation was provided years later when the house was pulled down to make way for Hobart House. Beneath the parquet floors of both the front and back drawing rooms was a ten-inch layer of cockle-shells. They must have been an enormous weight, but houses were built solidly in 1870 and seashells cost nothing.

Though I was then only involved in the debutante set, many different groups of people were in London for 'the Season.' The 'young married set' lived there practically all the time, as their husbands usually worked in the City or had some other London-based profession, like the Bar; and there were many other sets as well, including the 'Prince of Wales's set'. This was before the Prince took up with Mrs Simpson. Like most of the old noble families, my cousin, Lady Moira Cavendish, the daughter of my great-aunt Grace, Duchess of St Albans, was very much opposed to the Prince of Wales and all his friends. She had been asked by my mother to keep an eye on me, and she solemnly warned me, despite the fact that I had no opportunity to do so, against getting involved with the Prince's set in any way. 'They are a lot of jumped-up, tufthunters and degenerates who will come to no good,' she said. 'He has let down the monarchy. We can't have you mixing with people like that.'

Three months before Coming Out and becoming a deb, another landmark in my life occurred: I had attained the age of seventeen and therefore was officially a grown-up. Nobody talked of teenagers then and flappers had gone out with 'bright young things' in the twenties. First you were a child, then a schoolgirl, than an adult. The transformation came instantly on the relevant birthday. Being a grown-up had several advantages and few disadvantages. Because I had lived so much on my own in Ireland and latterly in Algeria, the freedom that grown-upness brought was not as wonderful to me as it seemed to be to most ex-schoolgirls. I had always been fairly free even when the family was at home.

I had only to say that my horses needed exercise and ride out the gates of Myrtle Grove and nobody could possibly know what I was doing or even where I was, and nobody seemed to notice when I came back.

The disadvantages were largely twofold. I had to do my share of entertaining the most boring guests, and I was told that I must either 'do up my hair all the time, every day, or cut it off'. I had very long, thick dark brown hair at the time, to which I was much attached and which my current young man said romantic things about. So for a while I struggled with hair pins, except for formal parties when my mother's lady's-maid welded my hair to my head in long plaits which stayed put, whatever my exertions. Left to myself, I sprayed hair-pins like confetti wherever I went and after ten minutes looked like 'mad Margaret'. After a while I gave in and sadly cut off about a yard of it, feeling all the time that in some strange way I was cutting off my whole past life and that I was starting off again as a quite new person.

Now, of course, I ate in the dining room all the time and took part in the frequent large dinner parties that my parents held when the family was in London. Even when there was no party, there was an absolute rule that everyone had to change for dinner. The men wore dinner jackets and the women long dresses, frequently of chiffon, with sleeves. One simply was not allowed in the dining room unchanged. If for some reason changing was impossible, a tray was brought up to one's bedroom. For these family dinners my father wore a velvet dinner suit of dark red or dark green with a little round hat to match which had a tassle in the centre of the crown.

A lot has been written about Edwardian food, the gist of which is that rich people at the time ate enormously. Although by 1931 we were way past Edwardian times, at our home we had more or less the same sort of menus – seven courses for dinner parties, five on other evenings – though one was only expected to eat a very small helping of each dish, and usually ended up having ingested about the same quantity of food as one would today. For dinner parties the courses ran like this: *hors d'oeuvre*, usually caviar or *pâté de foie gras*, or occasionally plovers' eggs; soup; an *entrée*, which could be a fish or egg dish or something such as sweetbreads, with sauces; a roast joint of beef, lamb or venison with two kinds of vegetables and potatoes; a sweet, which in turn was succeeded by savoury; and finally fruit and nuts. Never cheese – that was only eaten at luncheon. If we had game birds they were served between the *entrée* and the roast, making an extra course.

The food was handed round by two of the footmen while the butler opened the wine, carved the joint and generally supervised operations. The third footman served the wine. Sherry for the soup, then white wine followed by claret or burgundy, champagne for the sweet and then port.

An eighteenth-century Irish tradition which was observed in our house and in one or two other houses I visited was that the wine-footmen kept filling up your glass as you drank, except for the port, so that at the end of the meal, you had four full glasses of wine beside you. This wine was the perquisite of the footmen. They could drink it or pour it into bottles, to store or sell. Curiously enough, I can't remember ever having seen a footman drunk, though I do remember we once had a butler who disappeared mysteriously, much to everyone's consternation, just before a big dinner party. He was discovered as the entrée was being served, lying dead drunk under the dining table hidden by the tablecloth hanging down at the sides. My mother took it calmly, leaning down and saying, 'Stay where you are, Jones, and don't touch any of the ladies' ankles.' Despite the picture of butlers drawn by P. G. Wodehouse in his stories of 'Jeeves', alcoholism was always an occupational hazard for them, as it is for journalists and politicians.

For family evenings the *hors d'oeuvre* and the savoury were done away with and chicken or game was often served instead of the joint. Irish stew and casseroles or curries and similar 'made dishes' were eaten only at lunch.

The cook prepared these feasts assisted by the kitchen maid. The kitchen maid cooked for the servants' hall. Who cooked for the steward's room I don't know, but as she had to eat it herself I expect the cook kept a very sharp eye on its preparation. The scullery maid cleaned up after the cook and kitchen maid and scoured and polished all the copper saucepans.

My mother used to go down to the kitchen at 9.30 every morning and carefully write out the menus for the day. Once in Ireland, having watched her doing this every day for three years, I innocently asked her why she bothered, as I knew well that our current cook could neither read nor write. She showed considerable surprise but continued her routine just the same. She said we always got what she ordered anyway.

Both the servants' hall and the steward's room had quite different menus from us. Nothing would have induced the staff of the household to eat the 'mixed-up foreign food' that was served in the dining room.

There was also a hierarchy of food as well as people in our house. Though we were neither Jews nor Moslems, pork was never eaten in the dining room. As I loved roast pork with its delicious crackling, which I had eaten at friends' houses in Ireland, I once asked my mother if we could have some for lunch. 'No,' she said, 'pork is unhealthy – and in any case it is servants' hall food.' I asked her 'why, if pork was unhealthy, did we constantly eat pork sausages for breakfast? And why wasn't it unhealthy for the servants?' I received no reply.

There was a similar ban on T-bone steaks (steward's room) and steak and kidney pudding (ditto) and there were other dishes which I have forgotten which were only eaten 'below stairs'.

In later years, when I was studying the customs and beliefs of primitive peoples, I remembered the intricate customs and taboos of my own background which seemed to cover everything from food and clothes to the use of words and, in fact, one's whole general behaviour, and I had a strong fellow-feeling with these 'undeveloped' people.

After the Season was over we all went back to Ireland and were joined by some of my new London friends. They seemed strangely different when they got to Myrtle Grove, and I wondered what I had ever seen in them. Some of the White Russian cousins came to stay as well and proved much more sympathetic. They had all done well for themselves in the unfamiliar West European world into which they had been thrust. Prince George Chavchavadze had become an internationally known pianist, and Mme Volkoff had acquired two more houses in Earl's Court. The rent she got from letting the rooms in three houses, even though they were in a rather run-down section of London, brought her in a comfortable income.

For the first time I saw the point of Bernard Shaw's statement that 'No two nations were more foreign to each other than the Irish and the English.' The Russians, on the whole, seemed rather more like us.

Margaret Sheridan came to stay in August, with her brother Dick, who immediately became fast friends with my youngest brother Teeny.

The Sheridans were fleeing the fierce heat of Biskra in high summer. Everyone who had the opportunity to do so left the place, including the rich Arabs, who owned farms high in the Atlas mountains.

Margaret told me that Ali-ben-Gana had had another attack of liberalism and had tried to make his wives drive up to his farm unveiled. After long and bitter negotiation, Miza and Ziada had agreed to do so but only on condition that he replaced all the car's windows with dark blue glass. This he had done and everyone was happy, each side feeling that they had won.

I pondered a good deal on the women's strange determination to remain in purdah and I came to the conclusion that it was partly due to conservatism and a belief that unveiling would reduce their status, and partly because they well knew Ali's unpredictable and changeable moods. I had seen a prime example of these myself that day on the roof of his house. They must have figured out that if they did what he wanted, he was quite capable of turning round and divorcing them on the grounds that they were bad Moslems, bad wives and a disgrace to the ruling Ben Gana family. This he could easily do with the support of their own relations, who as they were all first cousins, were also his, and he could keep their share of the family inheritance.

Out of my dress allowance I, together with my brother Teeny, who was then at Cambridge, bought a second-hand pea-green Morris Oxford 'two-seater' car for the princely sum of £8. He taught me to drive, which extended the range of houses I could visit greatly and there were no more long, long rides over the mountains. My new mobility didn't last, however, as Teeny crashed the car into a speedily travelling funeral, smashing the hearse and sending the coffin flying into the ditch. The pea-green car was a write-off and he was lucky under the circumstances not to have been lynched by the mourners.

You never miss what you have never had. Before I owned a car I had been perfectly happy riding Isabella to wherever I wanted to go, but once having known the pleasure and speed of motoring, I found it intolerable to go back to this medieval mode of transport. After the episode with the funeral, my parents had placed a ban on either Teeny or myself buying another car until we were twenty-one, when we were promised a new one each. This affected me much more than Teeny. He was still at Cambridge and had no idea what he would do when he came down. Though very clever and able he was interested in such a large variety of things that he was like the proverbial donkey who starved to death because someone had placed two bundles of hay at equal distances from him on either side, and he could not decide which to eat first. In the end he put off the decision by taking a job offered by a very rich Dutch family to accompany their difficult son, a fellow student of his, round the world. It took over a year.

So it was partly due to lack of transport that, when autumn came and the annual migration of the Arbuthnots to London became imminent, I raised no objection when it was suggested that I should accompany them. This caused delighted surprise, as there was usually a battle royal when my parents tried to shift me to England.

It wasn't only the lack of car that made me want to leave home. I loved my Irish friends and I never tired of the beauty of the countryside. There was also a young Irish man who lived higher up the Blackwater River of whom I was getting very fond – though, unlike my fellow debutantes, I had no intention of getting married yet a while. My experiences since my hunting accident had given me a taste for adventure. Ireland is a very small country and the world is wide. If I wanted to spread my wings and fly, it seemed to me that London was the best available launching pad.

CHAPTER 6

Marriage

It was obvious to everyone concerned that if I was going to spend the winter in a city, I must have something to do or I would drive myself and the rest of the family mad. I would have liked to study marine biology or failing that, horticulture, as I have always been passionately interested in molluscs and all forms of plant life, but my lack of formal education would have prevented me from passing any form of entrance examination. So I fell back on my third interest, painting, and entered for a course at the Westminster School of Art, who accepted me after seeing my drawings of horses and water-colour landscapes. Vincent Square was within walking distance from Grosvenor Place, and every morning I set off with my paints and pencils.

It didn't take me long to decide that I was certainly no Michelangelo. The teachers agreed with me, so I switched to a course in design which proved a great blessing to me in later years.

At art school I met an entirely new section of the English people. They came from a wide variety of backgrounds and I found them a great deal more interesting than the upper-class debs I had known in the previous summer. It was a lesson in how dangerous it is to make generalisations about races. For instance, most foreigners who have worked and lived for years among factory workers in Lyons, often think that they understand the French. They don't. All they may understand is factory workers in Lyons. I am not suggesting that art students as a group were representative of the British people, any more than upper-class girls were. They were just one tiny piece of the mosaic which makes up the nation. But if one can get enough of these tiny pieces together, a pattern begins to emerge.

When abroad, in the U.S.A. or England, I am often asked to explain the Irish. I am always careful to say that I think I well understand the people of rural Ireland. I am different in culture from these small townsfolk and farmers, but I have lived among them nearly all my life and I am a part of the whole diverse community. I know very little about the urban population of Dublin and Cork who, though they are nearly all only second or third generation away from the countryside, have already developed, or are developing, all the characteristics of urban people everywhere. I couldn't begin to tell you what they will think or do next.

The girl who usually worked next to me at the art school was called Josephine. She was either a daughter, foster-daughter, niece or one of many mistresses of Augustus John, the famous portrait painter. I never did work out her relationship to him. At all events she lived with the Johns and she gave me a vivid account of the life in their household. It sounded like a serial in one of the more popular women's magazines and every morning I used to hurry to Vincent Square, eager to hear the latest instalment. Though there were many references to drink in her saga, I never heard anything about drugs, either from her or from any of the other students. If there had been any going about the art school in those days, I feel sure I would have known about it. Like a great many other people at that period, I had never heard of the use of any form of drugs until I went to Algeria, where I soon found that nearly all the men smoked hashish but not the women. I knew that old ladies of previous generations at home were always lapping up laudanum and that Conan Doyle thought it quite natural that his hero, Sherlock Holmes, should constantly inject himself with cocaine, but that did not seem to have any connection with real life as it was lived in 1931. I don't think my innocence was in any way unique. There just weren't many drug addicts going about then.

The best-selling novel *The Constant Nymph* was supposed to be modelled on the John family. I am sure, from what I heard, that this was so, but it seemed that the author had certainly toned down the colours a bit.

As the days went by Josephine grew more and more depressed. The reason was that she knew she couldn't really draw. She wasn't any better at it than I was – rather worse, if anything. In the John family art had been deified, as music had been in the family depicted in *The Constant Nymph*. To have failed as an artist was to have failed as a person. She didn't know what to do. I suggested that she should abandon any kind of representational painting and concentrate on some form of abstract art. I suggested that with her connections in the artistic establishment she would probably be declared a genius. She said that she hadn't realised I was so cynical, but eventually she took my advice and built up quite a reputation for herself as a painter. I lost sight of her just about the time she mounted her second successful one-woman exhibition.

Spending nights in one kind of environment and days in another almost automatically causes one to develop a sort of split personality. I felt that my art school friends would not have recognised me as the girl they thought they knew if they had met me at home. My family would have been equally surprised if they had suddenly descended on me at the Westminster School of Art. Teeny, who sometimes used to walk with me to Vincent Square when he was up from Cambridge, remarked that even my walk used to change as soon as we reached Buckingham Palace Gate. I think that this happens to most people, but they are quite unconscious of it.

As the whirl of the social season was now over, I spent many more evenings at home with my parents and so I got to know most of their friends among whom were many very interesting people. The majority were my mother's friends, as my father met his cronies at the Carlton Club in Pall Mall, where he spent a good deal of his time.

During the four years before she married, when my mother had lived as the Governor's only daughter in Hong Kong, the British Fleet seems to have visited the colony constantly. She must have been uniquely attractive, as half the junior naval officers had obviously been in love with her. Now they had risen in their profession, and become faithful friends. 42 Grosvenor Place was awash with admirals. One of them was Admiral Sir William Goodenough, who was President of the Royal Geographical Society – a charming, very slow-speaking man who liked enterprising young people and who made a point of encouraging me in every way. He was to have an enormous influence on my life.

There were also a number of elderly Ceylonese gentlemen who had been friends of my grandmother's when Grandpapa was Governor of Ceylon and who always visited us when they came to England. They all seemed to have had impossibly difficult names for Europeans to pronounce and were pain and grief to our butler. He could just manage Sir Solomon Bandaranaike but when it came to Sir Perambulam

Maranarshallum, he gave up and used to fling open the drawing door and announce 'the Sir'.

Sir Robert Ho Tung, the Chinese billionaire, used to drop in as well. He had been a friend of my grandfather's when he was Governor of Hong Kong and I suspect that they had made many deals under the table together. Every time he came he brought gifts for us all and introduced to us a new 'Lady Ho Tung'. My mother remarked that this was bad manners. 'He ought to call them his nieces.'

I made a secret plan to visit Ceylon and angled for an invitation from the Bandaranaikes which in the end I got. My father owned a tea plantation in the hills near Kandy, of which one day I would inherit my share. I suggested to my parents that it would be a good thing for me to visit it and see Ceylon, of course well chaperoned by the distinguished Bandaranaikes while I was still free to do so. I had nearly got the project organised when all my plans changed.

I had met a young Englishman called Arthur Byron. Arthur looked like a twin brother to Fred McMurray, the film actor. He had been born in Canada, near Calgary, where his parents had a ranch. They were not Canadians but had recently emigrated from England. His father came from the family of Lord Byron, the poet. They had a little money which they sank in the ranch, hoping to make their fortune in the New World. But both Arthur's mother and father had died when he was very young and he had been snatched back to England to be brought up by his aunt Miss McAffee. He was a first cousin of Robert Byron, the writer and historian, and it was through Robert that I met him, which was just a chance because Arthur was definitely not a member of Robert's set at all.

Though his parents had been hard up for cash, Arthur was not. His money had come to him in a rather curious way. His grandfather had owned a country house and a large estate at Purley, now a suburb of London but then deep in the countryside. This grandfather was also a keen hunting man, who kept his own pack of hounds. As London spread out, the area in which he could hunt grew smaller and smaller until he could only draw his own covers and hunt round and round on his own land. He continued to do this, refusing to sell even an inch of his, by now immensely valuable, fields though his children were forced to emigrate to earn a living. He lived to be very old, still clinging onto every blade of grass, and when at last he died his executors promptly sold his estate as building land and his heirs reaped the benefit.

Consequently Arthur could well afford to take me to the Café de Paris and other fashionable night spots, and he did so night after night. He was an excellent dancer and knew his way round the pre-war night life of London, though he was careful to take me only to the most respectable places. He was also a very good driver and loved driving powerful cars at a great speed, which I too found exhilarating at that age.

Altogether, to a girl of just eighteen, he was an extremely glamorous figure, and soon all my plans for the future were forgotten. Towards the end of the hunting season, I asked him to drive me to Leicestershire as I had been offered a horse there and wanted to see what English hunting was like. I was disappointed. I found it both tame and overcrowded. Arthur didn't ride; he followed round in his car all day, and during the party that followed the hunt he asked me to marry him. I accepted instantly and excitedly and I remember we drove all night in his big black Bentley, with the leather straps over the bonnet, to Cambridge, to wake up my brother Teeny and tell him of our engagement. Teeny wasn't very encouraging. He looked at us gloomily and sleepily.

'I hope you *both* know what you are doing,' was all he said.

We had a fairly long engagement and then in the autumn a very grand wedding at St Mark's, North Audley Street – and went on a month's honeymoon to Sicily.

The delay was caused by my mother. My father had been delighted with the engagement. He liked Arthur and though I'm sure he was very fond of me I think he was glad to get me off his hands so quickly and to someone who could support me, if not quite in the style to which I was accustomed, at least very comfortably indeed. I had sometimes seen my father look at me warily, like someone who owns a strange pet whose temper they are not quite sure of, and I felt he was relieved that at last I appeared to be doing something sensible.

My mother had many misgivings. She too liked Arthur but felt I was too young to settle down. She also said, "I don't think you should marry an Englishman. I am quite sure that when you have seen enough of the world, you will go back to Ireland and he won't like to live there permanently. Englishmen seldom do. You will also slide back into your old ways with your old friends in Ireland, and make him feel an outsider. Of course it is your decision, and as your father approves, I will make no objection – but think it over very carefully. Don't rush into anything.' I was deeply touched by her concern but gaily said I did know what I was doing. Which, of course, I did not. Nor could I have. I was in love for the first time and could not see that Arthur and myself had really very little in common beyond physical attraction and a mutual desire to have a good time. Having been brought up by an elderly spinster lady of limited education, he had never developed any intellectual interests. I hadn't had much education either, but I had had the advantage of a great deal of conversation with those that had, and also the advantage of my grandmother's library which I had devoured. Because of this, I found that after we were married, and for the first time were alone together for long periods, we had very little to talk about. I was bored with the things that interested him and vice versa. Arthur had been at a public school, Marlborough, which he liked, and after that to Cambridge which he adored. He had been very good at rowing and had moved with the athletic crowd, who were proud to be called 'hearties', as opposed to the 'aesthetes'. Like most of that set he was basically extremely conventional, and had not acquired the habit of thinking things out for himself, nor of taking the lead in any enterprise. This, of course, prevented him from making many disastrous mistakes, but it was very limiting. I don't regard his marrying me as a disastrous mistake from his point of view, as he always said that in the six years that we were together he had a wonderful time – and looked back to our life and travels with nostalgia.

He was good and kind and generous, and I am happy that after we were divorced he married soon again to Evelyn Blundel-Hawks, an ex-deb and acquaintance of mine, who was much better suited to him than I was.

Before we were married, Arthur had bought Little Clarendon House in Clarendon Place, off the Bayswater Road. It was a charming house, unusual in London in that it was long and low, and in the first few months of our marriage I had a happy time decorating and furnishing it in Art Deco style, the fashion of the early thirties.

Like most teenagers, I was trying to assert my own individuality by getting as far away as possible from the taste of the previous generation. Myrtle Grove was full of oriental furniture, the loot from my grandparents' colonial days, and Grosvenor Place was largely Louis XIV. In Little Clarendon House the big sitting room was decorated in black and white, with white walls and a black carpet. The furniture was largely made of looking-glass and the curtains and covers were either white chintz with black dots or black chintz with white dots. There were a couple of abstract pictures by Josephine on the walls. It was a boon to photographers. Colour photography had not yet come into general use, so that photographing some interiors was difficult. My black and white room was easy, and soon pictures of it were frequently featured in the glossy magazines, particularly after our house-warming party, where the drinks were restricted to 'White lady' cocktails and 'Black Velvet' – a mixture of stout and champagne – so that everything matched.

There were a number of disadvantages to this decor, which soon became apparent. One was that we had to spend a fortune on bright coloured flowers to cheer the place up, and another was that as soon as we got back from Sicily I acquired a red chow dog called Susan and two white Persian cats. All three ceaselessly shed their hair over every part of the black carpet, and it stuck like glue to the thick pile. Poor Squires, our houseman, began to resemble Mike Walsh, the man who raked the gravel at Myrtle Grove. As soon as he had succeeded in clearing the carpet of hair, he had to start again. He didn't seem to mind though, as he adored all three animals. Nor was it the sort of room in which one could comfortably spend a quiet domestic evening. It seemed to ask to be the background for a party. After a short time one became depressed and edgy and started ringing people up.

There is a saying among Irish farmers that if you want to make money from agriculture, all you have to do is go to fairs and cattle markets and listen carefully. When you hear enough farmers saying that there was no money in something, like pigs or maybe tomatoes, you should go in for this profitless line instantly, and in a big way. Everyone else will have gone out of it and in two years there will be a shortage and you will scoop the pool. The same is true of furniture. When we left Little Clarendon House we dumped or gave away all the 1930s stuff. It had quite gone out of fashion and nobody wanted it if they could possibly afford anything else. Not long ago I went to a sale in

New York at Sotheby's or Christie's and was saddened to see what was either my own old furniture from Clarendon Place or identical pieces going for hundreds of thousands of dollars. The fashion had come round again.

The same cycle operates for pictures as well as furniture. It makes me sick to think that I was once offered four very good pre-Raphaelite paintings for £10 apiece and that I didn't buy them. In the 1930s they were thought to be hideous and a drug on the market. The moral of this is to hang on to everything you own, except what is immediately fashionable. Sell that, as it may take a long time for people to consider today's treasures desirable again.

So there I was at eighteen, with a husband, a dog, two cats and a much-publicised London home, in fact a chic member of the 'young married set.'

I soon found that the life didn't suit me at all. I was dreadfully bored.

It proved to be an extension of the sort of thing I had done as a deb, and I was mixing with the same sort of people. The women still had no interest in anything except themselves, their clothes and local gossip. The only difference was that their fierce competition for husbands had temporarily abated.

Arthur was an underwriter at Lloyd's and every morning used to go off to the City. I am sure that there were many fascinating people working at Lloyd's but I didn't seem to meet them.

I went back to art school, but only for the mornings. In the afternoon I shopped and took Susan, the chow, for a walk. In the evening we usually dined with other young couples who lived a life similar to ourselves and at about 11 p.m. inevitably went on to a nightclub called the '400'. It was very dark. The lights were low and the walls and ceiling were entirely draped in a dark red material. It was also very crowded as it was the 'in' place at the time and there was great competition to get a 'good' table. The food was quite edible if you were hungry, which you usually were not, as you had just eaten a big dinner, but if you were so unwise as to order fish, you ran the risk of getting a mouthful of fish-bones, as it was impossible to see what was on your plate. I came to dread going there, but there was no escape.

'Let's drop in at the "400" and see who's there' was the cry. 'We needn't stay long.' I complained to Arthur that the place was too dark to see, too crowded to dance, and too noisy for conversation, and that we were losing our beauty sleep and our money to no purpose. I even threatened to take my knitting with me to the '400' so that at least the time spent there would not be entirely wasted. But Arthur liked it, so we tended to drift to the place with the rest of the crowd. Years later my second husband Claud Cockburn used to say to me that if you wanted to understand politics you should study the financial news, and if you wanted to understand the financial world, you should study politics. This is obviously true, but it did not seem to have got through to most of the City people I met.

Even the Great Depression had not shaken them and they seemed to believe that their way of life could continue indefinitely. In 1933 they ate, drank and were merry, entirely ignoring the hunger marches of the unemployed who were then slowly wending their way towards London. They also ignored the war clouds which, after Hitler came to power, soon appeared over the horizon.

Of course, most of them were extremely right-wing and thought Hitler was doing a good job in dealing with the German Communists; they appeared to be entirely unconscious of his other ambitions. Few of them bothered to read *Mein Kampf* when it came out – which I did – and even fewer studied his speeches. To give the Führer his due, he wrote and said exactly what he intended to do, and nobody should have had any doubts about the outcome.

Inexperienced as I was, the message got through to me and I put it to Arthur that if we wanted to travel and see the world, we had better do it quickly, before the coming war put an end to everything.

And so it was decided that we should set off and, taking our time, zig-zag around the world going from West to East.

Arthur was a partner in his firm of underwriters at Lloyd's and it was arranged that he should take a year or so off. Teeny, who had come down from Cambridge and returned from his world cruise, agreed to live in our house and look after the dog and cats and the two men servants.

I took this plan to Sir William Goodenough who, as President of the Royal Geographical Society, seemed to me to be the best person I knew to advise us about the most interesting places to visit – all, preferably, well off the beaten track.

I had met him often in the preceding months and it was partly his stories of strange, exotic places and people that had hardened my determination that Arthur and I should see the world while we still could. He was enthusiastic about the project and exceedingly helpful. He also said, 'Look, Patricia, next year the whole question of the Negrito tribes of the Far East will be coming up at the Geographical Society and frankly we don't know very much about them. If you would just make a rough list of their names and where their territories are, I would be very grateful. It would save a great deal of tiresome correspondence.'

I asked him what he meant by 'Negrito' and what exactly he meant by the 'Far East'. He said, 'They are the aboriginal tribes, who are usually but not always nomadic hunters and gatherers and who live in the forests of nearly every country east of the Persian Gulf. Well-known examples are the Vedas in Ceylon, the Sakë in Malaya, the Ainu in Japan, though the latter are not considered to be the original inhabitants. There are thousands of distinct tribes who have never been properly listed and studied, as most of them are constantly on the move.'

I said I would do what I could but I would rather concentrate on one country, so we settled on the forests in Northern Siam, now called Thailand.

After that, my afternoons were spent at the London Library studying primitive tribes in general and Northern Siam in particular.

CHAPTER 7

Over the Hills and Far Away

The journey was started in style. The liner *Empress of Britain* was reputed to be the last word in luxury. Her decor was designed by the most prominent and fashionable artists, and her food was considered to be equal to that of the very best French restaurants. What the advertisements for her did not say, however, was that, large as she was, she was most unstable. In fact she bobbed about like a cork in a cataract.

I was desperately seasick. I can't vouch for the *Empress*'s cuisine, as the only bit of it I sampled in the five days she took to cross the Atlantic was one cup of consommé, which I drank when the ship entered the St Lawrence river. In fact, so desperate was I to get my feet on dry land, that I insisted on disembarking at Quebec, our first port of call, instead of going on further as we had intended – which had the advantage that we were able to see that charming French city.

It is interesting to note what scientists and medical researchers can come up with when they really have to. Until the Second World War, there were no really effective anti-seasick pills, but when the invasion of Europe was planned, it became obvious that no soldier could possibly be in a condition to storm the beaches if he were, or had just been, horribly seasick. So the research laboratories were urged to concentrate all their efforts on inventing an anti-seasick pill which would really do what it was supposed to do.

We made our way from Quebec to Chicago, of which I have not many happy memories. In those days it was not as dangerous as it is today to wander about in towns and cities. In Chicago it seemed difficult to avoid the slums, as they were so close to the hotel district. I remember getting slightly lost and turning into a side street, to find a very dead horse by side of the road, which no one had bothered to take away. In general, the black districts were like Hogarth prints of eighteenth-century London. Even the faces of the people held the same expressions.

We had introductions to some of the 'Meat Barons' of Chicago and one of them invited me to see over his sausage factory. It was an interesting though horrible experience.

I had met this gentleman at a party, late at night, and had accepted his invitation for the next day. At 8 a.m. the hotel porter rang up to say that a car was waiting for me. I dressed hurriedly and, not feeling at all my best, was driven to the plant.

It was a model of efficiency and rationalisation. The pigs were headed up a circular ramp which went round the building to the top floor. On this floor they were slaughtered. The noise from the screaming, terrified pigs was agonising. By gravity the carcases went down to the next floor where they were gutted, down again to be cut up and so on, until they emerged at ground level as sausages and other similar products. I was very shaken and made a secret vow to turn vegetarian. This was reinforced at the conclusion of the tour by my host, who emerged grinning from his office with a brisk 'Now you have seen it all, it's time for breakfast,' and led me to a table on which was a silver dish full of sizzling sausages and bacon.

One of the most interesting things that I saw in that factory was on the floor that was given over to chilling the meat, which was kept at a very low temperature indeed. In fact, I was lent a fur coat before going in. The foreman told me that he had never been able to get rid of the mice who lived there – try as he would. 'Look,' he said, 'the pests have even grown furry coats to keep themselves warm,' and he produced a dead mouse in a trap, which had long silky fur like a miniature Persian cat. I was astonished and asked if he knew how many generations it had taken to produce this mutation. He didn't know, but said the mice had been there as long as he could remember.

I was tactless enough to mention this fascinating zoological phenomenon to the factory's owner, who was not pleased. He naturally didn't want the idea to get around town that his meat plant was full of vermin – whether their hair was long or short.

The rich people of Chicago, who were mostly 'old wealth', were very much what one would expect them to be. What surprised me was to find that some of the rich, respectable women had glamorised the gangsters who, at that period, had made Chicago a byword for murder and corruption. Just about the time we arrived in town, a notorious mobster had escaped from the police. He had killed about fourteen people in the process and was currently on the run, being hunted by every cop in the U.S.A. The progress of this chase was being followed eagerly by these ladies, many of whom openly admitted that they hoped he would escape and some made all sorts of silly excuses for this degenerate and heartless killer.

It is true that he was rather good-looking in a dark Latin sort of way, but they showed no contempt or disgust for any of the other leading members of the gangs that had given their city such a bad name. In fact, they almost seemed proud of them.

Although all have probably passed into history, I can never think of Chicago as the 'Windy City', but only as the 'Place of the Woolly Mice', the gangsters, and also, of course, that terrible pig factory.

After visiting Arthur's old home at Calgary – where we found the neighbours suspicious and unfriendly, causing us to think that there must have been some hanky-panky about the sale of his parents' ranch – we moved on to Banff in the Canadian Rockies.

Our idea had been to buy a second-hand car and drive over the mountains to Vancouver, but we discovered on arrival that this was impossible as there was then no road, only a railway line.

Sitting illegally in a small bar (people under twenty-one-years-old were not allowed in bars in Banff), I asked the barman how local people got about if there were no roads. 'In summer they ride horses or walk, in winter they ski or go by dog-sleigh. There's trails everywhere,' he said.

It is lovely early fall weather, I thought, and what would be nicer than riding over the Rockies? Arthur agreed and asked the barman if it would be possible to hire horses and a guide.

The man thought for a moment.

'You could try the postman, Ike Mills, he knows every path for a thousand miles round here and he's free just now – just done his rounds.'

That's how we met Ike.

He was a tiny little man and very Jewish-looking, which was not surprising as he had been born in Whitechapel. How he had got to Western Canada and become the most knowledgeable of frontiersmen,

I don't know. He was always pretty cagey about his past, but he had certainly earned the respectful admiration of the local community. He delivered the post, principally to the forestry's officials and fire-watchers over a large area – in the winter by dog-sleigh, and in summer on horseback. He also kept a fatherly eye on several odd characters who lived far away in the mountains by 'doing his rounds' about once every month or two.

He made extra money by guiding tourists who wanted to trail-ride round Banff and in winter he hired out his dog-team to film companies who were making Arctic films in the area.

He was a bit taken aback when we told him where we wanted to go. 'That's an awful long way, are you sure you are up to it?' And, he added, 'I can't be away too long.'

I explained my background and said I was accustomed to ride 40 to 60 miles a day, and had done so since the age of twelve and that once we reached the railway on the other side of the mountains we would pay for him and the horses to come back by train.

Arthur said nothing. It was only the day before we started off that he told me that he had never been on a horse before. I had just assumed he could ride. It seemed to me to be natural, like walking.

Another surprise on the morning of our departure was that all Ike's sleigh dogs had to come too. He had no one he could trust to leave them with. They proved an awful pest, always fighting among themselves and frightening the horses, and we had to take an extra pack-horse to carry their food. Ike said he always took them wherever he went as they were not reliable with strangers – a statement I remembered every time I left our tent at night.

So off we set. Three people, six horses and fifteen Eskimo dogs. Ike owned only three horses so he had hired or borrowed the other three. None of them would have won any prizes in a show ring but they were tough and mostly quiet, and all except one were well suited to their work. The exception, one of the pack-horses, was a mare called Cyclone who was a superannuated buck-jumper from a rodeo. Every now and then memories of her past would flash into her mind and she would start bucking. Saucepans, bags of biscuits and cans of meat would fly off, and we would have to stop and hunt for them in the undergrowth.

Top left: 1 Lady Blake, the author's grandmother; *top right*: 2 The author in 1917; *above*: 3 The author with her mother.

4 The author, aged fifteen.

op: 5 Myrtle Grove; *above left*: 6 The author as debutante, 1931;
bove right: 7 The author's marriage to Arthur Byron.

Top: 8 A curious carving on a Balinese temple; *above left*: 9 Watussi dancers in Ruanda-Urundi; *above right*: 10 Trained African elephants at the Niangara Elephant Training School.

Top: 11 Mud houses in Mousgoum. The one in the foreground is in the first stages of construction; *above left*: 12 A Zandi witch doctor; *above right*: 13 Pygmies in the Belgian Congo.

14 and 15 Andrew and the author out with the West Waterford Hunt.

'op left: 16 The author; *top right*: 17 Claud Cockburn; *above*: 18 One of the
uthor's shell pictures.

Top: 19 Claud Cockburn; *above*: 20 The author.

One pack-horse carried our 'tools for living' and most of our food. The second carried the rest of it, and also all the dried meat for the dogs, while the third carried the tent.

Ike was very proud of his tent. It was a real Indian teepee made of buffalo hide. On making camp each evening he would cut three poles, which he would carefully arrange in a standing triangle. Then he would throw the tent round them like a man throwing a lasso, prop open the chimney flap with a fourth pole and light a fire in the centre of the tent, over which we would cook our supper. We slept on the ground in a triangle round this fire wearing all our clothes and wrapped in a blanket, as the nights were already getting cold. We used our saddles for pillows. After riding all day in the clear air of the mountains we slept well.

Even in these rather spartan conditions Arthur was managing all right. He was athletic, and trail-riding with pack-horses is very slow and calls for practically no horsemanship whatsoever. At night the horses had collars of bells strapped round their necks, hobbles were attached to their fore- and near hind-legs to prevent them wandering too far away, and they were left loose to graze. As soon as we went to sleep some of the dogs, much to Ike's annoyance, invariably went off hunting. He said they would disturb the bears and make them 'edgy', but they always came back before dawn, and we never had any trouble with bears.

Riding through that empty mountainous forest gave me quite different feelings from those I had experienced on my long rides in Ireland. The scenery was equally beautiful – hundreds of small lakes and high rocky peaks glimpsed through steep dark ravines. The trees were conifers so that the delicious scent of pines was so strong that you felt you could almost touch it. I think it was the absence of people that made it all feel so different. I seldom met people on the Knockmealdown mountains at home, but the signs that they had been there were all around – a ruined cottage, its stone gable-end still standing, a barely discernible square of stone walls in the heather that had once enclosed a small potato patch. Sometimes I saw reminders of the remote past, neolithic ring forts, dolmens and standing stones. Ireland felt a very old land, and I felt myself to be part of its history. In Canada everything felt new. Everything connected with human beings was non-existent or just beginning. The land belonged to the animals and the plants and the fish in the lakes. Its history was about them, not us. It gave one a detached feeling, the freedom to admire and pass on.

We rode in single file down the narrow path, each one leading a pack-horse on a twelve-foot rope, and we only twice deviated from our route. Once, when the trail started to climb up towards a ridge, Ike, who always led the way, suddenly turned off to the right into the woods. I was leading Cyclone, who didn't want to leave the path and started to buck. As usual, her pack fell off and when we had gathered up all our equipment I asked Ike why we were leaving the trail.

'The trail goes up over that mountain and on that mountain grows a herb,' he said. 'I don't know its name, but it is a cure for the eczema that grizzly bears often get at this time of year, and the bears know it. When they get the itch they come here from all over, from hundreds of miles away, to eat the plant. The whole area will be packed with grizzlies right now, and we're not going to camp up there. They will be hungry and very cross – as you would be too, if you were tickling all over.' Arthur asked how the grizzly bears knew where the herb grew and that it would cure them. Ike shrugged.

'Same way a mountain sheep will travel hundreds of miles to get to a salt-lick, I guess.'

We skirted round the base of the mountain and rejoined the trail on the other side. The second deviation came when Ike said one morning, 'We're making good time, so if you wouldn't mind, I would like to visit an old man, a sort of hermit, who lives about a day's ride from here. I missed him when I last did my rounds. I was in a hurry and there was no mail for him, there never is. I'd just like to check he's O.K. You'll like him – he's educated, been to college, and you'll be surprised at his house.'

He was certainly right on both counts. The walls of the hermit's largish one-roomed building were entirely built of whiskey bottles with their bottoms facing outwards and their necks inwards. The chinks and the space round the necks was stuffed with clay, and the frame and the roof made of wood. Inside there was a large fireplace and chimney made of stone in which a blazing log fire was burning.

The hermit greeted us in a courtly way and seemed mildly pleased to see us, but worried in case we should stay too long. He said he had 'things to do tomorrow', but we were welcome to stay the night. Ike produced some whiskey from his pack, and Arthur and the hermit walked down to a little lake to catch some fish for our supper. All the water in these parts was teeming with trout, but normally we could not catch them, as we had no fish-hooks and only used the hundreds of small lakes for washing.

Our host talked slowly, as all people do who have not spoken to anyone for a long time. He told us nothing about himself nor why he chose to live in the wild, so far from the nearest human habitation, but he did like to talk about his house. He had built it himself, finding those thousands of bottles flung around a disused loggers' camp which had once been situated on the other side of the lake. He spoke enthusiastically of the insulation properties of whiskey bottles and how lovely they looked from the outside when the setting sun reflected on the glass. 'You would think the house was on fire,' he said. Ike had referred to him as an old man, but to me he did not seem so. His walk was springy and elastic, and his long beard was only just streaked with white. This may have been due to the healthy though solitary life he lived. He had made himself self-sufficient. The few stores he needed were brought to him twice a year in late autumn and spring by dog-sleigh and he saw no one except Ike and a very occasional forestry worker. No one wrote to him, and I saw no books around his room. Despite this, he seemed comfortable and contented, and not a bit lonely. He gave the impression of being a busy man who was kindly allowing us to take up some of his valuable time.

When we left next day he presented us with a fish-hook. Later on, when we were delayed by an early fall of snow, we were very grateful for that hook, as we were running dangerously short of food.

We arrived at our destination a couple of weeks late, but this was due to the snow, and not to us having lost our way. It was a miracle to me how well Ike piloted us: at times the seldom-used trail seemed invisible, but he never hesitated about which way to go and he was always right.

It was a sad moment when we came to say goodbye. During the whole trip there had never been a cross word between the three of us, which was remarkable considering we were living at such close quarters. Arthur and I had both become very fond of him. He was gentle, good-tempered and efficient and had that wonderful Jewish sense of humour which has made the fortunes of so many New York comics. I would have loved to have heard the story of his life which, as he never mentioned it, was probably dramatic and possibly tragic.

I also felt some affection for our motley collection of horses, even the idiotic Cyclone. They all had different personalities, but they had all done us well, given little trouble and plodded forward whatever the conditions. When the snow fell, as they were shod, it 'balled up' in their hooves until they had a snowball on each foot, which caused them to stumble and occasionally fall. I suggested an old hunting trick of smearing butter or lard on and around the soles of their feet, but we did not have enough fat to go round, so we just had to stop very frequently and clean out their hooves. It was also cold for them at night, as they had not yet grown their winter coats and we had no covers for them. We ourselves were as warm as toast, round the fire in our leather teepee, particularly as Ike showed us how to shovel snow up on the outside of it.

At the departure of the huskies, I felt nothing but relief. I normally love dogs, but huskies are different. To begin with, I had tried to endear myself to them by talking to them and offering morsels of food, but they only snarled or stared at me with a sceptical and suspicious look in their light blue eyes. This is not remarkable when you think of how humans have treated them. The Eskimos, whose lives depend on their dogs, are unbelievably cruel and even Amundsen, the Norwegian explorer, who wrote sentimental things about them in his diary, calling them 'his dear doggies', killed and ate them when they were no further use to him.

As was to be expected, Ike had a frightful job getting all his dogs and horses onto a goods train but miraculously no one was bitten or kicked, and when they were at last safely bolted in we had a last farewell drink with him in the station bar, and they all chugged away into the mountains and out of our lives.

CHAPER 8

South Sea Island

Now that we were on the Pacific coast we found that there were plenty of roads, so having collected our luggage at the rail-head, where we found it safely waiting for us, we bought a second-hand car and drove through the wonderful redwood forests to San Francisco. It is agony to me to read that they are now cutting these Sequoias down. They are indeed one of the wonders of the world, and look much more primeval than any of the rain forests that I have visited, such as the Ituri forest in the Congo, or the vast forests of South America. They looked much older than their 2,000–3,000 years, and it was hard to believe that on rounding one of their enormous trunks one would not meet a giant cave bear, a sabre-toothed tiger or a mammoth. I was disgusted to find in one place that a carriage way had been carved straight through the bole of one giant tree, which was still living. A large automobile could easily drive through it. A cheap and silly gimmick, like decorating the dome of St Paul's with tinsel and paper flowers.

Our plan was to get to the South Seas, the objective of all romantic travellers. We had discovered that there was a small boat that went to Tahiti from San Francisco once a month, and then on to New Zealand. It was the island's only link with the outside world except for a ship that sailed from Bordeaux via the Panama Canal, taking two and a half months to complete the journey.

When we arrived at San Francisco, we discovered that the boat had just left, so we decided to fill in the time till its next sailing by driving south towards Mexico. I was not sorry for the delay and the chance to go to Los Angeles, as Clare Sheridan had given me an introduction to Charlie Chaplin, her ex-lover, with whom she was still on good terms.

Charlie was extremely friendly, and as soon as he got our note enclosing Clare's letter, he invited us to stay. We regretfully had to refuse, as we were moving on next day, so he asked us to dinner that night instead.

He was then married to Paulette Goddard. I have been told that film stars usually look nothing special off the screen. If this is true, Goddard was certainly an exception. She was incredibly beautiful and greeted us in a long dress of green sequins, which made her look like a mermaid, and Charlie like something she had found in a rock-pool.

I am afraid that dinner was a bit disillusioning. Charlie Chaplin, that wonderfully sensitive and humorous interpreter of the underdog, seemed the biggest egotist that I have ever met in my life. He was also a bore. The entire dinner conversation consisted of a monologue by Charlie about his journeys around the world. The only thing that he seemed to have noticed about the countries that he visited was the size of the crowd that welcomed him on his arrival and their relative enthusiasm for himself. He only interrupted this travelogue to quote the immensely flattering things that important and powerful people had said and written about him. He sounded, on the whole, like a small and insecure boy boasting to keep his courage up.

There were also two or three other people at dinner, including a famous film director, King Vidor, but Paulette Goddard and I were the only women. As soon as we had finished eating, my hostess said, 'Let's be English and leave the men, and go and have some coffee upstairs.' I found this mysterious, as the large sitting room where we had been received was next to the dining room.

What she meant was soon clear. We went up to her bedroom where we sat chatting and sipping excellent brandy until it was time to go home. Having heard it all many times before, I guessed she was even more bored by the conversation in the dining room than I was. Afterwards I asked Arthur if it had continued in the same fashion after Paulette and I had left. He said that it had.

At last the small boat that was to take us across the Pacific arrived, and we set off for the South Seas. As usual, I was horribly seasick, but the first sight of Tahiti made up for the misery of the preceding fortnight. The scenery of the island still seems, looking back over the years, to be the most spectacular and beautiful that I have seen anywhere in the world.

It is a small island, shaped like a hand-mirror. The round main part is only 22 miles by 20, with the peninsula of Taiarapu, which is 11 miles by 6, tacked onto the southern end of it and forming the handle. In its centre, jagged, almost perpendicular mountains of volcanic origin rise to the double peaks of Mount Orohena, which is over 7,000 feet high. From the sea, the whole island looks like the painted back cloth of a Wagner opera, utterly unreal.

There is a flat strip all around the coast, mostly narrow but of varying width, on which the entire population lived.

Fifty years ago, the mountainous centre of Tahiti was unmapped and inhabited only by wild pigs. It was thickly wooded and full of oranges and other fruit trees, but difficult to explore because of the matted undergrowth. It was not always so. When Captain Cook first visited the island in the eighteenth century to observe the transit of Venus, people lived all over the mountains. As far as I can make out, the decline in the population of Polynesia is entirely due to the diseases brought by the Europeans and the Asiatics to which, having been isolated for so long, the Polynesians had no resistance whatever. The final blow, which wiped out a large proportion of the remaining inhabitants of Tahiti, was the world wide 1918 flu epidemic. I was told that there were still the remains of villages in the mountains where every single inhabitant had died, and as there was no one left to bury them, you could still see their bones lying about. I did not see these villages myself, as not unnaturally they were considered to be haunted, and no one would guide me to them, but many different people vouched for their existence, including some of the French government officials.

Papeete, where we landed, was the capital and the centre of the French administration. It was an enchanting little town composed of two-storey French colonial houses built of cut stone, or rather cut coral, shaded by enormous flamboyant flame-coloured trees which seemed to be permanently in flower, as were the countless bushes of hibiscus, bougainvillaea and tiare, a form of gardenia and the national flower of Tahiti.

A large flower-garlanded and singing crowd greeted our ship's arrival. This had not been organised by the local tourist board, because there wasn't one. Few people visited Tahiti in those days, as both the money and the time required were too great.

Europeans gathered at the quay to collect their monthly mail, and the Tahitians came for the fun of the thing, as an excuse for a party, and also to discuss the new arrivals, if any.

There was one small, comfortable hotel where we were the only guests, and after a few days, hearing that there was a road round the island, Arthur bought an ancient truck, and we set off to explore.

To call it a road was the grossest flattery. More than anything it resembled the long decayed avenue of a dilapidated Irish mansion. After about twelve miles, it petered out altogether and we came to a stop.

One of the nicest things about visiting a French colony was that the principal, in fact almost the only, activity of the administration was to teach the local inhabitants French. In Tahiti almost everybody could speak it, so that when we asked a Tahitian passerby if we could get any further along the coast, there was no language barrier.

He said, 'Certainly you can go further, but you will have to walk. But why do you want to go on? Isn't this a nice place? The lagoon is full of fish, the village of Punavia is just round the corner where there is an empty house and I, Iné, will be your friend. Why don't you stay here?'

We walked on and saw the house, which was a large oval hut standing ten yards from the beach. It was wooden, raised about two-and-a-half feet above the ground on stilts, and had a roof thatched with pandanus leaves. It was just like all the other houses in the village, except that it was larger, having three rooms made by a partition across the centre about five feet high, and a small satellite hut attached at the end for cooking and washing. It wasn't a 'village house', but belonged to a half-caste tradesman in Papeete who had originally come from Punavia; so after discussing things with the villagers, who had all gathered round, we drove back to Papeete, found the owner, hired the hut for a minute sum, and moved in.

It was a lucky chance: because of that haphazard meeting with Iné, I had the opportunity of living for six months in a successful, 'non consumer' society which has now, alas, vanished. The airport and mass tourism have seen to that. Nothing, I gather from friends that have visited it, remains of the Tahiti I knew, and the people; characters have totally changed.

We very soon knew all the inhabitants of Punavia, who were delighted to have us there. We had a truck, which they correctly thought would enable them to get in and out of Papeete without walking. Also, we seemed rich, and would give parties and feasts.

Correct again. Iné got a lot of kudos from having enticed us to settle there.

On the first morning he came round, bringing his wife, whom he introduced as Iné Vahini, or Iné's woman. I never did discover her name, which she kept secret for some reason. Iné said he would look after us and get us anything we wanted. Asked what he wanted in return, he looked hurt, and repeated he was our friend, and wanted nothing. Upon being pressed, he admitted that what he really longed for were new sets of teeth for himself and for Iné Vahini. So the deal was struck. We drove them into Papeete to the French dentist, who made them each an enormous set of false teeth, which must have been hideously uncomfortable, as they only wore them on ceremonial occasions.

The culture of the Polynesians differed in many ways from any of the other undeveloped peoples I was subsequently to meet. One of the most important differences was that the men did all the work. The women did nothing except sweep out the huts and prepare the food, which was supplied by the men.

Every morning, as it began to get light, all the young men of the village would go in their canoes into the lagoon carrying fishing spears. When they got to the middle they would slip into the water, almost without making a ripple and, swimming underwater, spear edible fish which lurked in the coral. These they threw into the boats. After about two hours, they would return, the canoes loaded with fish, which they tossed onto the sandy beach. Anyone could then go down and take what they wanted. There was always more fish than the village could eat that day, and the rejected ones were thrown back into the lagoon to be instantly devoured by other fish.

Apart from fish, the Tahitians' staple food was bread-fruit, avocado pears, a sort of wild spinach called *pota*, bananas, mangoes, pine-apples, and oranges, which the men brought down from the mountains together with limes. The limes were most important, as one of the usual ways of preparing fish was to cut it into small cubes and soak it in lime juice overnight, and eat it covered with coconut cream next day. The lime juice gave the fish the same consistency as if it were cooked. There were also a lot of scrawny chickens in the village who lived on coconut and insects.

All the cooking was done in pits, which the men dug. They were about three-and-a-half feet deep and four feet long, and lined with slabs of coral onto which coconut husks were thrown and set alight. These burned fiercely and heated the coral. When the husks were reduced to ashes, and the coral was really hot, parcels of food, chicken stuffed with pota, or fish with herbs, all carefully wrapped in banana leaves, were laid on the coral, and the bread-fruit tossed in as it was. More banana leaves were laid on top and then the earth was replaced. After about three hours, the food was dug up and unwrapped. It was always fully cooked and absolutely delicious.

The only money-making activity that went on in the village was gathering the coconuts, which were then split and dried and sold to a copra dealer. In this the women took no part.

Because of this there was practically no money in the village, there were no cash crops except copra, and there was no transportation for the surplus fish; but that did not seem to worry anyone. After all, there was very little to spend it on except oil for lamps, and an occasional new *pareu*. *Pareu*s were the universal dress. Nobody, man or woman, wore anything else on weekdays. It was a piece of cotton, two metres by one metre, always bright red, green or dark blue, with a large white floral pattern. These the women wrapped twice round themselves, knotting the covers at the waist, while the men twisted them into a sort of bathing trunks.

I always wondered when those three colours and that distinctive white pattern came to be decided on, and who decreed that all *pareu* cloth should be of that design. It obviously wasn't an ancient Polynesian tradition. Before the Europeans came, people wore tunics of brown 'tapa' cloth, which is made of pounded tree bark, and only the chiefs had wonderful cloaks of brightly coloured feathers. It wasn't an idea that came from the early, nonconformist missionaries either, as they would have disapproved of such scanty and brightly coloured garments. All *pareu* cloth was, and I think always had been, made in Birmingham, and was exported only to Polynesia. So it is possible that the exotic design came from England.

On Sunday all the women wore 'Mother Hubbards', sack dresses of any colour or pattern reaching to the ankles, a relic of the days when the islanders were bullied by the missionaries, who did their best to destroy the Polynesian culture and to introduce the people to puritan morals and the work ethic. In this they appeared to have been largely unsuccessful.

The only reminder of the dark days of theocratic rule was the fact that on Sundays everyone went to church and the women wore the 'Mother Hubbards', but going to church was considered fun. At 8 a.m. the whole village gathered and walked the mile to the 'Hymeny', as it was called, singing hymns in French to the tune of 'Daisy, Daisy, give me your answer do' and 'My old man said follow the van, and don't dilly dally on the way'. Once arrived at the church, we trooped in, like a school crocodile. The service was conducted in Polynesian and was largely choral. Most people stood the whole time, but if you felt tired you could sit on the mud floor without public disgrace. It went on for about an hour, then we went to the next village which was called Fa-a-a-a, to see friends, gossip and sing more hymns to the tunes of Victorian music hall songs. In the evening we returned, stopping on the way to bathe in a freshwater rock pool filled by a river, which flowed down from the mountains into the lagoon between the two villages.

No Tahitian would ever bathe in salt water for pleasure. Only the young men went into the sea to spear fish, while the small children splashed about in the shallow water. But Polynesians were all expert swimmers, and nearly every evening the small freshwater pool was full of women washing their beautiful, long hair, diving and swimming about or sitting on the rocks drying themselves and their *pareu*s, which they had worn in the water. Tahitians felt strongly about cleanliness, and soap was one of the very few presents you could give them that was really appreciated. When we went to Papeete, I used to stock up with it and pass it round on Sunday morning, so that our village was probably the cleanest in the island. To begin with, I bought a few bits of fashion jewellery, which I found in a Chinese shop, to give to friends but, though they thanked me politely, I noticed that it was never worn. The only decoration that I ever saw anyone wear were the *leis*, garlands of flowers that the women spent hours threading together, and were worn by men and women.

On the whole, I think the French ran Tahiti very well. They didn't interfere in the life of the Polynesians, and they kept a fairly sharp eye on who came to the island and what they did when they got there. You were not allowed to land unless you had a certain amount of money. This was an essential rule – otherwise the island would have been flooded with beachcombers and other free-loaders, who would have exploited the traditional hospitality of the Tahitians. If you were caught giving any form of distilled alcoholic spirits to the native inhabitants you were put on the next boat out. As for justice, there was practically no crime on the island: what cases there were seemed to be confined to Papeete, and involved disputes over property and administrative embezzlement.

The only real criticism I have was the lack of adequate free medical service and above all, a dental service. Despite their seemingly varied and balanced diet, Tahitians had terrible teeth, losing them at an early age. There must have been something missing in the diet, possibly calcium, as there were no dairy products. As they seldom ate anything that needed chewing – fish, bread-fruit, vegetables and fruit are soft – it didn't matter too much, but it certainly spoiled their looks. A wonderfully beautiful girl of sixteen usually became fat and toothless by the time she was twenty-six.

After we had been in Punavia about a fortnight, Iné gave us a strong hint it was time to give a feast. He said, 'If you would like to celebrate anything, the village will give you all the help you need.'

'The anniversary of our wedding is coming up. Tell us, what should we do?'

'Go into Papeete and buy a lot of sugar, some yeast and a live pig. I will go with you and show you where to get them.'

The sugar and yeast were for making pineapple beer which was quite legal, and as it was drunk fresh it was very strong and gave one a most terrible hangover. The village provided the tub and the pineapple, and Iné showed us how to ferment them.

There was only one pig for sale in Papeete, a small black one who had been captured in the mountains. Arriving home, we tied him by one leg by a long cord to one of the stilts under our house. Iné said I was to feed him well, and the day before the party he would come and butcher him. Of course, the piglet was terrified to begin with, but soon became very tame and friendly. Whenever he saw me he would come running and grunting up to me to have his back scratched. It would have been, for me, a quite impossible betrayal of trust for us to have killed and eaten him, but how to tell Iné? I worried about it all night. Then I remembered that before the missionaries came the Polynesians had believed in the transmigration of souls. Ancient pagan beliefs remain long in all people's conscious or subconscious minds. In Ireland, which has been Christian for fifteen hundred years, absolutely nobody will bring hawthorn blossom or flowering gorse into the house. Though few of them realise it, this is because both these plants were sacred to the Mother Goddess Bridget (no connection with the saint).

So next morning, I told Iné that I had had a dream that the pig was inhabited by the spirit of one of my ancestors, and that I must protect him or I would have great misfortune.

He accepted this without surprise, and said in that case he would ask the men to go into the mountains, and try to get another pig. In this they were unsuccessful, and we had to make do with chickens and lobster and some rather peculiar meat that I bought from a Chinese. Despite this, the celebration was a great success and as all Tahitians seemed to be able to play the güitar, we danced and sang till the sun rose.

So Pig remained under our house. To begin with, he was no trouble and made no smells: I lengthened his lead, and being, like all pigs if you give them a chance, very clean, he would go as far away as possible from his home to defecate – in this case, down to the beach where it was soon covered by the tide, but he grew fatter and bigger every day, and took to scratching himself against the piles on which the house was built. This made the whole building shake, as if it was about to fall down, and guests who did not know of his existence, would leap up shouting 'Quick, an earthquake. Get out into the open', and flee from the house. It also spilled drinks and knocked things over, so Pig was returned to the mountains. I hope he survived. I had done my best for him.

It is only fair to say that not all Europeans found the Polynesians as charming as we did. About once a fortnight, we took a truckload of villagers into Papeete to see the movies. These were shown in the open, on a portable screen, and consisted of silent films, old Charlie Chaplins, and the adventures of Pearl White. You wandered about among hibiscus and tiare bushes, or sat at small tables and sipped fruit juice while the show was going on. If you wanted anything stronger you had to go into one of the bars in the main street, and it was in one of these that I found myself sitting next to a small, stout, middle-aged American. I casually remarked what a beautiful place the island was, and how charming the inhabitants were. He almost exploded with rage.

'They are the most benighted, cruel, horrible, vindictive savages on the face of the earth,' he said 'May they all rot in hell.'

I was surprised, and asked him if he had had an unpleasant experience.

After nearly choking, he controlled himself and told me his story.

It seems he was a furrier from San Francisco who worked hard for his living, having to support a growing family. Despite his looks, he had strong romantic leanings and a fixation on the South Seas. He read any book he could get hold of about coral islands, but he could never get there. The fur trade was not all that good, he couldn't spare the time or the money. Every month he wistfully watched the little ship set off across the Pacific to the 'Isles of the Blessed'.

Then, when his children were almost grown up, he had a stroke of luck; an aunt died and left him her all. It did not seem to have been very much, but he felt that at last he could realise his dream. His wife, who was probably fed up with listening to him droning on about his obsession, agreed that he should take two months holiday by himself, if his brother could look after the family business.

He landed in Papeete, and was disappointed at what he found there. It didn't come up to his expectations. He said it was too tame. There was nothing to do but sit in the bars on the main street. He might just as well have stayed in San Francisco. Then, in one of these bars, he met a Norwegian sea captain. They sat there drinking together, and the Norwegian was most sympathetic. He said Papeete was not really the South Seas. He, Jorgansen, was the master of a small 'copra schooner' which went round the more remote islands collecting the copra for a wholesaler. He was setting out tomorrow, and if the furrier liked, he could go with him and they would have a great time.

So, full of rum and hope, the furrier set off in the small sailing boat. It was really an adventure – and this time he was not disappointed. His dream seemed to have come true.

About the second island they visited all the islanders collected to greet the 'copra boat'. It was a big event and, as was usual in Polynesia, it was celebrated by a feast. The furrier said it was wonderful: they danced and they sang, ate delicious food and drank gallons of pineapple beer under the brilliant tropical moon. He was in seventh heaven, so much so that when next morning the captain said that all the copra was loaded and it was time to be off, he implored him to stay just one more day. Jorgansen said that he couldn't do that since he had a schedule. But, ever obliging, he suggested that, as he had only two more islands to visit in this area, and as he had to pass this particular island on his way back, the furrier could stay here. The copra boat would pick him up in four days time. It was agreed that this was a perfect solution. The only thing was that the captain, like ninety per cent of the captains who sail their small schooners in and out of those tricky reefs to collect the copra, was a brilliant sailor, but a heavy drinker. Jorgansen simply forgot about the furrier and never came back, and copra is only collected once a year.

Nobody else came to the island, so for a whole year the poor furrier was marooned there. The furrier didn't get on with the Polynesians, whom he said were horrible to him. I don't know what he did to get on the wrong side of them. Perhaps in the beginning he tried to get off with some of the men's wives, never a popular move anywhere, but particularly ill-looked on in Polynesia, where permissive sexual morals were only acceptable among the single men and women. Once married, faithfulness was expected, and the only serious rows that took place in the community round Punavia, when I was there, were about suspected extra-marital affairs. In any case, the furrier had little to offer. His travellers' cheques meant nothing to them. He was physically unattractive, and could do no useful work. If he could have spoken French or Polynesian he could have told them stories, which, being illiterate, they would have loved, but he couldn't even do that. Still, they did look after him for a year, though with an ill grace.

When I met him he was waiting for the next boat home, which was due in a couple of days, wondering all the while what had happened to his business and his family, and how he would ever persuade his wife, if she was still his wife and had not divorced him, that he had not, in fact, voluntarily spent the last year and a quarter shacked up with some 'dusky beauty' in his 'Shangri-la.'

Arthur asked me what I had been talking about so earnestly with that 'funny little man', and when I told him the story, he nearly fell off his bar stool laughing.

I still regard it as a tragic tale.

And so we fell into the lazy, comfortable life of the islands. They really did cast a spell over you. To begin with, I made energetic plans to explore the mountains and to list the wild flora and the shells on the reef. I would start on Monday, well, maybe the Monday after, but I never achieved any of these objectives. We did walk nearly the whole way round the island and visited Robert Louis Stevenson's enchanting house where he lived before they moved to Fiji, but mostly I spent my time bathing and watching the brilliant coloured little fishes glide in and out of the coral, or weaving flower necklaces with the village women.

Nobody died in Punavia while I was there, so I never attended a Tahitian funeral, but we went to several 'house burnings', which were very dramatic.

Iné would say, 'I hear they are burning a house in Torahita the day after tomorrow, we must collect food and the young men will take it over.'

Tahitians built their houses out of native wood which they cut from the forest, and thatched them with pandanus leaves. After three of four years the thatch got full of insects, so the house was burned down and another built in its place – the family staying with neighbours during the week it took to replace it. A 'house burning' was always the occasion for a feast. People wishing to attend sent food in advance, which the villagers of Torahita prepared. We arrived about sunset bringing guitars and concertinas, and soon the oven-pits were opened. After the feast was over, the music and the dancing began. At about midnight the house was ceremonially set alight. It always burned magnificently, sending flames high up into the sky, and we danced round it, at a respectful distance, singing and shouting. As was usual in Tahiti, the party went on all night. If you got tired you just went down to the beach, lay on the sand and went to sleep, though in some places the mosquitoes prevented this, but they were not prevalent in our district.

In the morning a rather silent party slowly wended its way home.

We had never planned to spend so long in the South Seas. It was only the gateway to the Far East, but weeks followed days and months followed weeks. We were always going to leave by the next boat, and I think we should have been there yet, if an accident had not precipitated our departure. Arthur, walking on the reef, slipped and grazed his ankle. It didn't seem anything to worry about, but it didn't heal. He went to a French doctor who said, 'You have got coral poisoning. The coral insect is in the cut and it will grow. You must leave the island at the first opportunity and go to a cold climate and, above all, keep the foot dry.'

So that was that.

The entire village accompanied us to Papeete, festooned in flower garlands almost up to our noses. We hugged and kissed them all.

As the ship moved from the quay, they flung their flowers into the sea, singing 'Hawaiian' type songs. Then they suddenly changed to quite a different song, which I had not heard before, an ancient chant without melody.

A Frenchman, who was standing beside me at the rail, turned to his companion and said, 'Good God, they are singing the funeral song, the death chant. I hope that doesn't mean that they think the ship is going to sink.'

But I knew what they meant. They were saying a final goodbye. They knew we should never meet again.

CHAPTER 9

Oriental Journey

Our ship did not sink, but delivered us punctually at Wellington, North Island, New Zealand, where two things happened. We awoke from the dream-like daze that had enveloped us in the South Sea Islands, and Arthur's leg healed.

Before catching the boat for Australia, we stayed with friends in the volcanic centre of Rotarua, which is like a medieval picture of hell. During the night, there was a sizeable earthquake. But a large family dog called Butch was a pal of mine, and he consequently decided to sleep under my bed; when the house started to heave and shake, memories of Pig flooded back, and I thought it was due to Butch scratching. Next morning the family admired our stoicism in not leaping up and making a fuss.

From Sydney we moved on to Bali, Java and Sumatra. It was my first taste of the Orient, and of the effect it almost always has on one. I have a theory about Europeans in the tropics, which is based on observation and also on personal experience. Whatever characteristics you have will be intensified in the heat of an exotic land. If you are a bit lazy, you will become entirely supine. Conversely, if you are inclined to be a workaholic, you will become a ball of dynamic energy. This also applies to mental attitudes. The puritans will take on the characteristics of John Knox, and become power-hungry and bullying – while the permissive will emulate some of the lesser Byzantine emperors. The eccentrics become more eccentric, and the bores more boring – the tropics will seek out both your weaknesses and your strengths, and exaggerate them.

I am so glad I saw Bali before it became a tourist centre. There is all the difference in the world between seeing the famous 'monkey dance' done in a clearing by the local people, with the audience of Balinese sitting on the ground, all immensely moved by the religious significance of the ritual, and paying to see a performance of it. Maybe the dancers are better trained nowadays and their costumes are more magnificent, but the rows of chairs occupied by Europeans must destroy the magic.

Of course there were no hotels then, away from the main town, and you had to walk everywhere, but that only added to the sense of adventure and discovery. I was conscious all the time of the antiquity of the culture of these eastern islands, of how their civilisation had risen and fallen countless times over the millennia. They were poor and deprived materially, but they were not primitive. They made me feel primitive, awkward and newly hatched.

We landed on the west coast of Sumatra and made our way with some difficulty half way across to the Siak river, where we picked up a river boat. I have always liked river travel, but I didn't enjoy this one. The smell of the cargo of raw sago was so appalling, like very dead rats. Since that trip down the Siak river, I have never been able to eat tapioca pudding, which is made of sago.

In Malay we allowed ourselves to be delayed again, not in the places dominated by white expatriates. It would be hard to exaggerate the narrow prejudices of their ignorance. I kept thinking how right my grandmother had been when she, as the governor's wife, had feigned illness as an excuse not to have to entertain the wives of the English colonials. One tiny example of deep prejudice was shown at an English club, where we had been invited to a dance. I arrived in a purple evening dress, hastily made out of native silk, and to match it I had put some orchids in my hair. We had hardly arrived when a stout matron bore down on me. 'You must take those flowers out of your hair immediately. Only native women wear flowers in their hair.' She didn't actually tell me to take off the native silk dress, but I could see she disapproved of it.

Nothing that Somerset Maugham wrote about these people was an exaggeration. Even his most vitriolic descriptions were pale shadows of reality.

Having escaped from the horrors of the mem-sahibs and their equally boring husbands, we found a small cargo boat which would take us to Bangkok, stopping at all the little ports on the way to pick up freight. It had three European officers with the brightest blue eyes I have ever seen, and a Chinese crew who spent most of their time in the hold smoking opium. There were no other passengers. We had signed on as crew.

The officers were simple, kindly, fat Dutchmen, and the food was good, though I don't really like eating cheese for breakfast accompanied by Bols gin. The old boat was slow and smokey, and it was unbelievably hot. One day I was standing by the rail when the captain came up to me. 'Vot are you looking at?' he said.

'I am looking at that lovely, cool, blue sea with the flying fishes skimming over it. How I would love to dive into it and swim,' I said.

Next day the chugging of the engine suddenly ceased and there was an eerie silence.

'Oh God, now we've broken down. That's the last straw,' Arthur groaned.

But we hadn't. The captain came up, all smiles.

'You see, ve haf stopped ship, so the lady can have her bathe.'

I was horror struck. 'How would I get down there?'

'I haf put ladder over the side.'

Sure enough, there was a rather flimsy-looking rope-ladder hanging over the stern. It seemed a long way down.

'But what about sharks?' (The China Sea was said to be full of them.)

'I haf put man in the crow's nest, if he see shark, he will wave flag.'

He was triumphant. He had thought of everything.

I just hadn't the nerve to refuse after so much trouble had been taken and the ship stopped. Nervously, I put on my bathing dress, climbed down that frightening ladder and swam up and down a few times, watching out for sharks, and also keeping one eye on the Chinaman in the crow's nest, who appeared to be asleep.

The ship called at the village of Tumpat to pick up cargo. Tumpat later became famous as the place where the Japanese first landed for their invasion of Malaya in the Second World War, but when I was there it was just a small Malay village.

We had a letter of introduction to the only European inhabitant, and we almost did not present it, as we had been told he was a rubber planter, and we had seen quite enough of them in Kuala Lumpur; but when we did meet, we instantly felt he was a soul-mate and at his invitation we imitated the furrier from San Francisco, collected our luggage and moved into his house, while our ship sailed away.

Nigel was an unusual character, Scottish by origin and highly educated. He preferred to spend his life among the Malays, a people of an alien culture and totally uneducated. The 'mem-sahibs' in Kuala Lumpur would have dismissed him as having 'gone native', as he not only spoke Malay – so well, I was told, that no one could possibly guess he was a foreigner – but he nearly always wore the beautiful native dress of *bajou* and sarong. Despite all this he didn't correspond to the stereotype picture of a European 'gone native' in that he didn't drink and his charming house was kept in apple-pie order by his major-domo, Tiger, assisted by two younger Malays. He really loved the people of his village and they loved him, and proved it in the war.

When I heard that the Japanese had landed at Tumpat, I wondered what had become of Nigel. Nobody knew. His name was not among those listed as prisoners, so I assumed he was dead – but he wasn't. He had simply moved into the village and passed as a Malay. Nobody in Tumpat gave him away and he eventually emerged unscathed.

We stayed in Tumpat for a month, and it was one of the most enjoyable months of the whole trip. Among several things Nigel and I had in common was the fact that we had both kept animals under our houses, but I was completely upstaged, for whereas I had only kept a small wild pig, Nigel had a large rhinoceros called Hercules, whom he had been given as a baby and who was now nearly full-grown. Despite their ferocious reputation, Nigel swore that his rhino was as gentle as a kitten and as affectionate as a spaniel. He loved him deeply.

Hercules did not spend all his life in a cavern under the floor. Every morning at dawn, Nigel took him for a long walk. I never went with them. I didn't trust Hercules. He used to look at me with his little piggy eyes in a rather malevolent way. I think he was jealous, for he certainly adored his master. The villagers seemed to have got used to Hercules, and he never hurt anyone, and only once knocked down a small hut by mistake. Nigel, who was extremely knowledgeable about the local fauna, said that the reason rhinos were usually so cross was that in the wild they got thousands of leeches in the folds of their skin, which they could do nothing about, and which put them in a furious temper. Hercules was searched for leeches every day, and if one was found it was removed by touching it with a lighted cigarette – much the best way of getting rid of leeches, on both humans and animals.

Nigel took part in all the village activities, which mostly concerned some form of gambling, including fish-fighting and a humane form of cock-fighting, where the cocks wore no spurs and were snatched up by their owners as soon as they looked like losing, thus admitting defeat. All Malays are gambling addicts. They would bet on anything all the time, even on which dress I would be wearing the next day. I discovered this because one morning very early there was a gentle knock on our door. Arthur went to see who it was and came back looking puzzled. 'It's a little old Malay,' he said. 'He says will you please wear yellow today, and please not to tell anyone he asked.' I put on the yellow dress, and when I found Tiger I asked him why the old man wanted me to wear yellow. Tiger seemed very embarrassed. He apologised profusely and then explained: 'He is my grand uncle, and he has wagered a lot of money that you would wear yellow on Monday. He is a bad man, he wanted me to ask you to wear the yellow dress, but I refused. He should not have come to your room. I am very angry.'

There were two social events while I was in Tumpat. One morning Nigel asked, 'Have you brought an evening dress with you?'

'Yes, I had one made in Singapore.'

'Have you any jewellery?'

'No, I am not such a fool as to travel about with jewels.'

'What colour is the dress?'

'Sort of mauvish purple.'

'Good, I'll tell Tiger to get you some orchids. You can put them in your hair. The women do that here, they look lovely.'

'What is this all about?'

'We have been asked to dine with an old gentleman. He was quite a big-wig in this country in his day. When he retired he couldn't face going back to England, said it had all changed. He doesn't like the English people in Malaya either, says they have all changed too, so he built himself a house away in the jungle. He isn't a hermit though. He lives in great style, Victorian style, and he always changes for dinner.'

'Are you going to wear a dinner-jacket? I can't imagine you in one.'

'Well no, I haven't got one, but I shall wear my best gold sarong, and a turquoise *bajou*.'

So that evening we set off, accompanied by Tiger and the two house boys dressed in their best. It was apparently the custom to take your own staff to wait on you. The more you took, the grander you were. We drove for miles down a rutted track till we came to a large, white, two-storeyed Victorian house. We were announced by a Malay butler, and walked into a large drawing room furnished in perfect 1890 style, with draped curtains and gilded stucco work. Our white-haired host, who had the look of a retired ambassador, wore a stiff shirt, white tie and tails. He introduced us to the local rajah and his son, the 'crown prince', his daughter-in-law, and another English couple who, in his view, had apparently 'not changed'. Nigel, of course, knew everyone. The rajah looked at him with astonishment and hatred. He was wearing an identical gold sarong and turquoise *bajou*. He moved over quickly to the far end of the room to talk to Arthur.

As course followed course in the manner of a Victorian dinner party, a boy played Viennese waltzes on an antique gramophone, complete with a large horn.

The second social occasion arose out of the first one. The rajah asked us to dine with him at his 'palace'. Nigel was pointedly not invited. He had not yet been forgiven for wearing the same clothes as the rajah – who was convinced he had done it on purpose.

I did not enjoy that party at all, though it was very interesting. My hair had got blown about on the way over, so I asked the 'crown princess' if I could go somewhere where I could tidy it. When we were alone, she whispered, 'Be careful what you eat, the Rajah's second wife is trying to poison him.' How can one be careful when one is helped from numerous little plates of curries and side dishes?

When we got home, we told Nigel what had happened. He was soothing.

'I shouldn't worry, the princess is a hysterical girl who gets ideas. I don't think there is anything in it. It is true that the second wife has been displaced and is bitterly angry, but she would hardly dare to poison the whole company.'

Still, we spent a very uncomfortable night.

I liked the Malays. They reminded me of some of the people at home in County Cork. They seemed to like variety and to be averse to regular work, which is why the British employed the Chinese, an alien minority who have accumulated most of the money in circulation, and are therefore disliked by the Malays, who believe life is short and to be enjoyed to the full. They are great talkers, and love gossip and drama.

In Tumpat the men spent most of their time in the village street, gambling, spreading scandal and boasting – while the women did the necessary work including, of course, fetching the water. Water carrying, an enormously heavy and arduous task, is regarded everywhere in the Third World as women's work. You cannot go anywhere without meeting women, frequently pregnant, carrying gallons of water in large pots on their heads. You sometimes see a small boy helping, but never a man.

Tiger was an exception to the general run of Malay men, in that he worked hard and was so efficient. He really was just like Jeeves. Before the rajah's party, he had come to me and said, 'You will need a second evening dress. You cannot, for the honour of this house, wear the same dress twice. I have obtained some white and gold sari-silk, and know a woman who will make it up for you. I will bring her here in one hour.'

In one hour exactly she was there and made me an exact copy of my purple evening dress, which I have to this day.

CHAPTER 10

The End of the Voyage

Unlike the furrier, we were not marooned in Tumpat, but easily found another cargo ship to take us to Bangkok.

It was a beautiful city in those days, before there were any high-rise buildings, and deserved its rather hackneyed title of the 'Venice of the East', as there were few streets, the highways being canals, called *klongs* – which were a fascinating sight with all the market boats full of fruit, flowers and fish. I believe some *klongs* still exist, but most of them have been filled in and turned into roads. One of their disadvantages used to be that they were a breeding ground for mosquitoes, which in the evening were so thick as to resemble a fog. The buildings were nearly all one or two storeys high, so the fantastic temples with their golden roofs towered above them, and were visible from all over Bangkok. There were no motorboats on the *klongs*, so the only sounds in the city were the many voices of the people, the lapping of water and the flip-flap of sandals along paths.

I had an introduction from the Royal Geographical Society to a Danish professor at the University who, it was hoped, would help me in my job of listing the nomadic tribes, and he introduced us to a number of Siamese officials, as the best way of smoothing the path of my investigation.

I made several discoveries as soon as I arrived in Bangkok. The most important was that there were no roads; they all petered out eight miles beyond the capital. There was one railway, which went north to Chung Mai, little more than half-way up the country. Most commerce was conducted via rivers and canals.

Only three Negrito tribes were listed when I arrived – the Chong, the Sakei and Semang – but there were rumours that there were others in the forest in the northern part of the country. So north we went. After Chung Mai, getting around was quite difficult. If you couldn't stick to the waterways, you walked, and when we got up into the teak forests I was lent an elephant, my first experience of that most intelligent and charming of animals. The more you know of elephants, the more you will love them. This one had been stacking timber, and took a great pride in her work. After making a great pile, ready to be floated down the river, I have seen her go to the end and squint down the line to make sure that all the ends of the tree trunks were exactly level. If one stuck out a bit, she would go and carefully push it back. Riding an elephant has one disadvantage: after a time it makes you feel seasick, due to their rolling gait. At any rate, it had that effect on me, and I was told this was not uncommon. Once, for a change, I rode a water-buffalo, which was peaceful but very, very slow.

I listed the nomadic tribes by going about and asking everyone, from officials to timber workers to village elders what they knew about them. These people proved most helpful and always seemed to know a man who knew a man who knew something about some local Negrito tribe. These usually went about in small groups, almost extended families, each with their own distinct language or dialect. They were thought to be a very ancient people, the original inhabitants of the country which, because of invasions and migrations, is made up of a collection of different races – Han (Chinese), Khymer, Burman, Malay, Mohn, Daren, Annamite, Kach, Lawa and others, including some Tibetans as well as, of course, the Laos, who almost equal the Siamese in number.

I was quite proud that I managed to get a list of fourteen Negrito tribes, as well as the three well-known ones, and their approximate habitat. Most of them had not been seen by Europeans at that time, and some were even unknown to the Siamese officials.

When we were in the far north of the country, or we may have been in China proper, as there was no frontier marked then, we heard talk about a remarkable cave, of which everybody stood in great awe, and we decided to make our way there.

I went into the cave alone, as the Lao men who were with us refused to enter it, and Arthur sensibly said that it was safer for one of us to stay outside to get help in the unlikely event of that being necessary.

It was a very long cave and had obviously been used as a Buddhist shrine, as there were thousands of small golden Buddhas on every ledge of the rock walls. It was inhabited by billions of bats, who hung from the ceiling and must have been there for centuries, as the floor was composed of their droppings which in some places was raised in great mounds. When I disturbed the bats they flew out in such numbers that the wind from their wings created a gale.

I never reached the end and the innermost shrine, as my torch battery began to fade. I was not sorry to get out into the dappled sunshine of the forest, as apart from the almost choking stench of the bats, the cave had an immensely sinister and powerful atmosphere. There was a feeling of evil about the place, and I am not surprised that the Lao had refused to go in.

I felt that the cave must have been used in very ancient times for some horrific purpose which becoming a Buddhist shrine had not exorcised; but I still regret that I had not the courage to go in again with a new battery to my torch and explore it to the end.

When we returned to Bangkok, I made inquiries around the University about the cave, but nobody seemed to have heard of it. If it has not been investigated today, it would be well worth excavation and study. I would dearly love to know its history.

People have often asked me if I wasn't afraid of wild animals, particularly snakes, when I was walking in the jungle. My answer always is that I never saw any in Asia. The animals were just as keen to keep away from me as I was to keep away from them, and as for snakes, I only once had any trouble with them, and that was not the snake's fault.

It was in northern Siam. I had wanted to get some python skins to take back with me, with the idea of having them made into shoes and handbags. So when we arrived at a village, I would usually ask if there were any skins available that I could buy. One evening, when we returned from the forest, I was met by a man who could speak a little French.

'I got fine snake skin for you.'

'Good, where is it?'

'I put it in your hut.'

I hurried to the hut and flung open the rickety door. There was a large python skin there all right: the only trouble was that there was a large python inside it, and he wasn't at all pleased. I don't blame him. He had been captured, I don't know how, bundled into a sack and dumped on the floor. He had escaped from the sack and was just trying to find his way out of the hut when I arrived. He was probably frightened, if snakes can feel fear, and certainly angry. I fled, found the man who had brought him, and said, 'I wanted a python skin, not a live python.'

'All right. I kill and skin him.'

Showing no fear, he picked up a long bush knife and went towards the hut. I was relieved to find I had left the door open and the snake had slithered away into the jungle.

Back in the capital, we visited some Siamese friends, and I heard for the first time their side of the story of the original visit we had paid to them on our arrival.

When we presented our letter of introduction, they had invited us to a meal in their home. Remembering the lessons in oriental table manners that I had learned from the Arabs in Algeria, I thought that it would be considered very rude not to eat up any food that was offered. I had stupidly imagined that the same rules of etiquette would apply in Siam as in Algeria. I also told Arthur, who had no experience of non-European customs, that he must not leave anything on his plate.

Most rich Siamese had Chinese cooks, for two reasons. Firstly, because they liked Chinese food, and secondly because the cooks, not being Buddhists, could kill fish or chickens. Devout Siamese Buddhists are not necessarily vegetarian, as they would be in Sri Lanka, but will not personally take the life of any living thing.

At that first Siamese dinner party, the delicious Chinese dishes were not brought in all at once, as they are in a Chinese restaurant in Europe, but came in singly as separate courses accompanied by fresh bowls of rice. As course followed course, remembering Arab etiquette, we ate and ate, wondering if the dinner would ever come to an end. Finally, at bursting point, I laid down my chopsticks. If I ate anymore, I should be sick, right there at the table. However bad-mannered it was, I just couldn't eat any more. Soon after, we staggered back to our hotel.

It was only on our return to Bangkok, when we got to know our hosts better, that we learned that in Siam the reverse of the Arab convention applied. If an honoured guest finishes his bowl, more food must be provided. They had been astonished at our enormous appetites. We had stripped their larder bare. They had even had to send out for more food. They thought we would never stop eating. One evening, at our request, they organised a meal of real Siamese food for us. As they predicted, it wasn't a success. The dishes were so full of red peppers and chillies that our mouths and throats were on fire and tears poured down our cheeks. The only dish that I could eat with pleasure was called 'brother-in-law eggs', which was made of hard boiled eggs, onions, garlic and honey, which sounds peculiar but was really very good.

There was also a dish of crisply fried maggots which I did not sample.

After leaving Bangkok, it had been our plan to visit the Khymer ruins at Angkor, and then work our way up the coast of what is now Vietnam to China, but staying in a Chinese inn at Siem-Reap, close to the ruins at Angkor, I was unwise enough to eat a stew containing a lot of ducks' feet, and as a result developed a bad case of ptomaine poisoning. The nearest hospital being in Bangkok, I was rushed back there, and even after I recovered I felt very weak and unwell, so we decided to abandon the rest of our journey and return home. In any case, we had been abroad longer than we had at first intended.

I have always felt grateful that before I ate those poisonous ducks' feet, I had a chance to visit one of the most magnificent and beautiful ancient buildings in the world – Angkor Wat and Angkor Thom – and many other smaller temples which had been discovered but not yet cleared. These we found almost the most impressive and mysterious. They were lost in the forest, approached only by barely discernible paths. Great trees were growing in their courtyards, and flowering creepers festooned the enormous carved stone heads, as well as the supporting delicate carving. There was nobody about and we had them to ourselves. Only at Angkor Wat were there a few yellow-robed priests.

We went back to Malaya to catch the ship that was to take us back to England, and the first person I met on board was a retired Dutch doctor, who had been practising in the Far East for over fifty years. When he remarked how ill I looked, I told him about the ducks' feet and their disastrous effect on me. He said I was lucky to be alive, for Europeans die quickly of such things in the rain forests. He said that if I would do as he told me, I would quickly regain my strength. His prescription was strange. He said that for eight days I must drink nothing but water that had been boiled for two hours, and eat nothing but unpolished rice which had been simmered for eight hours and was in a mush. Feeling by then that I would try anything, I agreed, and he went off to instruct the ship's cook.

Whether it was the old doctor's cure or the sea air, I don't know, but by the time we reached Ceylon, I had put on weight and was bursting with energy. So much so that Arthur agreed that I should at last realise the plan I had made to visit my father's tea estate, which I had abandoned when I met him.

We left the ship at Colombo, and spent the next three weeks touring the island, visiting my grandparent's Singhalese friends, or at least those that were still alive, each one of whom insisted on driving me down Blake Avenue, named after my grandfather when he was governor, and inspecting the tea estate at Ithanside.

The visit to Ceylon had a big effect on the course of my life. Probably it was only the crystallisation of subconscious feelings that had been growing in me for a long time, possibly even since my childhood in poverty-stricken and war-torn Ireland – feelings of furious exasperation at the way the world was run, and the knowledge that if I were to meet a visitor from another planet, who asked me how we humans had organised ourselves down here on Planet Earth, I could only blush with embarrassment and change the subject. I was twenty-one years old, and before that time had accepted everything I saw with interest and sometimes disapproval. But I accepted it; it was my good luck to have been born into a privileged family and other people's bad luck if they had not been. That was the way life was. There was probably no alternative.

After my travels, and particularly our tour of Ceylon, I felt that there simply had to be an alternative. Unlike many young people, I had not the least idea what the solution was, but from then on I began to look for one.

I think it was the contrast between the beauty of the fertile island of Ceylon and the squalid villages filled with obviously deprived people that brought my indignation to the surface.

In the South Seas, thanks to the abundance of free food and building material for their comfortable houses, the property-less inhabitants were well off. Even the subsistence farmers I had seen in the Far East had in many ways a reasonable existence. They had food, work and an engrossing community life in their villages. In Ceylon there was much fertile but uncultivated land; many landless peasants; many malnourished children with swollen stomachs; many old, despairing beggars.

The uncultivated land had not always been so. In the jungle were the remains of great stone-lined canals, which had been built 2,000 years ago to irrigate the crops. They had now been allowed to decay.

Up at the tea plantations in the mountains, things were very different. The workers on the beautifully cultivated tea estates lived in neat bungalows with well-tended front gardens. I was proudly shown the company school and the company hospital, both triumphs of hygiene and efficiency.

The trouble was that there was not a single Singhalese in the entire outfit. The management and technicians were all English, and all the workers were Tamils, newly imported from Southern India, and trained by the company.

There are some old, established Tamils in Sri Lanka, who date from earlier immigrations and the time when there was an invasion and a Tamil king of ancient Ceylon, but the majority of the Tamil tea workers were brought in by successive plantation owners. They were well cared for and seemed, incidentally, well paid. Even so, Ithanside paid a dividend of 25 per cent to us in England. The average interest on shares then was 5 per cent.

Under these circumstances, it is not surprising that after independence the estates were partly nationalised. Unfortunately, probably due to ineffective spraying, a fungus disease decimated the tea bushes and their profitability declined.

The real losers were the Tamils. Poverty in India had driven them from their own country and they are now a large and unpopular minority in Sri Lanka. They are quite different in appearance from the Singhalese – very much darker, some almost jet black, with thin arms and legs – and are considered ugly by Singhalese standards.

They are hard-working, clever and ambitious, which causes them to be hated by the majority of the population, who have discriminated against them ever since independence.

Greeted in the local press as the realisation of a nation's dream, the dropping of English as one of the two official languages in Ceylon was a particular blow to the Tamils, as it meant that all examinations for government posts, however humble, had to be taken in Singhalese, in which few Tamils were fluent. Their language had always been English, so it was just one of many forms of discrimination.

It is a terrible mistake to think racist prejudice is a vice confined to the Europeans. I have met it everywhere, all over the world.

CHAPTER 11

Home and Away Again

Back in London, nothing had changed. My family greeted me with enthusiasm, and kindly listened to my traveller's tales without evident signs of boredom. My brother Teeny moved out of Little Clarendon House, and we moved back in. He said he had enjoyed living there, except for my horrible chow dog Susan who, on finding herself deserted by her owner, had become intolerably fierce and bitten anyone who came to see him. I think she must have felt that with us gone, it was up to her alone to guard the home, as she calmed down considerably after our return. Listening to my lyrical account of Tahiti, most of my family declared that they would visit it at the first opportunity, and the next year my father and mother did go, and stayed in the hotel in Papeete. They seem to have had a lovely time, but my sister Joan did not get there for many years, until after the airport had been constructed and the island 'developed'. Months later, I received a postcard from her. It only said 'What did I do to you when we were children that you have sent me half across the world to this horrible place?'

Sir William Goodenough thanked me for my report on the nomadic tribes and seemed well pleased with it. From his attitude, I got the strong impression that he had not really believed I would come up with anything useful. I had been careful to enclose a map of where I had been, and where possible gave the names and descriptions of my informants. I also suggested he should contact the Danish professor in Bangkok, just in case he was harbouring the unworthy suspicion that I had spent my time lazing in the sun, and had invented all those Negrito tribes and their habitats on the ship on my way home.

In 1936 my son Darrell was born, and we moved house. It seems incredible that a young couple living in a house with four bedrooms, two bathrooms and three reception rooms, plus a cocktail bar and a roof garden, should consider it too small once they had a child. But we did.

So we sold the house, got rid of all the Art Deco furniture and bought a large conventional Victorian house in Stanhope Place, just by Marble Arch. It had a floor for everything. A basement for the cook, a ground floor for the dining room and a library, a drawing-room floor, a bedroom floor, a nursery floor, and on the top of all, under the roof, were the servants' bedrooms.

It wasn't a lucky house; nobody was happy there.

Of course, I had a nanny for the baby, one of those square, middle-aged 'Hyde Park' nannies about whom people write nostalgic books nowadays. She looked a little like Nigel's rhinoceros Hercules, and the dark grey coat and skirt which she always wore was just the colour of his skin.

She was immensely competent and immensely possessive of Darrell, whom she always alluded to as 'my baby'. As a result we had several conflicts of wills which she usually won, as she was almost always right. I knew nothing about babies, and at twenty-two was not really responsible enough to be a good mother or, in fact, any mother at all.

One conflict I did win was over the pram. It was one of those very large ones, fashionable at the time, and designed more for the glory of the nanny when she met the other nannies in Hyde Park than for use and convenience.

My nanny demanded that we should have the family crest painted in miniature on both sides of the pram.

I said 'No, it would look pretentious', and in any case the Byron crest was a half-undressed mermaid holding a handmirror. I had had enough of people making jokes about that mermaid's breasts when they saw them on the forks and spoons.

Nanny was furious. She cited all the families she had been with who *always* had their crest on their prams. She was on the point of giving notice, but I stood firm, and she restrained herself.

It was just as if we had never been away. Arthur went to Lloyd's every day. Every night we went to cocktail parties, dinner parties and on to the '400', or some other night spot. In the summer we took a beautiful villa in the hills above Eze, in the south of France, while Nanny and the baby went to Littlehampton. She insisted on that. All the best nannies went to Littlehampton with their charges – the bracing air was supposed to be good for the children.

In July 1936 the Spanish Civil War broke out. To this generation that probably means very little, but in 1936 nearly everyone felt it was a watershed, the overture to the long expected Second World War.

General Franco, supported by Hitler, who needed a friendly, or at any rate a neutralised Spain for the furtherance of his plans, led a military coup against the new left-of-centre government of Spain, which had been elected in the previous February.

Most of the upper-class people we went about with supported Franco, if only tacitly. He would deal with those 'Bolsheviks' – which ignored the fact that of the 278 seats that the Popular Front won in the Spanish Cortes, only 17 had been won by the Spanish Communist Party.

By now, through my brother Teeny, I had met and made friends with a number of people who were more liberal and intellectual than my and Arthur's original friends, and they realised fully the implications of what had happened. They were what was known later in intelligence circles as 'premature anti-fascists', and many of them went to Spain to do what they could to help the elected Government. Though the full horror of Nazism was unknown to me, as it was to most people in England at that time, I had read enough Nazi literature and speeches to have a fair idea of what fascism stood for. So when it was suggested by a group of friends who were going to Spain that I should accompany them, I was in two minds as to what was the right thing to do.

I asked my brother Teeny if I should go to Spain with the Sheehans.

'Certainly not. There are quite enough liberal intellectuals cluttering up the place there already, eating scarce food and taking up the time of equally scarce organisational manpower. If you had some special technical or medical training you might be of some use, but if you went there it would really be to satisfy your love of adventure, and to be able to congratulate yourself on being noble and self-sacrificing. You would only be a nuisance.'

'Don't you think that it is a boost to the morale of the Spanish people that anti-fascists of all countries are coming to their aid?'

'I should have thought the International Brigades would have provided that, if it were needed.'

Feeling rather dashed, but knowing he was right, I returned home.

Years later, when I told my second husband Claud about this conversation, he laughed and said, 'What a sensible man your brother was. I had the job, in Madrid, of looking after those well-meaning liberals at one time, including your friend Clare Sheridan. She was one of the most pestilential of the lot, and that is saying a good deal.'

Very soon my alleged 'love of adventure' found a new outlet.

Admiral Sir William Goodenough rang me up.

'I have checked on your report and shown it to other members of the Geographical Society and we all agree that it is very useful. Congratulations, Patricia, you did a good job. Now, would you and Arthur like a much tougher assignment? Would you consider going to Central Africa?'

'To do what?'

'Too long to tell you over the 'phone. Come and see me the day after tomorrow.'

It turned out that the Geographical Society were considering financing a scientific expedition to Central Africa to study the various tribal languages. In the part of the Belgian Congo (now Zaïre) north of the River Congo and in French Equatorial Africa, (now the Central African Republic), there was then only very sketchy information to use as a basis for discussion as to where that expedition should base itself. What Admiral Goodenough wanted was for us to cross Africa, starting from the Province of Equatoria in South Sudan and moving roughly due west parallel to the OuBanqui River until we reached the point at Banqui where the river turns south to join the River Congo and then go north-west, finishing up at Lake Chad. We were to fly to Kampala and start from Uganda visiting the Ituri forest in the Congo where the true pygmies lived, and try and get some information on whether their language had a totally different root from the other languages spoken by the tribes settled along the rivers.

When I heard this I was astonished.

'Good heavens. Why me? I have no knowledge of languages – nor any natural talent for them.'

'There are absolutely hundreds of languages and dialects in that area. Nobody knows more than a tiny percentage of them and we have no contact with them. You obviously have a great talent for getting information out of people. We understand that there is a dry weather track which would take a light van most of the way. You could put your equipment on that and then walk north and south of the track to various areas using bearers whom you could pick up from the local tribes. We only want a rough language-map as a basis for discussion.'

I said I would discuss it with Arthur and come back to him.

Arthur was enthusiastic about the idea, but there were many difficulties. It was one thing to leave Little Clarendon House, two cats and a dog for a long period, but another to leave a household which contained a nurse and a baby.

I discussed the problem with my mother, and she had a suggestion. She told me that she and my father had decided to sell 42 Grosvenor Place – both to save money and because, with the children leaving home, they had no need of two large houses. It seems the rich Arbuthnots had been overspending for years – and now the family firm, Arbuthnot-Lathum, had wickedly lent money to Nazi Germany which was not being repaid, nor even serviced. The financial crisis cannot have been very serious, however, as after selling 42 Grosvenor Place they almost immediately bought an equally large house in Cadogan Square.

Her suggestion was that she and my father should move into Stanhope Place and look after everything and then take our whole household, nurse, baby, dog, and cats and servants, over to Myrtle Grove for the summer – putting a caretaker into our house. She loved small children, and was obviously delighted with the idea of being in charge of Darrell. I had a mental picture of the battles royal that would take place between her and the nanny. I don't know which of those dominant characters I would have backed to win. Probably my mother, for she had a great deal of my grandmother in her. It served Nanny right.

So it was settled, and I spent a lot of time with Admiral Goodenough studying maps and making lists of the stores we should need – principally items to barter, as money was unknown once we left comparative civilisation, including a great deal of salt, mirrors, iron arrow-heads and several cases of a revolting cigarette called 'La Cigarette Albert' which was coal black and enormously strong. Also we had to take canned food for ourselves, and a great deal of ammunition for the rifles, as to a large extent we would have to live on what we could shoot. We had to think of everything that was necessary – but keep it down to a minimum. These stores would be ordered in advance and picked up in Kampala, capital of Uganda. And it was thither that we finally flew, in one of those delightful old flying boats, now extinct, landing on Lake Nyanza.

We had an enormous piece of good luck as we drove westward from Kampala through the country of the Buganda – then the ruling race in Uganda. We picked up a daring, supremely intelligent young man of the Buganda tribe called Juma, who was to be our 'head boy'. He recruited the bearers and organised their feeding and pay. Juma had the added advantage of being a brilliant linguist, and if he could not speak a language, always seemed to be able to find somebody who had a smattering of some tongue that he could understand. Like most Buganda he was a fine figure of a man, looking like a Victorian illustration of the Noble Savage; coal black, tall and well-proportioned. One of the things that struck me most in Central Africa was the enormous physical dissimilarity of the different tribes that lived there. In Europe all the different nationalities look more or less alike, there are blondes and brunettes in all the races but in Africa you could not possibly mistake a member of one tribe for a member of another. They differ totally in height, shape, colour and face. Even after all these years, if I leaf through my photographs and I come across one that has nothing written on the back, I find no difficulty in saying who the people are and where they came from.

Juma was originally supposed only to stay with us for a short time and then go home, but in the end he accompanied us for almost the whole trip.

In the months that followed I spent a good deal of time talking to him. It is always difficult, if not impossible, to make real communication with someone from a totally different cultural background and I don't suppose I really succeeded, but the effort was intensely interesting.

Juma had not been to a mission school, and was consequently illiterate – and the days of black power and nationalism had not yet arrived, so that he was untouched by either European culture or the modern, largely urban, black ethic. His ideas and standards were the ancient tribal ones of the Buganda, fertilised by a good deal of common sense, a lively mind, and a great sense of humour, which was surprisingly like our own.

Not long after he joined us, he and I were standing on a hillside in Kivu province. I said,

'Have you a word for beauty? Do you understand what a thing being beautiful means?'

'Yes.'

Below us was a small lake backed by a panorama of high mountains. Groves of tall feathery bamboos grew from the bright red volcanic earth and swayed gently in the breeze. In the lake, which was fringed with blue water-lilies, a solitary naked man in a dugout canoe was fishing with a square net held open with crossed sticks. It was a scene of exquisite loveliness, reminiscent of a Chinese painting. I waved towards the view.

'Do you think that scenery is beautiful?'

He looked puzzled, paused, and then said, 'No.'

'What *do* you think is beautiful?'

He pointed to my rifle, which I was carrying.

'That is beautiful?'

'Is it beautiful because it is powerful and can kill things, or is it beautiful in itself? If, for instance, I had no bullets, would it still be beautiful?'

'Both,' he said.

Another time in the Ituri forest, when I had ordered him not to tie live chickens up by their feet to the branches of trees, I said, 'Why are you so cruel to hens, and yet so kind and gentle to my pet hyrax?'

He made an effort to explain himself. 'If the hens suffer it does not hurt me, but I love Turi-the-hyrax. If anyone hurts him, it hurts me – and if anyone hurts me, I kill them.'

'Well,' I said, 'if anyone around here is unnecessarily cruel to any animal, it hurts me, so you had better see they don't do it, and that includes you.'

After that he understood perfectly.

Before going down into the Ituri rain forest to look for pygmies we went up into the mountain province of Ruanda-Urundi, as we had heard that a very interesting tribe, the Watusi, lived there. Nowadays I hear that you can book a package tour to Ruanda to try and see the gorillas, but when I was there it was virtually unknown territory. Though in theory it was a Belgian protectorate, in practice there was no white administration or influence of any kind. The only Europeans who lived there were a family of German Protestant missionaries and they were away on leave when we arrived. It was in fact governed by the Watusi, a Hamitic tribe, under their king, Mutaga. They must have emigrated at some period from further north and they ruled the Bahutu – a Bantu people who must have been the original inhabitants – and also the Batwa, who were virtually their slaves.

After the Second World War, the Bahutu rose against their masters, the Watusi, and there was a civil war and appalling massacres. Newspapers in England reporting the conflict always referred to the Batwa as pygmies, which, of course, they are not. It is true that they are very small, though not nearly as small as the true pygmies of the forests, with whom they have nothing else in common.

The remarkable thing about the Watusi was their extraordinary height. They were very thin and were usually between six foot six inches and seven foot six inches tall, and I saw a few men of eight foot. They were very black, had negroid hair which they shaved in curious shapes and had handsome, finely cut features. They were a pastoral people, owning huge herds of native long-horned cattle, and their culture seemed to be rather similar to that of the Masai in Kenya. Their diet was dried beans, milk, and blood from the living cattle – they just opened a vein in a cow, drew off some blood and then closed it up again. Another curious feature of their culture was that they considered it to be just as indecent to be seen eating or drinking in public as we should think it to be seen defecating. Consequently there were lots of little huts dotted about where you could eat and drink in private, and there were no communal feasts. To celebrate they held ceremonial dances. The king had a trained troupe of dancers composed of young warriors, and their ballet, you could not call it anything else, was one of the most dramatic and exciting entertainments I have seen anywhere in the world. Most native African dances are fairly static, involving a lot of stamping and jigging and waving of arms, but with the dancers usually staying more or less in one place. With the Watusi it was quite different. The 'stage' was about the size of a football field and the forty dancers whirled about it at a tremendous speed like ferocious swallows, leaping high in the air and doing complicated manoeuvres while swinging about their ten-foot spears. It was a triumph of precision and timing that they did not spear one another.

The music to which they danced was produced by a band mostly consisting of drums of various kinds, including one sequence of drums ranging from very small to quite large that were roped together and played by a man who struck them with two bone hammers, like a xylophone. There were wind instruments made of cow horns and a six-foot-long straight bronze trumpet exactly like the ones found in ancient Egyptian tombs.

Many years later I was sitting at home listening on the radio to a programme on recent archaeological discoveries in Egypt. 'And now,' said the announcer, 'you will hear a sound that has not been heard for 3,000 years.' The eerie, impressive note of the long trumpet filled my room, and took me back, not 3,000 years, but to those days of my youth on the uplands of Ruanda-Urundi.

All the Watusi, men and women, wore a sort of Roman toga of white cotton printed with red stars, called a *kanga*. The rest of the population, Bahutu and Batwa, wore small loincloths of any material they could get hold of. Before we left Ruanda, I was determined to get a *kanga* to take home with me, and at last King Mutaga gave me one. On examining it I found 'Made in Birmingham' printed on the corner.

During the afternoons we usually watched jumping, the great sport of the Watusi – and they were quite excellent at it. I have seen a man jump a six-foot eight-inch pole almost from a standstill. If there are any Watusi left, I am sure that with a little training they could easily win the jumping events at the Olympics.

CHAPTER 12

Pygmies and an Erupting Volcano

Despite its geographical position I feel that Ruanda belongs totally to East Africa, and has nothing to do with the vast area of Central Africa. As we descended from the mountains into the rain forests we came into a new world. Few people in Europe seem to have any real mental idea of how vast it is. Having been brought up on Sir Roger Casement's *Red Rubber*, his exposé of conditions on the rubber plantations, and heard many stories of Belgian exploitation and maltreatment of the inhabitants of the Belgian Congo, I was surprised to find that few of the people we met on our way had even heard of their Belgian overlords, much less seen them. The Belgians never attempted to administer the whole country, an impossible task in any case, and only concerned themselves with those areas where it was possible to grow crops such as rubber and with the mountainous districts like Katanga where there were mines. The larger rivers, and particularly the Congo River, were used for communications. Only there could be found the settlements and even small towns along the banks.

Most of the country was too impenetrable for even Arab slave-raiders to have attempted to cross, so the people of the rain forests had been left on their own to lead hungry, short and disease-ridden lives. All, that is, except the pygmies. They alone seemed to be well adjusted to their environment. Everyone who has ever had anything to do with them seems to fall a victim to the charm of the pygmies. I was no exception.

Pygmies are nomadic and they move around in extended family groups of between forty and sixty. They are hunters and gatherers, living on what nature provides, eating roots, leaves and berries. Their protein requirements are satisfied by their being insectivorous, eating grubs which they find in rotten wood, and other insects, plus the occasional animal or bird that they manage to shoot with their little fur-covered bows. This diet seems to be an adequate one, as they were by far the healthiest as well as the jolliest people I saw in the forest. They can never stay longer than about a fortnight in one place, as by then they will have eaten all the available food within reasonable distance of their camp and they have to move on. By tradition when they move they take nothing with them except the sacred fire – and a few little gourds of the poison which they make from certain leaves and which is used to dip their arrow heads in if they are attacked. For huts they make temporary shelters of leaves and branches.

We camped at a small native village on a tributary of the Ituri river, made enquiries as to where we could find a group of pygmies, and waited.

Both Graham Greene in *A Burnt-Out Case* and Joseph Conrad in his *The Heart of Darkness* seem to have found in the great rain forests of the Congo Basin nothing but an atmosphere of evil, death and decay – and I have met other travellers who speak with horror of the primeval jungle, with its giant trees entwined with a million creepers and the strange fungoid growths on fallen branches. I did not have that impression at all, and found the forest interesting, exciting and strangely beautiful. Under the trees it is always twilight and no flowers are to be seen. There are plenty of orchids, but they grow on the tops of the trees far above one's head. Much colour, however, is supplied by butterflies which often descend to ground level and appear in the clearings in their millions, like fields of meadow flowers. There is always a feeling of life in the forest, with the sounds of monkeys and birds and insects, and the nights are wonderfully romantic, with the bright tropical moonlight shredded by the leaves and branches making patterns on the ground, and fireflies darting about in the undergrowth like shooting stars. When night falls the countless frogs set up their chorus – and the drums from the villages start their nightly programme of news and gossip. I have heard many people say that those never-ceasing drums and the croaking of the frogs are guaranteed to drive a European mad. I have never understood why. To me they were a delightful lullaby. They never got on my nerves. I only longed to know what the drums were saying.

Certainly the great rain forest did not depress either Arthur or myself or make us want to take to drink – an impossibility in any case, as we only carried one bottle of whiskey for celebrations, and a bottle of brandy for emergencies.

Juma was not depressed either, being delighted to get away from Ruanda. He despised all Africans not of the Buganda tribe as being physically and mentally inferior to himself, and had been upset and confused by the ruling Watusi, with their great height and arrogant bearing.

We did not find the pygmies: they found us. Apparently one of the items of news that the river people of our village beat out on their drums had been that a white man and woman had arrived, and that the woman had astonishingly long hair. (I had grown mine again in Tahiti and it was now well below my waist.) Nobody had ever seen hair like that in the Ituri forest, and a large family group of pygmies who happened to be in the neighbourhood heard the drums, which they could understand, and came to see the sight, as people used to flock to see the bearded lady in a circus at home. We woke up one morning and there they were. Juma, who had made contact with someone in the village, came and told me why they had come, so I went out to where they were gathered and brushed my hair, then plaited it, undid it and brushed it again. They stood round me in a circle, looking up with intensely serious expressions on their faces, and when I had finished burst out laughing. My 'act' had been a success.

They were much smaller than I expected, the men being about three feet six inches high and the women three feet. The babies, which the women carried on their hip supported by an arm, were enchanting, like tiny little brown dolls. Both men and women were naked, and their only ornamentation was a steel spike about an inch and a half long which came through a hole in their upper lip horizontally. Pygmies evidently did not kiss.

They all looked fit and healthy in contrast to the river people and though certainly not beautiful they had kindly, good-humoured faces. After watching the hair-brushing they went and examined all the things that we had brought with us. They were excited by the small mirrors, so I gave them some. Then they spotted an empty can, which had held peas, and pounced on it with joy. I soon discovered that that was what they really wanted. It would be invaluable for carrying water, or collecting grubs to bring home. We had lots of tinned food, so as soon as a can was empty we gave it to them and they soon had quite a collection.

The pygmies were on very good terms with the villagers and some appeared to speak the river people's language, but among themselves their talk sounded quite different. Mindful of Admiral Goodenough's directions I asked Juma to try to find out from his contacts among the river people whether the pygmy language was related to any other tongue, but he had no success. I was not disappointed, as I had always thought tracing their language was a hopeless task, which could only have succeeded if we had happened to meet someone who had had long contact with them and could make himself understood to us, and the chances of that were minimal.

The pygmies stayed around for about ten days, both men and women disappearing into the forest by day to gather food and talking, laughing a lot, and dancing by night. Their dance consisted of jigging round slowly in a circle to the beat of a drum which they borrowed from the village. They were friendly to us and the leader of the group gave us his little bow, which was made of wood covered with tan-coloured monkey fur and strung with the sinews of some larger animal.

Then one morning we got up and found they were gone, silently as they had come, and in a neat row were laid out all the things we had given them, the tin cans, the mirrors and the other odds and ends. True to their tradition, they carried nothing with them when they moved on. They allowed themselves no possessions.

After the pygmies left we moved north, recruiting porters at villages and taking them only a short distance, so that they could get home without danger. Had they left their own territory and strayed into that of a hostile tribe they would have been killed and eaten – or so they thought.

Our progress was always announced in advance by the 'local radio', i.e. the drums, and as soon as we arrived anywhere we were greeted by a deputation from the nearest village headed by the chief who always brought a present – usually eggs, which were frequently rotten – and we reciprocated with salt and spear heads. They were always glad to see us, and always had a request, which was invariably the same wherever we went. It was to ask if we would please shoot a leopard, which was hanging about the place and had already killed some women and children as they went down to the river to get water. If it wasn't leopards it was crocodiles. They had no guns, but they seemed to know all about them.

Remembering these pathetic requests, I can never really sympathise with those conservationists who wish to ban the sale of leopard skins. It seems to me to be one more example of the arrogant lack of understanding that the rich section of the world has for the poor one.

Some years ago the newspapers in England were full of the story that a puma was loose in the Surrey woods. People became absolutely hysterical. Armed police were sent out to hunt the beast. Nobody would go out at night.

One puma in the whole of Surrey – and these are the people who campaign that Africans should co-exist with leopards and crocodiles. I am not suggesting that all leopards and crocodiles should be exterminated, but I feel that they should exist only in game parks – where people are not allowed to live. Pumas are the least fierce of any felines, and in any case the 'Surrey puma' turned out to be a large dog.

We managed to shoot four leopards and dried the skins in the sun, and when we returned to England I had them tanned and made into a coat. I wore it with pride.

The people in the forest were very miserable, suffering from malnutrition and disease; and as usual the women were the chief sufferers. In the forest, where the tribes were very primitive and there was little agriculture, women did not have to work quite as hard as they did further north, but such work as there was had to be done by the women. They were in fact slaves.

When we hired porters in the village each man would arrive with his wife. He would carry some of our stores, and she would carry his food and whatever else he wanted to take with him. Frequently her load was much heavier than his and she often had a child to carry as well. This enraged me, but there was nothing I could do about it.

Among the many diseases that beset these unfortunate people, one of the most universal was malaria. Almost everyone seemed to have bouts of it, and it always seemed strange to me that after having lived for so many thousands of years in that malarial environment the people had not developed an immunity. Even rabbits are developing an immunity to myxomatosis. Although they were at first decimated by foreign diseases, now the Polynesians react to them in much the same way as Europeans and Asiatics. The same applies to Central America. After the Spanish conquest the people of Mexico declined by two-thirds. This is usually put down to the brutality of the Spaniards, but it is now established that a great majority of the deaths were due to the new germs that the foreigners brought. But by now the Central Americans are no more susceptible than anyone else.

Perhaps in Central Africa people's bodies could not adjust and develop immunities because of their totally inadequate diet. They have always suffered from a desperate shortage of protein and vitamins. Many of the tribes lived on manioc, and some on plantains which grow wild. This is chiefly because they have nothing else to eat, but also because they are as desperately conservative in their food as they are in everything else.

Most of these primitive peoples lived their whole lives in fear, not only of a hostile environment and of neighbouring tribes, but of a thousand evil spirits and malign influences which could only be countered by the power of the witch-doctors and with elaborate rituals. Many things and activities were taboo, including items of food.

I saw a fine example of this. Juma announced one day that the porters were starving to death.

'That's ridiculous, we have plenty of rice, boil it up for them.'

'They won't eat it, their tribe eats nothing but boiled plantains. They have eaten the last plantain that they brought with them yesterday. And there are none growing wild around here. Tomorrow they will be dead.'

This may sound absurd, since it takes about two months to die of starvation, as I knew very well it had taken more than that time for the Mayor of Cork and other hungerstrikers to die during the War of Independence, but if a member of a primitive tribe in Africa is convinced he is going to die, he dies. There is no doubt about that. It accounts for a great deal of the power of the witch-doctors. They can curse a man and, believing totally he is doomed, he dies. We were in a very serious situation. The problem was how to get the porters to eat the rice.

'Look, Juma, boil the rice and then go and talk to them. Tell them that, as they know, there are lots of different kinds of bananas, big yellow plaintains as long as your arm, small sweet pink bananas you can eat raw, and many other kinds. In the country we come from, the bananas are very, very small and light-coloured. You boil them like the big plantains. We eat them all the time and that is why we are so powerful.'

How Juma got it across to them I don't know, but he did; they ate up the rice (small white bananas) and we got them back to plantain-growing country, where we picked up a new lot of porters who liked eating frogs.

Not long after that I added another example to my collection of hermits, people who for one reason or another had turned their backs on civilisation and humanity and had gone to live in the wilds by themselves. These were a couple of White Russians, who having escaped from Russia after the Revolution with a little money or jewels, had gone to the remotest place they could find – the Congo side of the Mfumbiro mountains – and built themselves a home in a clearing in the jungle. They, and the local tribesmen that they recruited, had proved themselves excellent handymen. They had an enchanting bungalow with a lovely garden. Years of thought and ingenuity must have gone into its construction, for it had polished parquet floors made of beautiful local woods arranged in an elaborate pattern. The furniture was also made of local wood and covered in leopard and other skins; flowering creepers climbed the pillars of the verandah and the garden was full of flowering shrubs. There was water laid on for showers from a nearby stream. As there was a track to their house we arrived in the van, but they had no car. Instead they had an elephant. They grew a little coffee which was sent by elephant to the nearest trading post to sell. In this way they earned the small amount of money they needed to send for things, such as tools, that they could not make for themselves.

We were invited to stay, and the elephant was sent fifty miles into the mountains to a lake to fetch fish. She (for it was a cow) and her 'mahout' did the journey so speedily that even in the equatorial heat the fish were quite fresh on their return, and were a real treat for us after a diet of canned food and tough game. I was astonished at the sight of a trained African elephant. I had always believed that African elephants, unlike the Indian ones, were untrainable.

'Where did you get her? Who trained her?' I asked.

'We got her at the Elephant School at Niangara. Elephants are very cheap, and cost nothing to run. She is just let loose in the forest at night to graze.'

'Doesn't she run away and join a wild herd?'

'No, never. She is always here in the morning waiting for her breakfast of sugar cane. We grow it specially for her, she loves it and she adores her 'mahout'. He came with her from Niangara. She likes us too.'

We had never heard of the Elephant Training School and decided at once to go there, though we were running a bit short of time. The menace of the rainy season was approaching and if it caught up with us we would never get across Africa. We did however make one detour on the road to Niangara, which, as it is in the north-east corner of the Congo (Zaïre), did not take us out of our way on our journey to the South Sudan. The detour nearly cost us our lives.

We had camped near a White Fathers' Mission close to Mount Nyamaragira, which is a semi-active volcano, and the Fathers told us that, growing near the summit, there was a very strange collection of plants, including varieties of giant groundsel, which grow nowhere else. So, not wishing to miss our only opportunity of collecting some rare seeds, we decided to climb the Nyamaragira. When we were about three-quarters of the way up there was a tremendous roar. The ground shook and the sky darkened.

The volcano had erupted.

Fortunately for us the eruption had created a new crater on the far side of the mountain, but it was terrifying, much worse than being out in the streets of London during the Blitz, which it somewhat resembled.

Our first instinct was to get down the volcano and away as quickly as possible. But it turned out that the new crater was oozing out red hot lava, the streams of which were rolling down and partly encircling the whole volcano.

We could not go very fast or far on our feet, so we decided that it would be safer to wait and see which way the lava streams were going. I shall never forget those three days camped in an old non-active crater waiting for the eruption to abate, or for something worse to happen, while the whole mountain shuddered and red-hot stones and ash fell from the sky. I remember sitting in the choking sulphur fog, thinking of the trivial things I had worried about in the past and swearing that if we ever got out of this alive I would never bother about anything again.

By volcanic standards it was a very mini-eruption or we should not have survived, and after two nights we were able to skirt the hot lava streams and return to the White Fathers. We asked them if they were surprised to see us again, and they said not: they had all prayed for us and were sure their prayers would be answered.

Later I told this story to my second husband, Claud, and for years, whenever he and I were particularly worried about some difficult situation in which we found ourselves, we would say to one another, 'Well, at any rate it is not boiling lava.'

CHAPTER 13

Making the Language Map

The Elephant School at Niangara, when we finally got there, was no disappointment. Although I was not alone in thinking that the African elephants had nowhere been domesticated, the School had in fact been going for a long time, ever since the time of King Leopold of the Belgians. The commandant who was running the place when we got there told me its history.

In the first half of the nineteenth century a young Belgian officer on leave was visiting Rome. Wandering round a museum he was struck by a large relief carving of Hannibal's Carthaginian army. Depicted in that carving, as well as horses and soldiers, were many war elephants, and it was on these that he focussed his attention. They all had big ears and therefore must have been African elephants, not Oriental ones. As the museum had dated the relief as being contemporary with the second Punic war, i.e. about 200 B.C., the chances were that the sculptor had carved those elephants from life. If so, Hannibal's war elephants, with which he crossed the Alps, had been African. And as he had so many, it must have been common practice in those days to domesticate them. Why shouldn't that practice be revived? What the Carthaginians could do, the Belgians could do. Trained elephants would be tremendously useful in the Congo for transport and timber work. The young officer was determined to start the first Elephant School in Central Africa.

It was a long time before he realised his ambition. The belief that African elephants were untrainable was rooted in people's minds, and he could not raise the money to get the project off the ground. Finally, through a relation of his at court, he managed to put his idea before King Leopold, who was intrigued by it and gave him the money to found the Elephant School at Niangara, which had been training African elephants ever since.

The young Belgian officer had begun by importing two Indian

elephants, as well as several Indians who were used to working with elephants. These had now, of course, long gone and the workforce, like the elephants, were all African.

The young, half-grown elephants were captured at the start of the rainy season when the great herds always moved north from the rain forests to the savannah country, and then trained, largely by the already domesticated adult elephants.

There were about thirty of them, mostly cow elephants, when I was there. The few bulls had had their tusks removed so that they would be no temptation to ivory thieves – who existed even then. The elephants spent most of the day exercising or being trained, and at night they stood or lay on cement platforms chained by one leg. Every morning they were loosed, and galloped down to the river, which flowed below the farm, for their daily bathe.

It was delightful to watch them playing in the water. They behaved like kittens, ducking each other, squirting water with their trunks and pushing each other over. After about an hour they would all come back to their individual platforms, where a breakfast of sugar cane was waiting for them.

Each elephant had its own keeper, to whom he or she became deeply attached, and who always went with his charge for a period after it was sold. The school was supported by a government grant and it also made money by selling trained elephants and by hiring them out for special jobs and to any film companies who were making African films in the area.

The elephants enjoyed this, and proved excellent actors. They would demolish a fake village with the utmost ferocity, uproot trees, or do anything else that they were told to do by their keepers, who always stood by, hidden from the camera. There was one cow elephant called Marie whose speciality was being shot. She put her whole heart into her dying act. A supposed white hunter would fire a blank cartridge at her. She would, stop, shudder, fall on one knee, rise, stagger a few steps, then collapse and lie on her side as if dead, until her keeper came forward with an orange or a bunch of sugar cane – then she would jump up and proudly receive the applause of the company.

I got very fond of Marie, and made quite a pet of her. She got into the habit of coming up after her bathe to my hut and sticking her trunk in through the window for an orange. The commandant, however, told me that I was creating jealousy among the other elephants, and that if I gave a titbit to her, I must give one to all the others as well.

I had many interesting talks with this commandant, who was enthusiastic and extremely knowledgeable about his job and, indeed, about all African wild life. He kept a pet lion whom I did not trust, so he kindly sent it away during our visit. He told me, among other things, that he believed there were still unidentified animals in the great forest – in fact, the pygmy hippo, mentioned by Stanley in his account of the first expedition to cross the Congo, had only just been officially established as existing as a separate species.

He also told me that he believed there were pygmy elephants and that he personally had seen two skulls of elephants which had had four tusks each, two on each side.

I don't believe that conditions in Zaïre have changed much in the last fifty years. The place is so enormous that the colonial power made little, if any, impression on the majority of the territory, away from the major rivers, and I don't see that the present administration, with fewer facilities and trained personnel, could make any either. Recently there have been rumours that some kind of dinosaur still exists in a remote area, and two expeditions have been mounted to find it. While the existence of such a creature seems unlikely, I don't regard it as being by any means impossible.

The commandant offered to give us Marie, in exchange for our van, and I was very attracted by the idea. But Arthur said it was daft; what would we do with her and her keeper when we left the forested area where food for her was easily available, and how would we get the keeper home?

Still, on our journey north into the Sudan I constantly wished she was with us. We had been given maps from the Royal Geographical Society which were said to have come from the War Office. These maps marked tracks which had no existence in reality, and where tracks did exist the maps made no reference to the rivers which crossed them. We had to cut trees and tie them together with creepers to make rafts on which to float the van in order to cross them.

Arrived at the Sudan in the province of Equatoria, we made for the home of a British District Commissioner called Logan Grey. He had been told to expect us and he was quite worried that we had not appeared before.

The British District Commissioners in the Sudan ruled their little kingdoms as absolute monarchs, and certainly Logan Grey ruled his very well. He was just, kind and pragmatic as well as being totally dedicated to his job. Of course, his rule was entirely paternalistic. He never allowed a trace of democracy to creep in. This had the advantage that the weaker sections of the people, particularly the women, were protected as far as possible from those who were more aggressive and powerful, and the disadvantage that the Africans were in no way being prepared for independence. The entire population of Logan's district were illiterate. To get any form of education an African had to go to a mission school, which were few and far between. To attend them the pupil or his parents had to become Christian, whether they understood the religion or not. Nor were there any medical missionaries in the district. The many sick people could only go to the local witch-doctor or the District Commissioner, neither of whom had any medical training. One of the first things that we learned about Logan was that he hated missionaries. He repeatedly said they were the bane of his life.

I had a suspicion that possibly his dislike owed something to his not wanting to share authority with anyone in his little kingdom. But he explained his aversion to them by saying that they were trying to change the culture of a people without ever really understanding what that culture was and the physical conditions that had given rise to it. In sum, they didn't know what they were doing.

The day we arrived, after he had installed us in his house, he left us and rushed off with a troop of his soldiers. The reason for his haste was that he had just heard that one of the neighbouring chiefs had been converted by a German Protestant missionary and that this chief had been told that now he was a Christian, he could only have one wife. The chief, who had six wives, had selected the most attractive and hard-working one, and then driven the other five out into the jungle to be eaten by lions and leopards or die of starvation.

Logan succeeded in rescuing three of them and arrived back in a furious temper, with the chief in chains – and deploring the fact that he couldn't arrest the German too.

Polygamy was universal among the tribes and it created many problems. Though this time the missionary had obviously made a stupid mistake and thus caused the death of two women, I still think he was right in principle, quite apart from the effect on the unfortunate women.

Originally, when there was constant war between villages and raiding parties were common, a great many of the young men were always being killed, and most villages had a large surplus of women; but now that there was an imposed 'Pax Britannica', the sexes were usually more or less equal in numbers, so that if one man had three wives two had none at all, which didn't make for peace among neighbours.

I had travelled enough before I went to Africa to fully recognise the appalling condition of women in the poorer countries of the world, where the vast majority were slaves, and, what is more, slaves that were often treated as badly, or worse, than those in the eighteenth-century cotton plantations of the American Southern States.

But for the first time, among the African tribes, I saw a society in which the women did all the work without exception. They tilled the crops, built the houses, cut the trees, fetched the water, ground the corn, tended the stock, cooked the food and looked after the children.

The reason for this unequal division of labour was not hard to guess. In a tribal village everyone's function in society was marked out for them from birth. Boys helped the women until puberty, when, usually after a horrible initiation ceremony, they became warriors, whose job it was to defend the village or tribe. This had been necessary from time immemorial until about the last century. Being warriors was a full-time job; they had to be constantly on guard, and if they survived they eventually retired and became elders who did nothing but sit under a tree talking, electing the chief and settling the affairs of the community.

Consequently all the chores of everyday life devolved on the women – a state of affairs that had become petrified in African culture, though the original reason for it had long disappeared.

I believe that the independent African governments are doing their best to correct the situation, and that in the urban and the more civilised areas they are succeeding. But Africa is vast and the majority of the population rural – and women still do most, if not all, of the work. It is one of the major reasons why subsistence farmers will not grow a surplus of food to sell to the towns. The fact that nearly every one of the newly independent African states has to import food is not solely due to the climate and the infertility of the soil: the women cannot cope with the extra work involved in producing food for sale and carrying it to market. They are already working as hard as they can to sustain their own villages. It seems to me that the only solution is for the men to work as hard as the women, to really divide the labour. It is little use waiting for modern methods of agriculture to evolve, i.e. capital-intensive rather than labour-intensive farming. This already exists on the land developed by the original white colonialists, but in the vast backward rural areas the people have not the expertise to work or service the machines, nor their governments the money to buy and fuel them.

Logan Grey was bitterly opposed to our projected map-making trip westward. He knew everything about his own district, spoke at least four of the local dialects (British District Commissioners got a rise in salary for every extra language they knew), and was familiar with the personalities of most of the elders and all the chiefs he ruled over, but he knew nothing about what went on beyond the frontiers of the Sudan. To him French Equatorial Africa was cannibal country, and he was certain we should not survive. He cursed Sir William Goodenough and the committee of the Royal Geographical Society as irresponsible idiots. He accompanied us as far as the frontier, imploring us not to cross over.

'The French have no control. There is chaos in their territory, there are few District Commissioners, and what there are never leave their houses.'

'How do you know? You say you have never been there.'

'I hear stories,' he said darkly.

After three or four days when we reached the post of the nearest French administrator, which we did without difficulty, he was astonished to see us.

'Where on earth have you come from?'

We pointed behind us, eastwards.

'You mean to say you came from English territory? You are lucky to be alive, it's chaos over there. The English don't understand *les indigènes*.'

He was a talkative young man, as well he might be, having been there for five years all alone, with no one to talk to, as he could hardly speak the local language – it being French policy to teach *les indigènes* French.

He also had bad toothache, so I gave him all my aspirin and oil of cloves, a generous act which I bitterly regretted later when I myself got raging toothache and was reduced to stuffing the hole in my tooth with cotton-wool soaked in brandy. Monsieur le capitaine was, however, a great help to us, marking our map not only with White Fathers' Missions – there were several dotted about the country – but also the habitat of anyone who could speak French, from administrators to witch-doctors. We zig-zagged on our way from one to the other, gathering information. With so much help the job proved less difficult than I thought it would be.

In the country of the Zandi tribe I acquired a dog. As in the Congo, when we arrived at a village in the evening we were always pre-announced by the drums, and a reception committee awaited us headed by the chief bearing a gift. When we got to Zandi country the first chief that met me gave me, not the usual eggs, but a puppy. He said it was a lion hound from his personal pack, which was surprising as it was so very small. I asked him if it had a name. He said, 'Yes, she is called Ammatangazig,' whereupon all the accompanying Zandis burst out laughing. I asked what that meant but no one would tell me. I gathered it was something frightfully indecent.

So Zig became a member of the family and remained with me for several years. She proved to be a Basenji, a breed of dog common to several African countries, though varying slightly in each. The ones from Kenya are bigger – she looked a little like a fox terrier but with a pointed nose and curly tail like a pug. Like most Basenjis she had a bright reddish tan coat on her back and head and was white underneath. Her tail was tan with a white tip. She could not bark, only yodelled. She grew up to be highly intelligent, devious and rather malign and I loved her dearly. At that first moment, however, she was rather an embarrassment. It was, by then, getting difficult to find gifts to give the chiefs in return for theirs, as I had developed a taste for 'la cigarette Albert' and had foolishly smoked most of them myself, and we were running short of mirrors and spear heads. The porters were paid with salt. Anyway, the Zandis all seemed to have plenty of long spears, made entirely of iron. However, we found that, like the pygmies, most tribes valued empty tin cans and we still had some of our original stock of disgusting tinned peas which no one would eat, however hungry. So the chief got a tin can in return for Zig.

The Zandis were a war-like tribe who in the past were always attacking their neighbours. Now they satisfied their aggressive instincts by hunting lions. The little dogs were not meant to attack the lions, only find them. The pack, who always had bells round their necks, scented the lion and made a circle round the scrub where he was lying, ringing their bells and yodelling with all their might. The warriors then also ringed the lion, chanting and slowly closing the circle. At some point the lion would spring at one of the warriors, who fell on one knee and speared the lion from underneath. If he got the spearhead well embedded and could hold on to the other end of the shaft whatever happened, he had nine foot of iron between him and the lion. All the men on either side of him instantly thrust their spears into the lion, but it was the warrior who had broken the first spring who got the lion's eye teeth, which he wore round his neck ever after as a badge of honour. I saw men wearing necklaces of twenty or more lions' teeth. I also saw the graves of the ones who could not hold on to the end of their spears. In all Central African countries lions were listed as vermin; you got a bounty if you brought their tails to an administration post, but the Zandis didn't bother. They hunted for sport and to clear their territory of lions.

As we journeyed westwards, the peoples whose territory we passed through were almost untouched by the twentieth century; they lived as they had lived for thousands of years. If I had ever had any illusions about the benefits of the simple life, of getting back to nature, they would have been quickly shattered. Their primitive lives were miserable and it was a credit to their spirit that they survived at all. The disease rate was appalling. Every morning there was a crowd of hopeless invalids waiting to see us, pathetically believing that we would have some magical cure for them. The knowledge that this confidence was misplaced was heartbreaking. All I could do was to give them aspirin while our stock lasted, and tell them firmly that it would drive the evil spirits away. I hoped that just as the conviction that they were doomed caused them to die, they might equally be able to cure themselves by faith.

The only European objects that I saw in those villages were home-made deck-chairs, which seemed universal – the canvas replaced by skins – and once I saw some boys playing a game with a gourd that looked remarkably like football. No tribe except the Sarra were completely naked; most wore bunches of leaves fore and aft. When we left the forest areas and went north up the Shari river some Arab influence became noticeable and woven cotton replaced the green leaves. We were approaching what is now Chad, a bare country of dried mud. The only trees were laburnums of which there were thousands. It was so unpopulated that the numerous flocks of guinea fowl were so unafraid of humans that you could nearly catch them with your hands.

There was one Hamitic tribe, of great interest in that they spoke a tonal language more akin to an oriental tongue than an African one. I heard about them from a French administrator, Colonel Porreau, with whom we stayed for a week. The visit was a welcome rest, as I was beginning to suffer badly from lack of sleep, and had gone down to about six stone in weight. I wasn't getting enough rest because of Zig and the sentries.

Making camp each night involved a good deal of administration. Fires had to be lit at each corner of the encampment and a rota of sentries arranged to feed the fires all night, which had to be kept burning brightly to keep off lions, leopards and thieves. Dinner had to be cooked or heated and then all stores counted. This had to be done every night to prevent theft. If guns had been fired that day, and they usually had, they had to be cleaned, and there were diaries and reports to write. So it was around eleven o'clock or later before the day's work was done. I had a narrow canvas campbed which I had to share with Zig and my rifle. We had to take our guns to bed with us, as in no other way could we be sure that they would not be stolen while we slept. The ammunition was stored under Arthur's bed. Zig was supposed to sleep under my bed. This she absolutely refused to do – and made such a fuss when I tried to force her to, by tying a rope from her collar to a bed post, that it was less trouble to let her curl up on my feet. All night the lions grunted around the camp – you could hear them for miles – and every time a lion grunted Zig yodelled at the top of her voice. I couldn't stop her – she was just doing her job as a lion hound. In any case, I slept in the open, and so lightly, that if the light of the fires died down, I was instantly awakened and had to get up, shake the sentries and make them feed the fires.

I told Juma over and over again to explain to them that if they went to sleep, being on the edge of the camp, they would be the first ones to be killed, by humans or animals. He just shrugged and said, 'Yes, they know, but they are tired and often sick.' Which unfortunately was true. Another time he told me that the porters always alluded to me as 'she who never sleeps'. They were about right.

Arthur, who slept like a log, would leap up just before sunrise, about 5.30 a.m., and say briskly, 'Come along, time to start breaking camp. Where's breakfast?'

The French commissioner with whom we stayed was a typical Parisian. He had an intellectual interest in Africa, but loathed the lonely life and longed for home. Like a long-term prisoner he had a large calendar, on which each evening he thankfully crossed off the day past, saying like Goncharov's Russian serfs, 'Another day gone, Thank God.'

He was a great gourmet and at 11.30 a.m. each day we had a seven-course dinner. It was astounding the meals he produced with the scant local produce. He had even developed a way of making dik-dik, a sort of gazelle, delicious. One of the troubles of living off the land in Central Africa in the days before refrigeration is that if you shot a deer and ate it at once, it was so tough you couldn't get your teeth through it, but if you kept it twenty-four hours it had gone bad. What Colonel Porreau did was to have a pit dug about five feet deep. The fresh gazelle was laid in it and all the earth put back. After three days the gazelle was dug up again skinned, cut up and roasted. To my surprise the meat was fresh and tender.

He loved variety, and was always experimenting with different kinds of meat. One of his favourites was python, with garlic and coconut sauce. He would not tell us what we were eating, until we had admitted that the dish was very good. I was careful not to disclose to him that the pygmies got most of their protein from fat white wood-maggots as I was sure he would send people out to look for them, and we should get maggots for dinner next day.

It was interesting to see the difference between French and British administration on the ground. Both Logan Grey and Colonel Porreau were intelligent men conscientiously doing their job, but whereas Logan was emotionally involved with his people, had his own opinion about everything, and settled all problems by common sense, Porreau worked by the rule book. There was a directive, it seemed, as to how to deal with any given situation. And he stuck to it, whatever his own personal opinion might be. He was quite detached, and only longed to get back to France. Logan was always dashing all over his district dispensing justice personally. Porreau stayed at his headquarters and ruled through intermediaries. The two systems were diametrically opposed, but I didn't find that it made much difference to the people governed – conditions in both districts appeared to be very much the same, or so it seemed from the local gossip and complaints as related by Juma.

The people on the Shari river, which flows into Lake Chad, had for centuries suffered from Arab slave raiders, who used to capture all the women. In defence, this poor people devised a scheme to make the women hideous and deformed. Baby girls had their lips pierced and a reed inserted in the hole; as they grew, larger and larger pieces of wood were put in until in the end a disc about three inches in diameter was worn, which made them look like some strange sort of water bird with broad bills. Though Arab slave raiders, when I was there, had ceased their activities, the practice had not been abandoned, since by then a large beak was considered a thing of beauty and no girl with normal lips would be wanted by anyone. This is not so strange when you think of the fluctuations of fashion in Europe, of Victorian young ladies desperately lacing themselves in to obtain eleven-inch waists, which are equally unnatural – or the bright young things of the twenties strapping down their breasts to appear flat, while the brassières of the sixties were padded out to make them appear huge.

As there was little timber around the Shari, this tribe, who lived principally on fish from the river, made beautiful houses of mud shaped like artillery shells, decorated outside with complicated patterns. Whether it was the shape or the material used I don't know, but they were remarkably cool and comfortable inside.

CHAPTER 14

Across the Sahara

Our return route lay across the Sahara. It was wonderful to get back to the Great Desert, which I had first fallen in love with when I was wintering in Biskra. The dry air and the cool nights soon gave me back my energy and I loved lying in my camp bed at night looking up at the brilliant stars which, because of the dry air, never twinkle, and listening to the silence, which was absolute.

Most of the Sahara is dried mud and rocks, many of them enormous and thrown about haphazardly or piled in great heaps. There are also, in the Hoggar Mountains, cliffs of great height and plateaus as flat as a billiard table. There are, of course, two large areas of sand dunes as well, which move about, making road-making difficult. To me the scenery was beautiful, moonlike and strange as an abstract painting, the colour of the dried earth and the vast boulders changing with every hour of day as the sun rose and set.

There was no road, but the French had thoughtfully put cairns of stones every hundred yards or so, so if one was careful not to drive at dawn or sunset, when the light was bad, and never in a dust storm, one would have had to be incredibly stupid to get lost.

There was, in fact, a bus, which crossed once a fortnight, mostly carrying French officials, and we were advised to start off three days ahead of it so that it would pick us up if we broke down.

As much as I loved the desert, Zig hated it. She punished us as much as she could for bringing her there by being as annoying as possible. Her pet trick was to wait until we had everything loaded and were about to start off in the morning, and then run away. She watched us until all was ready and then at my first call of 'Zig, come here', off she went. I soon found that the only way to deal with her was to totally ignore her, to pretend I had forgotten her existence. We also had a cheetah cub, who had to be settled in his box. (The tree hyrax, Turi, had died some time back.) As soon as that was done we drove off – Zig, seeing herself deserted would gallop after the truck, stopping occasionally to throw back her head and yodel. We had to keep going for quite a long time to tire her, otherwise as soon as we stopped and got out to pick her up, she ran off again. Quite quickly she learned her lesson and ever after got into the truck before daylight and sat there waiting for us to move off.

We passed several families of Tuaregs in the South Sahara, that celebrated nomadic desert people with their finely cut features, coal black skins and bright blue eyes. The only other passers-by were a surprise. About 4.30 one afternoon we came round a small hillock of boulders to find a large shiny black limousine driving towards us. It was driven by a chauffeur in navy-blue uniform wearing a uniform cap. In the back were two elderly ladies dressed in black. They had smart little hats with eye veils and were wearing black gloves. The limousine did not stop, as is the custom when people meet in the desert, but slowly and steadily came on. As they passed us the two little old ladies, who were sitting bolt upright, bowed to us in a formal manner. When they had gone Arthur and I looked at each other,

'Did you see what I saw?' we said in unison.

Next day we stopped at a French Foreign Legion post. They were dotted along the route at 300- or 400-mile intervals, and we were having a drink with the captain in charge. Rather nervously we told him of the apparition of the black Rolls-Royce, wondering if he would send for a medical officer to examine us for sunstroke. He only laughed. 'Yes, I know who they are. They stayed here the night before last. They are the grandmother and great-aunt of a high French official in West Africa. Every year they get into their automobile in Paris, dressed in their best Parisian clothes, and drive across France, Algeria, the Sahara and Nigeria to visit him. It is said that he is absolutely terrified of them, and is always blind drunk for a month after their departure.'

After the war the English newspapers were full of stories about brave and enterprising 'overlanders' who drove across the Great Desert to get to East and South Africa, and of the difficulties and dangers they encountered. The stories were rubbish, and on reading them I couldn't help thinking of those two aged Parisian dowagers.

Our only other unusual and interesting experience occurred not long after we had left Fort Lamy. While there, I had visited a doctor attached to the French Foreign Legion, as I was running a temperature. We made friends, and after he had assured me that I had nothing to worry about, said that if we were going to take the Hoggar route across the desert, he would be most grateful if we would deviate to the east after Tamarasset and visit a young officer in a remote fort whom he knew to be desperately lonely, and perhaps suffering from '*le cafard*'. If we thought this lieutenant was really in a bad way, we were to let him know when we got to Algiers, and he would take steps to have him moved on medical grounds.

The doctor said the route to the fort was well marked with stone cairns.

I promised to do as he asked, and after leaving the track north we drove all day, even during the hottest midday hours, but saw no trace of the fort, which was said to be only a fairly short distance from the main route. When dusk began to fall we decided to camp and continue the search in the morning, but at that moment we saw ahead of us, not a fort, but a small town built in a traditional Arab style and constructed of the red earth of the desert. We were astonished as we had heard nothing of any town or village. On arriving in the main square we saw that this was no ordinary Arab village. The houses were clean and neat and new-looking; there were no wooden doors anywhere and there was absolutely no sign of life. It did not seem like a place that had been abandoned, for there was no sign of previous habitation. In the centre of the square was an elaborate fountain modelled out of dried mud, from which no water came. The desert wind whistled eerily through the empty doorways.

'There is nobody here,' Arthur said. 'We had better sleep in one of these houses.'

'Certainly not,' I replied, 'this place is sinister, haunted. I don't believe it really exists. We'll push on and camp in the desert beyond.'

We drove on a fine unrutted road out of the village and over a causeway of rough stones with a balustrade of decorated and filigreed dried mud. It crossed a dried-up wadi and at the end of it was a triumphal arch. As we passed under the arch we saw ahead of us a scruffy little French fort with the tricolour flying from a rather crooked pole on the roof. On either side of the central doorway stood two black Senegalese sentries, unquestionably alive.

We had arrived at our destination. The young French lieutenant was so overjoyed to see us that he positively babbled. Over a bottle of excellent French wine he asked a thousand questions about who we were and where we had come from. He took us over the fort and introduced us to his only companion, a mynah bird, who repeated 'Vive la France, vive la patrie' over and over again. We asked how long the young man had been here. He replied instantly, 'Three years and fifty seven days.' He got mail every month or so, and was in communication by wireless with the nearest military post, but he lived quite alone in command of a troop of Senegalese – with whom, for reasons of military discipline, he could have no companionship.

We then asked somewhat shyly about the ghost town across the wadi. He swelled with pride. 'I made that. It is the fruit of my genius. I will conduct you over it tomorrow. It is the boredom that is so terrible here. Not only for me but for my men too. We are here to keep order in this part of the south Sahara, but always all is quiet, peaceful. There are no people to be controlled. We never even see any wandering Tuaregs. We are not on the route to anywhere. We cannot spend all our days drilling and fighting mock battles, so I decided to make 'sand castles'. There is a very good well in the fort so we take water down there and mix it with the earth and dry it in the sun to make brick and I build my beautiful city. I am just about to start on a fine 'Palais de Justice'. See, I have the plans here.

'It keeps the men busy, and avoids trouble and perhaps some day an artesian well will be sunk, people will live in my city, my fountains will flow with water. In any case it will be a fine puzzle for archaeologists in the future when we are dead and gone.'

He then asked how we had found him and I told him of the Legion doctor who had suggested we pay him a visit.

'Do not say a word about my sand castles – it would do my career great harm. Say you found me in good shape, and well adjusted to conditions here. As you see, my mental condition is perfect. It would be absolutely tragic if I were moved before I have finished all my administration buildings.'

He became extremely agitated at the very thought of it.

And so we continued our journey northwards and left Africa behind us – the Africa of half a century ago: fascinating, beautiful and in some ways horrible. The amount of human suffering I had seen, against a background of nature in its most powerful and dramatic form, affected the whole of the rest of my life. I have never forgotten it, nor ceased to relate the condition of its people to that of the Western world I live in, just as I have never fogotten the day when I was nearly entombed in boiling lava. It has helped to put things in perspective.

CHAPTER 15

The Shadow of Death

On arrival back in London we found that my whole family, including Darrell and the nurse, had gone to Ireland and we planned to join them as soon as we had delivered our photographs and reports to the Royal Geographical. My animals were, of course, in quarantine and I was worried about Zig as most Basenjis died when they were transferred to a cold northern climate. But the kennels where she was quarantined were very interested in her, as she was the first Basenji from the Congo that had been imported, and took great care of her, installing a special infra-red lamp in her kennel. In any case she cleverly grew another half inch of fur almost at once, with more beneficial results than those Australian ponies that I knew of, who for three years after they had been imported into the northern hemisphere grew heavy coats in the summer and shed them in the winter, causing immense trouble to their owner.

Then, after a few days, disaster struck. My mother telephoned from Myrtle Grove to say that Darrell was gravely ill, and would we come at once.

He had fallen in the garden and scratched his nose. The graze had turned septic and he had blood poisoning.

We found him lying in the Bons Secours Convent Hospital, where I had spent so many months when I was sixteen. There were no antibiotics in those days, and from the first the doctors held out little hope.

He lay in his little white cot, semi-conscious. Thank God at least he was not suffering. I sat by him watching his life slowly ebb away. I was frozen with despair and guilt. I had seen so little of him in his short life: I should never have left him. It was no good my family saying that this could have happened whatever I had done. Despite being true it did nothing to relieve my feeling of responsibility and regret at not having been a more devoted mother. In Africa I had been so busy and interested in the new places and people I was seeing that I had hardly given a thought to those at home.

After the funeral Arthur and I returned to London. I fell into a deep depression, refusing to see anyone or go anywhere.

Nowadays, when someone is in that condition, a doctor is consulted and the person is treated with drugs. But in those days one was supposed to have enough strength of character to overcome all such blows of fortune. To begin with everyone was immensely sympathetic, but after a bit my whole family became extremely irritated with me – and ceaselessly told me to pull myself together. The Royal Geographical Society put on an exhibition of my photographs, but I didn't even go to it. I could take no interest in anything.

I was still very thin and it was thought that perhaps I had picked up some bug in the Congo that was causing me to behave in this, for me, untypical way, and I went to the Institute of Tropical Medicine. The doctors there were very interested in me, not because I had anything wrong with me, but because I hadn't. They were particularly interested in the fact that I had never had malaria. They mapped out where I had been and asked me endless questions. Had I taken quinine as a preventative? No, I had taken nothing. Had I slept under a mosquito net? No, it had got torn early on. Had anyone near me had malaria? Yes, most of the porters had it intermittently. They also asked me about the water I had drunk. Did I always boil it? Usually I made tea, which involved boiling, but if for some reason that was impossible I always put a slug of whiskey in it to kill the germs.

This almost made them fall over with laughter. They told me that only equal quantities of pure alcohol and water left standing for at least eight hours would have the effect of sterilising the water. There followed more tests to see if I had picked up a waterborne germ, but the answers were all negative.

By then I was fed up with hospitals and doctors. Also I had a dark suspicion that as they were so interested in why I had not got malaria, they wanted to keep me at hospital just to study me, and maybe even try to give me malaria. So I discharged myself.

Then one morning I woke up and knew exactly what I must do. I must go off somewhere by myself. Of course I knew I was running away from problems and situations that I simply didn't feel strong enough to handle. But there are occasions when running away is the sensible thing to do. I wasn't doing myself or anybody else any good by hanging around, hating London, and getting on everybody's nerves.

I asked Patrick Balfour, an old friend who worked on the *Evening Standard*, if his paper would be interested in articles about some remote place. I suggested Ruthenia, the extreme eastern tip of Czechoslovakia which is now part of the U.S.S.R., and after a delay of about a week he telephoned me and said, 'Yes, the editor would be very interested.' He added, 'I gather there is a good deal of trouble there, which is apparently what you want, so do be careful.'

There was trouble all right, as I soon found when I got to the Carpathian Mountains, of which Ruthenia is composed. The mountains run north and south, forming a barrier between East and West, but there is a pass – the Pass of the Tartars, over which first the Huns came flooding into northern Europe, and after them Genghis Khan's Golden Horde. The inhabitants called themselves 'Little Russians' and spoke Ukrainian.

They were woodcutters. For a thousand years they had lived by felling timber, floating it down the rivers to the plains of Unvaa and Munkas in the spring. They followed the timber on rafts and remained all the summer in the lowlands working on the land, returning home in the autumn with money and grain to last them through the long cold winter. Now, in the autumn of 1938, the plains had been given to Hungary and the frontier closed, so there was no outlet for their timber and no possibility of their earning any money. The tiny patches of potatoes and rye in the valleys would not feed even one tenth of the population.

There was unemployment pay, for men only. It amounted to 10 crowns a week, worth 1*s.* 6*d.* or 7 new pence, and was only given in exchange for a day's work on the roads. Not surprisingly, eighty-five per cent of the people were starving. I felt I was back in Africa again, except that it was so cold.

The capital, Chust, an untidy overgrown village, had a gay, rather hysterical and very raffish atmosphere, which contrasted sharply with the silent suffering of the countryside.

Cafés and cabarets of the most squalid kind were crammed with soldiers. Not only was the Czech army there; there was also the 'Sitch', a Free Corps who called themselves the 'Army of Greater Ukraine' and was composed of White Russians and Ukrainians from Poland and Roumania. They claimed that they were 30,000 strong and openly admitted to being financed and armed by Hitler. In fact they were fervent Nazis in every respect, including rabid anti-semitism, and never tired of describing the pogroms they would like to inflict on the Jews who made up ten per cent of the population of Ruthenia and who were largely very small farmers who lived in the few arable districts of the country.

Altogether Chust was a horrible place and I was glad to get away from it.

Getting about the country was not easy, since the whole of Ruthenia was under martial law and there were sentries posted on all bridges and at ten-mile intervals along the roads. One had to have a permit to move from one village to another.

One afternoon I was arrested on the grounds that my papers were not in order, but managed to get off by waving a letter from a friend who was a peeress, and who had a coronet printed on both envelope and writing paper. I had brought the letter with me because a journalist friend had once told me that he had got out of a difficult situation in a foreign country by showing the top of a writ that had been served on him for non-payment of a debt, and which had 'On His Majesty's Service' printed on it. In those affluent days I had no writs, but I did have the peeress's letter. Knowing that the officer could not read English I declared it was from the King of England, of whom I was a close relative, and that terrible things would happen to him if he did not assist me in every way. It would be a diplomatic incident of the gravest kind.

Surprisingly enough, it worked – and he ended up by giving me dinner and providing me with an escort to the next village.

Driving along the mountain tracks I watched the peasants hard at work gathering in the last of their crops from their tiny patches of arable ground. One could easily tell the Ruthenians from the Jewish farmers, as the latter all wore their traditional dress of black coats and flat-topped, wide-brimmed black hats. They wore their hair, which was either black or red, in long ringlets. I discovered that they were just as uneducated as their Slav neighbours, and quite ignorant of all political movements. They were busy trying to get enough food in for the winter, unaware that they and their families would soon be swept away by the Holocaust. With the help of a 'village hetman' who interpreted for me, I asked five men what they thought of Hitler. Three had not heard of him, one thought he was a Hungarian general and only the last said, 'I know of him. He is bad for the Jews.'

One evening I drove into a village in a remote valley and suddenly realised that I could understand what the people in the café were saying. They appeared to be Ruthenian peasants, but they seemed to be talking a kind of French. I went to look for the local rabbi, who was likely to be the only educated man in the village, and when I found him, I asked him for an explanation. He told me that the majority of the villagers were the descendants of a troop of Napoleon's soldiers, who, on the retreat from Moscow, became separated from the main army, got lost in the Carpathian Mountains and, on reaching this valley, decided to go no further, and settled down. Though they all could speak Ukrainian, the inhabitants of the valley always spoke a slightly archaic French at home and among themselves.

As soon as I had gathered enough information for my articles for the *Evening Standard* I was in a hurry to get out of Ruthenia. It was a depressing place, cold and bug-ridden, with an overpowering atmosphere of misery and fear and the pervading presence of the horrible White Ukrainian irregulars, vocal in their impatience to create a greater Ukrainian state modelled on Nazi Germany. It was also necessary to get out quickly before the last link with the West, a narrow mountain track, was cut – either by snow or marauding Free Corps action. The railway and the main road ran through Hungarian territory and had been closed for some time.

Despite the roughness of my solitary expedition, when I got back to London my health had improved and my depression lifted.

It was no good brooding about the past. The past was dead. I was still only twenty-four and I must look to the future, though the future in the spring of 1939 did not seem very promising.

Two things were obvious.

My marriage to Arthur was ending and World War II was about to begin.

My mother had been right. I had been far too young to get married.

Arthur and I had been good comrades on our travels together, but now we were home we just could not get on even reasonably well. There was no foundation on which to build. After Darrell's death there was just nothing left to hold us together and the shock of his death had brought everything to a head. One thing we agreed upon – the certainty of the coming war, and the necessity for both of us to get some training for useful war work. I could have just 'opted out' and gone to Ireland, but that was the last thing I wanted to do. Being passionately anti-Nazi I wanted to play my part, however tiny, in helping to defeat Hitler, who seemed to me, and still seems, the personification of all evil.

Arthur joined the army, and went off to the country for training, and I signed on with the Air-Raid Precautions organisation, the A.R.P., which was just beginning to be formed, and was assigned to the 'Northern Control Centre', which meant I was to work in a large cellar, deep underground beneath Praed Street in Paddington.

CHAPTER 16

Claud Cockburn

I met Claud Cockburn at a very grand party given by a rich American woman called Connie Bainbridge at Arlington House, just below the Ritz.

He had read my pieces in the *Evening Standard*, and asked our hostess to introduce him to me, as he wanted to do a piece on Ruthenia in his paper, *The Week*.

I had never met Claud before though we had many mutual friends. This was probably due to the fact that he had been in Spain all through the Civil War, and when he returned I had been on my travels. But I had heard a very great deal about him. He was a famous and highly controversial figure, said to be either a hero or a villain, according to the speaker's political persuasion. Everyone agreed that he was brilliant and unpredictable. Brilliant he certainly was, but not unpredictable. In fact he was in all things utterly consistent. In the forty-one years we were married I never knew him deviate one iota from his principles.

He was Scottish in origin, being the great-grandson of Henry, Lord Cockburn, the great advocate and judge, a civilised and humane man, always well in advance of his time.

Claud's father had been a diplomat, who had been Counsellor at the Peking embassy in China during the siege of the legations by the Boxers in 1900. Claud was born shortly after the siege was raised by an international force, who had taken fifty-five days to fight their way up from the coast.

His first two years had been spent with his parents in Peking, and then, being a sickly child, probably due to the malnutrition and nervous tension of his mother during the siege, he had been sent with a Chinese nurse back to his grandmother in Scotland.

The nurse could not speak a word of anything but Chinese, and Claud saw little of his grandmother, so that when his parents came back on leave two years later they found that their little son could speak nothing but Chinese – a language that his mother could not understand, though his father was fluent in it.

Horrified, his mother immediately sent the nurse back to Peking, a stupid act, which I believe had a big effect on Claud's life.

It certainly had a big effect on his relations with his mother, for he had, naturally, loved the nurse, who was the only mother he knew, and he never grew to like his real mother, though he adored his father. I never met his mother, and of course she may have been an eminently dislikeable woman, but she always sounded pretty harmless to me, and I have always felt sorry for her.

For some reason that I have never understood, his father, who retired early, settled not in Scotland but in the south of England, never buying a house, but renting them and moving about until Claud was of school age, when they took a house at Berkhamsted, so that he could go to school there.

It seems to have been a good choice. It was a small but ancient public school and the education must have been excellent as so many of his school fellows seem to have distinguished themselves in one way or another. Charles Henry Greene was the headmaster, father of Hugh, Raymond and Graham Greene, and the latter became a lifelong friend of Claud's. Claud really loved him and in the holidays they used to go on little trips together, including one with a barrel-organ which they hired. He told me that it was astonishing how much money householders gave them just to go away.

Claud always said that one of the nicest things about Graham Greene was that all his life he had retained the enthusiasm and energy of an eighteen-year-old. In fact he said that he never really grew up, a statement that in some ways also applied to Claud himself. Claud always regretted that in later life their paths so seldom crossed, though they did occasionally correspond.

After the First World War, when Claud was sixteen, his father got a job, by way of the old-boy network, heading a commission sent to sort out the tangled finances of the defeated Hungary. He knew nothing of Hungary, and even less of finance, but the previous incumbent, who was an expert in both, had been sacked because he had been seen picking his teeth with a tram ticket in the lounge of the best hotel in

Budapest and was therefore considered a disgrace to Imperial and Victorious Britain.

Claud spent his holidays with his family in Central Europe. It was his first introduction to the horrible effects of war and political upheaval. After the defeat of Germany and her allies there had been a revolution and a counter-revolution in Hungary. Thousands had been slaughtered, everything was in chaos and now inflation was astronomical and the survivors were starving. The Four Freedoms which were supposed to prevail when the Western Allies had won their 'war to end war' were not in evidence. Certainly not Freedom from Want and Freedom from Fear.

It was an eye-opener to one who had lived all his conscious life in the cosy embrace of the English Establishment.

Having obtained a scholarship to Oxford, where he studied for a degree in classics – Greats as it was called – he joined his cousin Evelyn Waugh in moving with the flamboyant set which included Harold Acton, Robert Byron, Christopher Hollis and Basil Murray.

Until it was suppressed by the college authorities he was a member of the committee of the Hypocrites Club. He was not seriously political at that time, though he was for a period secretary of the Liberal Club and the editor of *Isis*. He marched about Oxford in mauve Oxford bags, with a magenta satin cummerbund, drinking, getting into debt and generally having a good time. Despite an apparent disregard of his studies he did well in his final exams and then won a travelling fellowship from Queen's College, Oxford which took him first to France and then to Germany.

It was in the Germany of 1926–7 that he first really studied the works of Karl Marx and Lenin, but at the same time he met many highly informed people and read many authoritative books which held that what was happening in the United States in the boom years of 1926–29 made nonsense of the economic theories of Marx, Lenin and Bukharin. He felt he must go to America and see for himself if Americans had miraculously solved the contradictions which Marx held were inherent in the capitalist system. While in Berlin he had been working for *The Times*, and when the two years of his travelling fellowship ended he applied for the job of assistant correspondent of *The Times* in New York and Washington and was appointed. Hardly had he got there when, on 24 October 1929, the New York stock-market collapsed and the great slump began. He felt that the American miracle had been a delusion.

After three years as *The Times* correspondent in the U.S.A. he resigned, came back to England, and joined the Communist Party of Great Britain. *The Times* was very reluctant to let him go. He had been a brilliant success as a correspondent. Malcolm Muggeridge, in an introduction to one of his books, has described him as being one of the greatest journalists of all time. When he resigned, the editor of *The Times*, Geoffrey Dawson, simply thought he was having a nervous breakdown due to overwork, and offered him six months' paid leave to get over it. But his mind was made up. To raise money for the start of his new life he wrote a book on the social and political set-up in Washington called *Hi-Lo Washington*. This he completed in only six weeks. Then he set sail for Europe.

A great deal has been written about Claud. No account of the political and literary life of the thirties in England seems to be complete without a character sketch of him, and I am always astonished by the fact that almost invariably they get him wrong. For instance, Harrison Salisbury, a famous American journalist, describes Claud in his autobiography as 'one of the most cynical men I have ever met'. Whatever Claud was, it certainly wasn't cynical. Quite the reverse – if anything, he was almost adolescently romantic, and retained this characteristic to his dying day.

He always used to say that he thought that the origins of his move to the extreme left in politics arose from the fact that he had to recite the Magnificat from the Prayer Book every day at morning prayers at school. The lines about 'the mighty being cast down from their places, and the meek exalted' made a deep impression on him.

In a queer, rather convoluted way, he was a product of the nineteenth-century Victorian ethic. He believed in honesty, hard work and loyalty, as well as in good and evil, though he did have his own interpretation of the former. During the Spanish Civil War, which he was reporting for the *Daily Worker* and some American papers, he was much criticised for inventing occurrences which did not, in fact, take place – for instance, the revolt at Teruel. He defended himself on the grounds that all journalism was, in essence, propaganda, if only in the selection of the news reported. He was fighting against the evils of fascism for the good of humanity, and was therefore fully justified.

Claud was an emotional man who felt passionately about practically everything. He was also uninhibited. From the early days of our relationship I refused to go to the theatre with him – or if I did go, insisted on sitting in a different row of seats – because if he liked a play he was inclined to stand up and cheer, and if he didn't he shouted 'Balls' at the top of his voice – quite a contrast to the stony-faced 'apparatchik' many who did not know him imagined him to be.

Claud has always been described as a brilliant journalist and propagandist, but his real interest was in writing novels and short stories, and I am delighted that his works are now being reissued. I once heard him say to a fellow novelist that if he were in some way prevented from writing ever again, he would rather be dead.

All those who knew him well loved him deeply for his understanding, wonderful sense of humour and general charm as well as his brains.

Even Evelyn Waugh, who disagreed with Claud's opinions in every possible way, refers to him in his diaries as 'My poor, dear, mad cousin Claud'. He is almost the only person mentioned that Waugh is never bitchy about.

Claud loved children and animals, though he was hopeless at training his dog and cat, not being consistent enough. There was never any 'generation gap' between him and his three sons, or, in fact, any other adolescent. He would always listen to their views, however outlandish, with respect, and many came to him for advice on questions that they would never have dreamed of discussing with any other member of the older generation.

Claud's plan in returning to London in 1933 was to revive the eighteenth-century English tradition of the newsletter. In the 1930s the sort of facts – political, diplomatic and financial – that were discussed openly in clubs, embassies and among people who were near the centres of power, never got into the national newspapers. The newspaper proprietors automatically adopted an attitude of 'not before the children'. Many conscientious foreign correspondents often tried to file stories that did not fit in with the accepted view of what was going on that was being purveyed to the mass of the population, only to have such stories blue-pencilled by the editor. It had constantly happened to Claud.

Starting any form of newspaper required, and always has required, an immense amount of capital. Also the owner had to belong to the Newspaper Publishers' Association to get his paper on the newspaper trains. So the dissemination of information was virtually a closed shop.

Claud saw that the invention of the hand-operated mimeograph and the use of the postal system could overcome these barriers. And so he started *The Week*. Since then there have been countless newsletters produced in the same way, all over the world. But Claud's newsletter was the first since the eighteenth century. He started it with a capital of £40.

In my book *The Years of the Week* I have described how his venture succeeded. Though never large in circulation by newspaper standards, *The Week* was soon enormously influential, and became required reading for all serious journalists and politicians. Later the *Observer* newspaper wrote of it:

> It was one of the half dozen British publications most often quoted in the press of the entire world. Included among its subscribers were the foreign ministers of eleven nations, all the embassies and legations in London, the leading banking and brokerage houses in London, Paris, Amsterdam and New York. All the leading foreign correspondents in London, twelve members of the United States senate and thirty members of the House of Representatives, fifty M.P.'s and a hundred members of the House of Lords. The secretaries of all the leading Trade Unions, Charlie Chaplin, King Edward VIII and the Nizam of Hyderabad.

Claud was what was known after the war as one of the 'premature anti-fascists' and, of course, those powerful sections on the right wing of the Conservative Party, who were working hard for a deal with Hitler, hated him. Ribbentrop, then German ambassador in London, tried to get *The Week* banned.

Claud invented the name, 'The Cliveden Set' after 'Cliveden', the home of Nancy, Lady Astor, for all those around her who were striving for such an accommodation with the Nazis, and the name stuck. It infuriated Lady Astor; correspondents and politicians refused to come to her house on the grounds that they might get labelled as being members of 'The Cliveden Set'.

It wasn't only the right wing that were worried about the success of *The Week*. The G.B. Communist Party weren't too pleased either, basically because they had no control over it. Each week Claud banged it out on an ancient typewriter the night before it was duplicated and sent out. There was no time for a committee to brood over it to make sure if he was really purveying the 'milk of the Word' and the party line.

Such was the background of the man that I met and fell in love with at Connie's party. When I told my family I was planning to marry Claud Cockburn, they really hit the roof. He was not only the notorious owner of *The Week*, but the foreign editor of the Communist *Daily Worker*, which he also wrote for under the name of Frank Pitcairn. They regarded him as a 'traitor to his class' (my mother's phrase), and altogether undesirable; also he had no money. In fairness, I don't think that the latter fact played a major role in their objections, except perhaps for the unworthy thought that he might be after mine.

My elder brothers were sent in rotation to try and reason with me. Teeny refused a demand that he use his undoubted influence, holding to his opinion that whom I married was my own affair, and nobody else's. Also he liked Claud. When the brothers failed in their objective my father came himself. Poor Daddy, red and embarrassed. I shall always remember his last remark, shouted with exasperation, 'Don't you realise, Patricia, that if you go ahead with this mad plan, you will never be allowed into the Royal Enclosure at Ascot again!'

At the end of it all my family retired defeated, cut off my allowance, declared they were disinheriting me, and broke off diplomatic relations. As far as they were concerned, I became, for the time being, a non-person. Except, of course, for my dear and loyal brother Teeny and his wife Helen.

I doubt if an English family of the same class would have made such a fuss. In the old Anglo-Irish culture marriages were not just the business of the parties most nearly concerned. They were family matters involving settlements and legal contracts. It was, after all, only one or two generations since arranged marriages had been the rule rather than the exception.

My own friends, largely members of the literary and artistic intelligentsia, were sympathetic but vaguely apprehensive. Claud had been married twice before, firstly to Hope Hale the American writer, by whom he had a daughter, Claudia, who later married Michael Flanders, of the theatrical team Flanders & Swann of *Drop of a Hat* fame; and secondly to Jean Ross, the model for Christopher Isherwood's Sally Bowles in 'I am a Camera', which was afterward turned into the musical *Cabaret*. They had a daughter, too, Sarah, now a distinguished barrister and writer.

Claud, tall and thin, with his vitality and charm, had always been immensely attractive to women; in looks he slightly resembled his distant cousin Raymond Massey, the actor, who eventually became Governor-General of Canada. He also had the reputation for having a roving eye. The most apprehensive of my friends was Connie Bainbridge, who had introduced us and therefore felt responsible. She was devoted to Claud, but felt the marriage would not last, and advised against it. I suspected she was annoyed that I, whom she had always regarded as a social asset, might very easily become a social liability to her, hanging about, deserted and penniless.

She need not have worried. Claud and I remained happily married until his death at the age of seventy-seven in 1981, each year growing closer and more devoted to each other.

CHAPTER 17

When the Bombs Fell

With the outbreak of war, most people I knew felt that the end of their world had arrived, and that they would shortly be blown up or gassed. Many of them had been to see the film of H. G. Wells' book, *The Shape of Things to Come* and believed that if they did survive they would be living in holes in the ground. Despite this belief they clung onto things they knew, hence the interest in my marriage to Claud. They were like people who, endeavouring to escape from a house which is on fire, dash back into it to save some memento of their past lives. I certainly had no time for social considerations, as I was working full time in the Control Centre under Praed Street. There were two teams, A and B, and we did twenty-four hour shifts, alternately changing at 10 a.m. each morning. This in itself was a ridiculous idea, obviously thought up by some bureaucrat. If the Germans had continued their raids on and off for twenty-four hours, the entire rescue and fire services of London would have collapsed. Nobody can continue to work at that intensity for twenty-four hours on end indefinitely. On our twenty-four hours off we were supposed to go home and sleep. But as everyone had their household chores to see to, shopping, cooking and so forth, no one really went to bed when they came off duty, and during one's nights off one was kept awake by the noise of bombs and the anti-aircraft guns. Even I, who have strong nerves, found it hard to sleep, tired as I was.

Apart from that, the system was a good one and worked very well once some of the initial wrinkles had been ironed out.

Sixty of us sat in the large underground room, each at a narrow desk on which were four telephones coloured white, red, green and black. There was also a flat, lidless box with three divisions in it. In one division were a number of rings attached to white discs; these represented ambulances, the exact number you had at your disposal. In the next division, rings with red discs which were fire engines, and in the third rings with green discs which were representing heavy rescue machines – a kind of bulldozer with a claw. On the wall in front of the desk was a board with nails sticking out of it in rows, numbered vertically from 1 to 20 and horizontally marked, 'On the way to the Occurrence', 'At the Occurrence' and 'Out of Service'. Above the nail board was a very large-scale map of the area one was responsible for.

The black telephone was for communicating with the Chief Warden of one's district, who 'phoned you when a bomb fell, saying 'H.E. [high explosive] at the corner of Acacia Street and Watt Crescent. Casualties and fire. Request four ambulances and two fire engines.' You then picked up your white telephone and ordered two ambulances to go to Acacia Street, and your red telephone and told one fire engine to go there too, at the same time taking out two white discs and one red one and hanging them on the nail under No. 1. if it was your first bomb of the evening, and on a level with 'On the way to the Occurrence'. When you were notified that they had arrived you moved the discs down to 'At the Occurrence', and so on. You never gave the warden all the machines he asked for. If you did you would run out of ambulances and fire engines long before the raid was over. If any of them were blown up or broke down when they were out on the streets you moved their discs to 'Out of Service'. When you were informed on your white or red telephones that the ambulance or fire engines were safely back in their garages, you took the disc off its nail and put it back in your box ready for the next errand of mercy.

It was exactly like a child's game – and required about the same skill in playing it. Success was largely a question of temperament. At one time I had sitting at the next desk on my right a spendthrift whose district adjoined mine. In an emergency you were allowed to lend equipment across boundaries, and she was always asking me to lend her ambulances or fire engines, having been too prodigal with her own early in the night. To my left was a miser. Anyone unlucky enough to be fire-bombed in his district was likely to be burned to a crisp. I used to overhear him say to his Chief Warden, 'I haven't got any fire engines available at the moment. Try putting it out with stirrup pumps,' and I could see out of the corner of my eye that his tray was full of red discs.

I don't know how those telephones worked – most of the telephone system in London was destroyed in the Blitz. All I know was that the lights on them never stopped flickering – I suppose they were some kind of wireless.

The staff was largely composed of women, though there were a few middle-aged men as well. The superintendent, who was so fair he could have been mistaken for an albino, if he had not had large, slightly protruding ice-blue eyes, had been the manager of a nitrate mine in Chile. He had lived in South America for years, but though over military age had come back to serve his country. He was not popular, but I liked him very much, and he seemed to like me, which was lucky as the first time I met him, it was as the representative of the staff, to announce that the whole lot were about to go on strike.

We had been practising for weeks before war was finally declared; in fact we started practising before there was any equipment to practise with. So to occupy our time they gave us first-aid lessons. The first lesson was on what to do in cases of poisonous snake bites. Not tremendously useful to people who were expected to spend the war in a bomb-proof cellar under London.

Three days before war was declared we had received an order that we were to wear our gas masks at all times. As all our work was done on the telephone, and the chief wardens and ambulance and fire services had received the same order, the result can be imagined. Nobody could understand a word anybody else said.

After shrieking ourselves hoarse through our gas masks for an hour, and receiving only grunts and glug-glug noises in reply, we downed telephones. I was asked to go and see the superintendent and announce a strike.

I was sure the order could not have come from our superintendent, and it hadn't. He saw the point immediately, got on to the relevant ministry, and we were given permission to be gassed if there was an attack, which at that time was thought extremely likely. I heard later that in the original plans for the Control Centre there had been a provision for airtight doors and an elaborate air-purifying system, but they were never installed.

The superintendent spent a lot of time brooding on philosophical matters, and had a habit of talking to himself, which worried people. I remember I came into his office once to complain that the tea, which came round in a wagon at 2 a.m., was always cold. As I entered I heard him say, 'The past is a myth, the future a dream, only the present exists. I wonder . . .'

But his thoughts were not all philosophical. He had practical ideas as well. It was he who installed a ping-pong table so that during the days when nothing was happening we could get some exercise, instead of sitting around knitting and quarrelling. During the period when there were no night air-raids he obtained some rubber pads and gave them to us, saying, 'You can put these pads on the floor and lie on them and get some sleep, but remember, three reliable people must at all times be sitting up, awake, watching the light; if it turns yellow they are to rouse the others and have them at their desks instantly.'

The light that he referred to was a large globe in the ceiling operated from the Air Ministry. It usually glowed with a rather sinister green; when enemy planes were spotted crossing the coast it turned yellow; when it was established that they were heading for London, it turned red, and the air-raid sirens were sounded. The superintendent had left it to us to arrange who should sit up on guard, and we decided to put all our names in a hat and draw the three responsible for the first night guard duty. My name came out first, then a quiet middle-aged woman, and then, to my horror, Mr Smith's. Mr Smith was a young man, exempted from military service because of a limp. He was a nice enough boy, but a fanatic, and a very voluble one at that. What he was fanatic about was the Douglas Social Credit System, which he passionately believed was the only thing which would cure all the world's ills.

'I am so glad we have been drawn together, Patricia, now I shall have all night to really explain the System to you. I am sure you will be utterly convinced that it is the only thing that will save us from chaos.'

And explain it he did for at least eight hours, non-stop. He maddened me by seizing handfuls of red and white discs from my box and saying, 'Here', he put a little pile of ambulances on the corner of his desk, 'is Capital, and here', he put another pile of fire-engines on another corner, 'is Labour.'

'Don't do that – if there was a raid they might get knocked on the floor and lost and then I couldn't know how many ambulances I had available.' He waved his hand crossly, and went on with what he regarded as the much more important business of explaining the Social Credit System to me in its entirety.

Despite that all-night sitting I still don't understand the Douglas Social Credit System: I only know that they have tried it once in the province of Alberta in Canada, with disastrous results. Of course, Mr Smith said that the Canadians didn't operate it properly.

One day, after my shift was over, I decided to walk home instead of taking the bus. It was a lovely sunny morning, having rained in the night. There was little traffic about and the world felt fresh and renewed. I overtook a man who was walking in the same direction as myself. As I passed him, I heard him say to himself 'And the glaciers, breaking and falling into the sea with that doom-laden crash.'

It was, of course, the superintendent and we fell in step.

'Tell me,' I asked, 'what is Chile like?'

He paused for so long that I thought he was not going to answer me. Then he said, 'It's like the world was when it was young. Everything is clear and vivid and intense, from the barren southern tip where the wind always blows, to the tropical rain forests. It's full of passion, misery and exhilaration. It's wonderful.'

'If you liked it so much why did you come home?'

'I had been there for so long I expect the spirit of the place had got into me. I felt that I was British and if Britain was at war, I had to come back, even if only to get killed.'

I am sorry to say this gloomy prediction of his came true. After I had left, a high-explosive bomb fell through an air shaft and killed everyone on Shift B, including the superintendent.

The last time I saw him it was to tell him that I was leaving the Control Centre. I was pregnant, and therefore debarred from working there.

'I'm sorry,' he said, 'you were doing a good job, and I liked having you around, you remind me of home.'

I have two other memories of the Control Centre. The first relates to one night during a heavy raid. The telephone flickered and a girl's voice said,

'My ambulance is on fire, do I have permission to abandon it?'

'Have you any patients inside it?'

'No, we are on the way to an Occurrence.'

'Have you a full tank of petrol?'

'Yes.'

'Don't ask any more questions, get out and run like blazes.'

I have always admired that girl's calmness in the face of an emergency, even though she did show a certain lack of initiative.

The other occasion that I treasure happened just after Prime Minister Neville Chamberlain had finished his radio speech to the British people telling them that they were now at war. We had all listened to it on a transistor provided by the superintendent. The great globe in the ceiling turned yellow then red. The air-raid sirens were sounded. We were all extremely tense. After practising for so long this was the real thing.

Nothing happened, and then my telephone flickered. A hysterical voice screamed at me, 'This is St Mary's Hospital. What shall we do? We have lost the key of the mortuary.'

There was no raid that day. It was a false alarm.

CHAPTER 18

Life with Claud

I had many problems to solve during my first year with Claud. There were enormous changes in my life that I had to adjust to – one of the most obvious ones was that after a lifetime of having enough money to do almost anything that I wanted, I now found that we had almost no money at all. Claud got £7 per week from the *Daily Worker* and I was paid £2 for an eighty-four-hour week by the A.R.P. Claud got a little extra by writing for some other papers, but not very much and very irregularly.

It seems absurd nowadays that two people could live on £9 per week – but we did it. For one thing there was practically nothing that one could spend money on. We had taken a furnished house in Clifton Gardens in St John's Wood, for which I paid £2 a week. The owners, who had fled to the country, were glad to have anyone live in it. It was a comfortable two-storeyed Victorian villa, with a basement and a quite large garden. All food was rationed; two ounces of butter per week, one shilling's worth of meat per week each – roughly one cutlet. I can't remember exactly how much bacon, tea, sugar and milk one got per week, but it was pretty minute. I remember one could get two smallish potatoes per day. Fish was off the ration, but you could never get it, except sometimes in the form of a white rectangular brick which was just labelled 'Frozen Icelandic Fish, as recommended by the Ministry of Food', and was so nasty that only the very hungry would eat it. I always found the bread ration adequate but most people complained. Of course, every other day I was fed by the A.R.P.

One did not have to spend much on gas or electricity, as it was mostly cut off by the bombing. When that happened I cooked on an open fire, fed with pieces of wood from bombed houses. It reminded me of Africa. One had to spend a bit on candles. Buses only cost pennies in those days, and nobody could get taxis except Zig.

Zig was another problem. Dogs are creatures of habit, and they don't take to disruption of their way of life. Zig didn't like the war and she didn't like Claud. In her sly way she did her best to make us quarrel. Her usual ploy was to try and make me think that Claud was secretly maltreating her. If I was out and Claud was in, as soon as she heard my key going into the lock of the front door she would set up the most pathetic yelping as if someone had kicked her. I would come raging in, shouting, 'What are you doing to my dog?'. Claud would say, 'Absolutely nothing. I have been sitting here reading, and she was asleep on the sofa. When she heard you coming she set up that yowling.'

Several times, before opening the front door I crept up and peered through the window, and thus proved he was speaking the truth.

She had the garden to run in, but she yearned for Hyde Park and last year's daily walks with other dogs and the delicious smells, and she was always trying to slip out the front door to get back there. Little walks to the shops on a lead were no substitute. One day she succeeded in slipping out and galloped off out of sight. I thought I had seen the last of her. About four hours later a taxi drew up at the door, the driver lifted Zig out of the back of the cab and proudly presented her to me. He had found her miles away, down by the river, sitting on a corner looking lost.

Seeing the medal on her collar, with our address on it, and thinking correctly she was a valuable dog, he had put her in the cab and brought her home. I had to pay the fare, of course, and give him a large tip. It took up most of my housekeeping money.

The implications of her adventure were not lost on Zig. She had found a way of having a delightful run, and then when she was tired, getting driven home. She redoubled her efforts to escape. About a week later she did it again. This time the taxi man said he had stopped to pick up a fare, when this dog suddenly jumped into the front of the cab next to him and sat down. When he had dropped his fare, he brought her home.

Altogether she repeated this performance four times.

This couldn't go on. We just couldn't afford it. There were other reasons as well for getting rid of Zig. She was completely devoted to me and passionately jealous, and I knew that when the baby arrived, she couldn't be trusted not to harm him. I was lucky in finding a good home in the country for her, through a friend who was connected with the

Kennel Club. It was with a woman who wanted to breed Basenjis. She offered me a large price, but I said I wanted only the assurance that Zig would never be put in a kennel but would be always kept as a housedog. Later I suddenly got an unexpected cheque from her for £120, an enormous sum in those days. The enclosed letter said it was 15 per cent of the price she had got for Zig's first litter of puppies. She also said she really loved Zig who always slept on her bed.

Apart from money and dog troubles I also had a great many other adjustments to make in my life. The friends Claud and I had in common were mostly political journalists and the literary establishment, most of whom were away on some form of war work. The only two that I can really remember coming to our house at that time were Patrick Hamilton, author of the plays *Gas Light* and *Rope*, as well as many wonderful novels, including *Hangover Square* and my favourite, *The Slaves of Solitude*. For a long time he was certainly Claud's most intimate friend. Together they would spend hours discussing the art of writing, and they also had a mutual passion for con-men, collecting newspaper cuttings about their activities from all over the world and exchanging them amid roars of laughter. At one time they had the idea of collaborating on a book about them to be called *Larceny in the Blood*. Claud had a theory that if you were absolutely honest you were quite immune to being taken in by a con-man. They always relied on a person being willing to obtain money or something desired, in a slightly underhand way.

Patrick Hamilton was nervous and tense to the extent that he was almost painful to be with, and his sensitivity was such that he had only to listen to a person's conversation for half an hour to be able to tell one all about them, their background, character and past. It was really uncanny.

I always feel nervous with neurotics and alcoholics, and Patrick was certainly both. He, for some reason, was obviously terrified of me so I kept out of the way as much as I could when he was round. Despite this, in the end, I grew almost as fond of him as Claud was.

Maurice Richardson, another character from the literary world of the thirties, was always bounding in and out, full of grandiose schemes, which almost, but never quite, came off. Full of vitality and enthusiasm, he lived in a fantasy world where every girl he went out with was as beautiful as Helen of Troy and as brilliant as Madame Curie. He was seldom downcast when things went wrong, as they constantly did, and he was absolutely sure that quite soon he would be fantastically rich and powerful. He certainly did have streaks of brilliance which shine out through some of his writing, particularly his short stories, and he was great fun to be with.

Claud knew an enormous number of people on the Left and these could be roughly divided into two categories: the 'radical chic', large numbers of whom lived in Hampstead and seemed to be connected with the law, and the working-class Communists. On the whole I found the latter more interesting. An exception was Alice Astor, daughter of J. J. Astor and one of the richest women in the world. She didn't fit into either of these catalogues. She had married as her third husband, after Prince Trubetzkoi and Count Reventlow, Philip Harding. Philip was the brother of Archie Harding, Claud's B.B.C. friend, who, if not a Party member, was a Marxist. Alice lived at Hanover Lodge, a vast house in Regent's Park, like a country mansion, with an avenue and a gate lodge – and, even in wartime, lots of servants. She still managed to keep them because they were mostly elderly White Russian refugees, relics of her marriage to Prince Trubetzkoi. She was not politically inclined, and before meeting Philip had lavished her money and her enthusiasms on the Arts, supporting the Sadler's Wells Ballet. Philip decided to change all that, and to convert her to his way of thinking. I remember visiting her one morning and finding her in bed, propped up with lace-fringed pillows. She had an expression of sheer desperation on her face, which was understandable, as on her lap was an enormous and heavy volume of Marx's *Das Kapital*. She was trying to interpret Marx's impenetrable prose and asked my help.

After a short time, having been temporarily converted to socialism, she announced she could no longer live in her fairy palace and moved into the tiny gate lodge. The servants still lived in the big house. I remember Claud and I were lunching there one day and I was sitting at the table facing a window with a view of the avenue. It was winter and it was snowing. Suddenly down the avenue from the house came a little procession. It was headed by the butler carrying a big dish with a huge silver cover, behind him was a parlour-maid holding an umbrella over his head, then a footman with the vegetable dishes and lastly another footman with the plates. They slowly wended their way down to the gate lodge, and arrived stiff with cold, as was the food.

Poor Alice! She really was a silly woman. After a while her marriage to Philip broke up and she returned to America to marry yet again, to a Pleydel-Bouverie. She never had any luck with her husbands, or anything else for that matter. While in London, she lived in fear that her brother, Vincent Astor, would have her kidnapped and put under restraint; and when she died, I am told, her will got lost in the New York subway.

What most people have forgotten, or are too young to know, is that in the 1930s there was not the hysterical fear and hatred of Communism that exists today. It was regarded by most intellectuals, except those of the extreme right, as simply an alternative, if eccentric, economic and social system for managing the world's affairs, and most of them would argue perfectly rationally about its pros and cons. This, of course, was before the days of McCarthyism, and before the international media had over the years built up a picture of degradation and general devilishness for anyone who believed that the production and distribution of the world's goods could never be organised in a rational and equitable way under capitalism.

Of course all societies need a devil, and the devils chosen are usually the people who seem most likely to interfere with the way of life of a powerful section of any community. I remember during Britain's 'Cod War' with Iceland there was a short-lived effort on the part of the media to depict the Icelanders as devils. As soon as an agreement was signed about the territorial limits where British trawlers could fish for cod, the Icelanders became civilised and courageous Vikings again.

Of course the details of the Russian labour camps were not then generally known. But sadly I don't think that horror at brutal behaviour and oppressive systems really influences people. Otherwise why did the Indonesians not attain devilship? The Javanese, after the war, were just as savage as the Russians and probably slaughtered nearly as many of their inhabitants. And there are a great many other nations whose behaviour is equally oppressive, as Amnesty International is never tired of pointing out. Torture was supposed, when I was young, to be confined to the distant past. It is now standard practice in a large number of countries. I think an understanding of the intellectual climate of those days before the war goes a long way to explain why people, including the highly educated young in the universities, became Communists.

Though the capacity to produce was increasing enormously, goods were not getting to the people who needed them, as I had seen for myself all over the world. In other words, the capitalist system was not working for the benefit of humanity. What was not so obvious was that the socialist system in Russia was not working either. Lenin's 'new kind of man' had not arrived.

Those few people I met who had been to Russia excused the Spartan, chaotic and restrictive conditions that they found there as teething trouble, largely due to the short time that had elapsed since the devastation of the Revolution and the counter-revolutionary wars.

They thought when things settled down an era of peace and plenty for all would be achieved. What they didn't grasp is that a centralised system needs a vast bureaucracy, and that all bureaucrats inevitably work for, and owe loyalty primarily to, their own organisations and not to the whole community; or at any rate they feel that whole community will be best served by their department becoming more and more powerful, important and rich. International conglomerates do the same thing.

One tiny example of this characteristic of all such groups I saw, or rather heard, during the early years of the war:

I was at a small party given by a friend of mine, whom I knew to be in MI6. In the corner of the room two other intelligence officers were in deep conversation. It was a small room and I couldn't help hearing what they were discussing. One was proposing various lines of action, and the other kept saying, 'No, no, we couldn't do that, that would be giving it to the enemy on a plate.'

It was some time before I realised that the enemy they were alluding to was not the Gestapo, or Nazi Germany, but their own country's Naval Intelligence. And England was at war.

The working-class comrades from the *Daily Worker* were pretty chary of me at first. I was an unknown quantity, who would probably be a bad influence on Claud. Harry Pollitt, who was then General Secretary of the C.P.G.B., refused to meet me. He had been a great friend of the beautiful Jean Ross, Claud's second wife, and had been upset by the breakup of their marriage. But Bill Rust, then editor of the *Daily Worker*, became a friend and gradually the others came to accept me. Bill was a tubby little Cockney, full of energy and determination as well as organisational ability. He had spent some years in Russia, and had there married Tamara, who had been a tennis star. Unlike the Russian wives of British soldiers stationed at Archangel who had been married during the war, she had had no difficulty in getting a visa to leave Russia and had settled down in London. After Bill's death she married Wogan Phillips, who inherited the title of Lord Millford, and thus she became England's only communist peeress.

Many of the Comrades I met in those days in London had a quality that I recognised instantly, coming as I did from early twentieth-century Ireland. It was that of the religious bigot. Either you believed utterly and completely in the obvious truth of the milk of the Word – so obvious indeed that it hardly needed discussing – or you were forever damned. Of course there were some honourable exceptions, but that was the general rule.

I got to know most of the Marylebone Branch of the Communist Party, which covered St John's Wood. It included about forty middle-aged Polish Jewish tailors who lived, suitably enough, in Poland Street. These men had been born in London and lived all their lives there. Their parents or grandparents had come to England as refugees from some early pogrom. The interesting thing about them was that not one of them could speak a word of English. They lived in a little enclosed community. They were all Communists and they had to take an interpreter with them to party meetings. They proved a nightmare to the A.R.P. wardens. This percolated through to the Control Centre and the superintendent came to me and said, 'Do you know anything about these people – they seem to live in your district? The Chief Warden says he can't make them understand about the blackout, and about the importance of telling the local warden each night how many people are sleeping in each house.'

'Yes, I know them. They can't speak or understand English, but there is one man' – and I wrote down his name and address – 'who is bilingual. Tell the Chief Warden to make him local warden, and you will have no more trouble.'

The superintendent looked at me a bit oddly. 'What curious people you know,' he said.

One day, when I was walking down the street, wondering what on earth I could buy to feed not only Claud and myself, but ten friends whose houses had been bombed and who were consequently living with us, sleeping in rows on the basement floor, who should I meet but Connie Bainbridge. There she was, tottering along in her high heels and wrapped in a mink coat. I was seven months pregnant at the time, a fact that she took in instantly.

'Darling Patricia. How wonderful to see you. How are you? You are going to have a baby. How nice. Where are you going to have it? Are you still with darling Claud?'

'Yes, I am, and the local hospital is, I understand, still functioning.'

'But you can't stay here, with all these terrible air-raids, it's impossible. Come and have a drink at the Ritz and we'll talk about it.'

While we were having our drinks, she went away, telling me to wait for her. When she returned she said,

'It's all fixed. I've talked to Claud on the 'phone, and I've talked to my husband. You are coming with me on the train to Scotland tonight. There is a good local doctor in our village and the wife of our gamekeeper was a matron in a hospital and is a mid-wife. It's an excellent plan. Go home and pack your things. I'll pick you up in a car at 6 p.m.'

And so I was whisked back into a life of luxury.

CHAPTER 19

'The Week'

Connie's home, Gledfield, was a very large Victorian mansion located in a glen in Ross-shire in the far north of Scotland. It was so far north that in winter it got dark at 3 p.m. and didn't get light again until 9.30 a.m.

When Connie had married Emerson Bainbridge she had 'done over' the interior of the house in her best New York style so that the rooms resembled a film set – or rather several film sets, as the style of each room represented a different period. The local Scottish landowners hated its flamboyance and I could see their point, but the house was very, very comfortable.

That first evening, sitting by a blazing log fire, on the soft velvet-covered sofa in the library and listening to the silence of a night without bombs or anti-aircraft fire, I felt really relaxed – doubly so because I had just eaten a delicious dinner of roast grouse, accompanied by a liberal amount of Emerson's excellent burgundy. He was justly proud of his cellar. Life was really looking up.

I wasn't the only evacuee. The household included a couple of other women and their children, one of whom, Elizabeth Laurence, I had known slightly in my deb days. She had been staying there for about a month before I arrived. I remarked to her how good the food was at Gledfield, a great change from what I had been eating recently in London. She looked at me sourly and then said,

'Maybe. That is, if you can stomach salmon and grouse.'

'Oh, I love them, I can never have enough of them.'

'Don't worry, you will.'

As day followed day, she was proved horribly right. It was salmon for lunch and grouse for dinner every single day – except when it was grouse for lunch and salmon for dinner.

The Bainbridge cook, who was a good one and had been with the family for years, did her best to vary the menu. We had salmon pie and even curried grouse, but it really made little difference. The trouble was there was nothing else to eat. Rationing was as strict in Ross-shire as in London.

The game-keeper, who was long past military age, was having the time of his life. Having always worked long and hard to preserve game for his employer to shoot and catch, he now had a chance to do it himself – and he was an excellent shot and fisherman. I dare say the local people, and the 'Scottish lairds', had many ways of obtaining farm produce, including some of the black-faced sheep I saw hopping about the heather, but, coming from New York, Connie was very much an 'outsider' and an unpopular one at that. Ignoring her warmth, kindness and generosity, they saw only her brashness, unsuitable clothes and heavy make-up. Also she had the, to them, intolerable habit of wearing tight trousers made of other people's family tartans. I was with her one day in the village shop when we met a crusty old gentleman in a kilt, who was known at Gledfield as 'the Monarch of the Glen'. He glared at her and announced,

'Mrs Bainbridge, you are wearing the McLean tartan.'

Connie gave him a beaming smile and said, 'Isn't that nice? Kinda makes us related.'

Apart from the food, the days passed pleasantly enough. Tiny items of excitement provided endless topics of conversation as they always do in isolated households – small mysteries, such as a dog who carried a basket in his mouth and who always galloped past the house and down the avenue on Saturday mornings and two hours later passed going the other way. We puzzled about the dog until, by asking around the village, I was told,

'He's old Willy's sheepdog, who does the shopping on Saturdays. Old Willy writes a list and ties it to the basket. Andy Mac in the shop puts the goods in, and the dog takes them home. Once a month Old Willy comes down the mountain and pays the bill. Old Willy used to come himself every week till the rheumatiz got him.'

I was determined to meet this remarkable animal trainer and in the end I did. Though the climb up the mountain in my condition nearly killed me, it was well worth the effort.

Old Willy looked rather like Old Father Time. He had been a shepherd all his life and lived in a little stone croft with only his dog for company, subsisting on oatmeal porridge which he cooked in a haybox, as Scottish people have done for centuries. He was now retired, being a very old man. His eyesight was still good and he spent most of his time reading, getting his books from the Carnegie library as he had been able to make an arrangement to have them delivered at the village shop which he visited on his monthly journey down the mountain. Although he was obviously an extremely intelligent man, great credit must be given to the local village school where he had been educated long ago. He told me that it was his schoolmaster who had first introduced him to history, archaeology and poetry, which became for him a lifelong interest. Scottish public education had also proved excellent for his three sons, who had all done well for themselves, one being a doctor, one a wireless operator on a liner, and the youngest 'in business' in Edinburgh. All three and their wives were always trying to get him to leave the croft, but he had no intention of moving.

'I've lived here, and I'll die here,' he said. When I left to go down to Gledfield, he always stood up, raised his hand, and gave me a blessing.

'May the Good Lord take you in his arms and care for you and the bairn.'

As I looked back up at him, standing against a background of rocks and heather and speeding clouds, his long white beard blowing in the wind, I was deeply moved.

Alexander Claud was born punctually and easily, and nine days later I returned to London. It was considered safe to take the baby home as the air-raids had for the moment ceased and also because I was not returning to Clifton Hill, which Claud had given up when I left, but to my parents' house in Cadogan Square.

Some time back my family had reversed their decision to cast me out. When Teeny, home on leave, had told my mother of Alexander's impending arrival, she broke down, and told my father in no uncertain terms that she wanted diplomatic relations restored. He agreed. He always did agree when she decided to put her foot down, but he didn't restore my allowance. We were both asked to a ceremonial lunch, which was an enormous success. The family were completely charmed by Claud, so much so that it was arranged while I was in Scotland that on my return Claud and I should both live at Cadogan Square till we found a place of our own.

I rather sadly said goodbye to all my Scottish friends and, thinking that, thank God, I never would be forced to eat salmon and grouse again, took the train south. I found a very different Arbuthnot household from the one I had left so many years before to marry Arthur. Gone were the footmen and the ladies'-maids, the butler and the chauffeur. There were no servants at all. My mother didn't seem to mind. She rather enjoyed doing the cooking, regarding it as a temporary condition due to the war, and looked forward to the day, after the West had won, when things would return to normal. She never did get over this feeling and for the rest of her life was always waiting for the Modern World to blow over.

The political situation had also changed, which made our life much easier.

When Stalin signed the Non-Aggression Pact with Hitler the *Daily Worker* had been banned – and also *The Week*, as Claud had followed the party line, which was that this was an imperialist war, like the 1914 one.

I was aghast, and we had our first real quarrel. It seemed to me a betrayal of everything that I had thought he stood for. He did not defend the Pact but just said that if you voluntarily joined an army you couldn't keep arguing with the strategy of the generals. Finally, we agreed to differ. I think now, with hindsight, that Stalin knew the Nazis would attack, but he also knew that the Russian army was in no condition to resist. He was trying to buy time, particularly as he had just shot a very large proportion of the army officers during the terrible purges of the 1930s, and was thus short of trained personnel.

With Germany and Russia at war, the party line changed, and the ban on the *Daily Worker* and *The Week* was lifted, as they were now supporting the war effort. The attitude in the West also changed. Even people on the right, like my parents, to whom Russia, which, to quote President Reagan's phrase, had always been 'an Empire of Evil', welcomed her now as our 'Gallant Ally'. Everyone admired the courage and tenacity of the ordinary Russian soldier. 'Little Ivan' became a popular hero.

This feeling was abetted by the fact that the Resistance movements in Europe were largely Communist-led, certainly at local level, and everyone knew it. For this reason it was no longer an embarrassment to the Arbuthnots to harbour us and have us meet their friends. My mother even encouraged me to help out occasionally at *The Week*.

The Week office was situated in an attic at the top of a rickety building in Victoria Street, and was inhabited, when I first went there, by Crystal, Claud's secretary, and her grumpy Pekinese, 'Pig'. By a coincidence, I had met Crystal years before with her ferocious mother, Lady Blois, who was always dragging her three daughters round the seaside resorts of France. She had been married to Archie Harding of the B.B.C., an Oxford friend of Claud's, but the marriage had broken down, and now, left alone, she had invested all her emotional capital in *The Week*.

Without office experience, and politically naïve, it hadn't been easy for her. But she struggled on, loyal and hardworking. *The Week* was her baby, and nobody else was going to change its nappies. She had invented her own accounting system which resembled something the prehistoric Chinese might have thought up, and which only she understood. But it seemed to work.

Nobody but Claud would have attempted to run a newsletter with the only permanent staff a secretary who could neither type nor take shorthand, and it was staggering that his influential sheet ever got out at all. There was an added complication in that the stencils for the duplicating machine had to be cut by an extremely efficient typist, called Margaret, who was the girl whom Archie, Crystal's husband, had run away with, and whom consequently Crystal could not meet. So Margaret had to come and do her job in the middle of the night. Someone always had to be there to let her in, as the building was locked at that hour. Crystal never discovered who cut the stencils – Claud told her it was someone who would lose their job if it became known that they were associated with a scurrilous left-wing paper like *The Week*. It was probably true at that.

On Tuesdays, dozens of unpaid helpers flooded in to fold and put the paper in envelopes in time for the evening mail. They could barely fit into the tiny office, reminding one immediately of Groucho Marx's cabin in the Marx Brothers' film *Horse Feathers*.

I remember that once on a Tuesday afternoon a distinguished foreign correspondent of a world-famous newspaper arrived at the office to see Claud about a sensational political scandal which he was passing on to *The Week* as he felt sure his editor would not allow it to be printed. Claud wasn't there, and as nobody knew or cared who he was, he was seized on, handed a pile of envelopes and copies of *The Week*, and told to 'get on with it'. This he did for hours, with a bewildered look on his face.

Claud had campaigned long and hard for the ban on *The Week* to be lifted. He had tramped the country, making thousands of speeches and writing hundreds of pamphlets demanding he should be free to publish again.

When he had succeeded, after the Labour Party, which was then part of the National Government, had passed a massive vote at its annual conference urging that the ban on both *The Week* and the *Daily Worker* should be lifted, he was frankly aghast.

He was perfectly right to be aghast. It was not only that he had lost interest in *The Week*, which he certainly had, campaigning for the ban to be lifted only as a matter of principle, but times had changed. *The Week* had always been an opposition paper, giving the news that no one else would print. In wartime there was little that he could write about the stupidities and duplicities of those in power – though there were certainly plenty of these – that would not give aid and comfort to the enemy, or that other papers with more resources were not covering already. However, he had shouted from the rooftops that he wanted to publish, so when this was allowed he hadn't the nerve to say that, on second thoughts, *The Week* was better dead.

One evening, early in 1945, he came home in a great state of excitement and pleasure.

'I'm going to San Francisco to cover the founding of the United Nations Organisation for the *Worker*. I'll be away about six weeks.'

He was beside himself at the idea of revisiting America, which he had loved and where he had felt so much at home.

'And who will edit and write *The Week* while you are gone?'

'Why, you will, of course.'

I was frankly horrified, not feeling at all equal to the task, and also realising that the problems of producing *The Week* in wartime had now been dumped on my plate.

'But I've never edited anything, and only written reports for the Royal Geographical, and a few feature articles for newspapers. I haven't got your background knowledge of world politics and personalities.'

'Oh, you'll do fine, and in any case there is no one else I can trust. Just be careful not to print stories that may be planted on you with some ulterior motive, such as those that are totally false, and highly libellous. If you fall for that, you will be sued and go bankrupt, or you might possibly be sent to jail.'

With these cheering words he went off joyfully to make his preparations for departure.

Some time before this, as soon as we had found a place to live, my parents had closed up 47 Cadogan Square and gone back to Ireland more or less permanently. We were very lucky in the house that we rented. It was in Acacia Road, and had been a farmhouse when St John's Wood was still countryside. The cowsheds were still standing at the end of the wooded garden, as was the dairy with its great stone slabs to stand the milk churns on. It was a peaceful and rural island surrounded by the ruins of bombed houses – in one of the cellars of which lived a costermonger with a small pony, of great use if I wanted to move anything heavy. I had worked hard on the garden, growing vegetables and tomatoes, and had filled one of the sheds with rabbits, bred originally with the idea of supplementing our meagre meat rations; however, the rabbits had rapidly developed into Alexander's and my much loved pets, and none was ever killed. Claud's view was that I could edit *The Week* from home, so continuing to look after Alexander, as well as the house, the garden and the rabbits. He dismissed such tiresome domestic details with a wave of his hand. He always ignored practical problems – it was both his strength and his weakness.

Realising that if I was to edit *The Week*, I had to be around and about where people in the know gather, as well as in the office, I hired a German Jewish refugee to look after Alexander as soon as Claud left for America, and set to work.

I had been worried that I would not be able to get enough copy, but I need not have bothered. My telephone never stopped ringing. It seemed that every crackpot in England, as well as quite a few of the malign types that Claud had mentioned, had got the idea that with Claud's wife in charge, now was the time to get some free publicity, or alternatively to destroy *The Week* once and for all. There were also a number of genuine friends, mostly journalists, a few M.P.s and civil servants, who did their best to give me a helping hand. My trouble was to figure out which was which.

I brought my worst difficulties on myself. Disturbed by Claud's reference to libel actions, I had hired a left-wing lawyer to check the paper for libels – one Geoffrey Bing, later Labour M.P. for Hornchurch. He had married Crystal, who had now left us, but he was always hanging about *The Week* office and had thought that Claud would make him editor while he was away. He was a great admirer of Claud's and also extremely jealous of Claud's international reputation. Barrister Bing told everybody that he was really running *The Week* and that I was just a figurehead.

Realising that he would consequently be held responsible for the success or failure of the paper during Claud's absence, he knew it was essential that it should be more sensational and brilliant than ever.

As a result of this, far from cutting out any possible libels, he added them, often trying to slip in the wildest stories. I tried to get rid of him tactfully, saying that we really couldn't afford a lawyer. He said he didn't want any money.

There was no shifting him. He was always bobbing up just before press time, arguing and trying to introduce some of his own handiwork.

In desperation I turned for help to Bill Rust, the editor of the *Daily Worker*. Many people regarded Bill as a stony-faced 'apparatchik', resembling the popular idea of a N.K.V.D. man, but I always found him warm-hearted and humorous. Anyway, he laughed very much at my wails about Barrister Bing and said to leave the problem with him. I don't know what he did, but the lawyer ceased to haunt *The Week* office. Later Bing went to Ghana to help Nkrumah destroy the legal system there.

Crystal had been replaced by a really splendid Jewish girl called Miriam, who looked like my idea of Scheherazade in the *Thousand and One Nights*. She was as efficient as she was beautiful, and so managed to decipher and decode Crystal's accounting system. This done, she came up with the announcement that *The Week* was broke. The trouble was that we had gone over to printing after re-publication, instead of using the old mimeograph – a disastrous decision, since the printing bills were enormous.

When Claud returned from the founding of the United Nations with a host of hilarious stories, I told him of the financial situation of the paper. And with a good deal of relief he closed it down for good. Being kept busy assisting in the last days of *The Week* had been therapy for me, as before that I had been in a very low state. I had received a body blow with the news of the death of my adored brother Teeny. He had been with the Eighth Army all along, rising from private to major in three years. The army had trained him as a signals expert and when the victorious Eighth Army had swept across Africa and was poised to invade Italy, the War Office had ordered him back to Alexandria to head a signals school. This distressed him, he wrote to me, because he wanted to be with his friends and comrades to finish the job. So he asked General Montgomery to use his influence to have this order rescinded. Montgomery, who liked enthusiastic young officers, agreed. Teeny was with his comrades in the invasion of Italy, survived the first battles and died of cerebral malaria in the marshes before Rome. He is buried in the military cemetery at Bari.

I went to his grave on the way to Yugoslavia at the end of the war. It was just one of the thousands of little white crosses that stretch down the valley and up over the hill. I found it a shattering experience. The immensity of the grief that all those little crosses represented seemed to sweep over me like a tide – a tide that encompassed the whole world. It wasn't just the inadequacies and stupidities of the world leaders that had caused this tragedy, though they, in the short term, were to blame. It was the complex situation of ordinary people who could see no alternative but to follow a path that led to war. All through history they had done so, and no doubt would continue to do so. Claud had thought that he had the answer, that by changing the system a new world could be created, that the causes of wars could and would be eliminated. At that moment I envied him deeply his belief in the future, but I need not have done so; unbeknownst to me his certainties were becoming less certain.

Some time before going to America Claud had briefly visited Algiers with a party of diplomatic correspondents. It was just before the Allied landings in Italy. The American and British military, horrified at his appearance at this crucial moment, tried to expel him, but they had reckoned without General de Gaulle who, as leader of the Free French, was officially Head of Government of Algeria, the only piece of France so far freed. Claud knew and greatly admired de Gaulle, who also esteemed him, and the General was outraged that anyone should try and expel a friend of his from his own territory and so protected Claud.

Also gathered in Algiers were the leadership of the pre-war French Communist Party, a parcel of ex-M.P.s recently let out of jail. They seem to have given Claud quite a jolt. Later in his book, *Crossing the Line*, published in 1958, he wrote

> Guided by hindsight, I should say the attitude – mean, rigid and out-dated – of these quarrelsome and querulous Communist Deputies in Algiers may have effected in my subconscious mind a basic shift in my own attitude to Communism. It took a lot of gilt off the gingerbread. Revolutionary organisations which are deemed, as a matter of course, to be living in the future, are often more inclined than others to be living in the past.

Another factor which may have nudged that shift a little bit further was the influence of General de Gaulle himself.

One day at lunch he asked Claud directly why he was a Communist; when Claud told him, he listened sympathetically – he always preferred disembodied theory to solid fact – and then said that he understood how Claud felt, and why he felt it, but added, 'You don't think your view is somewhat romantic?'

Later, back in London, Claud kept his worries and doubts to himself. I only noticed that he seemed dispirited, and put it down to a feeling of anti-climax after the excitement of trips abroad, and the frustration of having to work with people he disliked and despised in the General Election which followed immediately after his return. He was always deeply antipathetic to the British Labour Party for whom, still following the party line, he was forced to campaign.

After the demise of *The Week* I was also feeling restless and depressed. The war had gone on for so long, and during it we had all yearned so desperately for peace, that when peace finally came the relief was mingled with a feeling of disorientation.

At this moment, when we both felt that something drastic had to be done to lift up our spirits, Bill Rust suggested that Claud should go to Yugoslavia, Bulgaria and Roumania, spending a month in each, and that I should go with him. He had fixed me up with a commission from the Australian press.

I was anxious to get Alexander to Ireland in any case, as rationing was still severe. He had had glandular fever and I felt the good food and fresh country air of my home would do him good. My mother was delighted with the plan and came over to fetch him.

It may seem odd that after Darrell's death I should again leave my son and go off travelling, but with us the tradition of the extended family was very strong. Grandmothers had a big role to play in the bringing up of children; I, myself, had been partially brought up by my grandmother and had certainly never regretted it. What had happened to Darrell was a chance in a million, and certainly not due to any neglect in my family's care for him.

CHAPTER 20

In the Balkans

Arrived in Belgrade, the first thing that happened was that Claud's shoes were stolen in the night as we slept – and my thimble. Nothing else was touched, which shows the priority of useful articles in that deprived city.

Claud had only one pair of shoes and was due to meet a high government official that morning. Feeling he couldn't go out barefoot, I rushed out to try and get him another pair, which were, of course, unobtainable. Finally I had to go to the ministry where he was due later that morning and explain why he would not be able to keep his appointment. My news was not taken well. After the extraordinary struggle of the Yugoslav partisans, all Yugoslavs considered themselves heroes, even if they had done nothing but sit in an office during the Occupation keeping their heads down – and heroes, I was told, firmly and crossly, did not steal. Claud must have just lost his shoes.

However, after some delay a pair was produced, probably stripped off some protesting underling, as they were well worn. I dashed back with them in triumph.

The atmosphere in Belgrade was very tense. Tito was working up to his split with Stalin, and the place was buzzing with rumours and alive with political police. Claud said our situation was getting too complex and perhaps dangerous and that he wanted to go to Albania. However the Albanians would not give us an entry visa until the Yugoslavs had given an exit visa, and *vice versa*, so we went to Montenegro instead with three other Communist newspaper correspondents, a Russian, a Swiss and a Yugoslav. Echoing their leaders, the Russian and the Yugoslav quarrelled bitterly the whole time, arguing which of their respective countries had suffered most in the war. They were only united by their mutual hatred of the Swiss, who had a bland air of national superiority and was incredibly well equipped with every kind of gadget to make life easier. He even had a miniature pair of windscreen wipers attached to his spectacles, run by a battery which he kept in his pocket.

After a terrifying flight to Montenegro – the girl pilot was too young, and the small plane too old – we made our way on foot and in the back of a lorry to Cetinje, the capital, and found ourselves immediately at home.

Montenegro had been a centre of Resistance activity, and had been fought over again and again. All the bridges had been blown up, either by the Germans, the Italians or the partisans themselves, and a very great number of the inhabitants killed. It was a surprise to me that the country could support even those that were left, as the mountains are composed of bare rocks. An old *Encyclopaedia Britannica* which I had consulted in Belgrade said a 'fine road gives access to the richest parts of the interior, but there is little trade'. If there was a rich part in the interior I never found it, and there wasn't just 'little trade', there was no trade at all.

Cetinje was a charming little town, which surprisingly enough did not appear to be damaged at all. The heart of the place was a plaza surrounded on three sides by houses which had been foreign legations when, at the turn of the century, Montenegro had been considered a key-point of European diplomacy by the jostling empires of Britain, Germany, Russia and Austria-Hungary.

On the fourth side was the palace of the last king, left exactly as it was when he departed, full of Victorian furniture and model railways, which the king liked to play with. His library, which Claud made a bee-line for, was mostly composed of boys' books and frontier novels like *The Last of the Mohicans*, muddled up with volumes of the American Congressional Records of 1908.

The legations had been put to good use as schools and government offices and one, the ex-British legation, was an hotel, where we stayed.

The entire Montenegrin Cabinet took their meals there *en pension*, both at noon and in the evening, and we all sat at a long wooden table together.

All had been partisans, and they were a fascinating lot. They reminded me of home. Most of them looked like Irish mountain farmers come to town for a cattle fair, particularly the chief of the police who wore a belted mackintosh, rain or shine, and always carried an umbrella which was neither quite open nor quite shut; his hair stood up on all sides of his head like a brush. Two exceptions were the Minister of Transport and his wife. They were young, good-looking and well-educated in a Western sense. They looked romantic, and their story was even more so, sounding like something in a cheap women's magazine, but true nevertheless. She was an American from Dallas. Before the war she had won, in some American competition, a scholarship to study music in Europe, and had chosen to take it in Yugoslavia. On a visit to Belgrade, he had gone to hear the singing in the cathedral, and was immensely struck by the beautiful and talented soloist. After the service he had introduced himself. They met several times, fell in love and became engaged to be married. Then came the German invasion. He joined the partisans in the mountains, and later, unbeknownst to him, so did she.

One day they were both crawling up opposite sides of a hill in Croatia, each believing that the people on the other side were German soldiers and planning that, when they got to the top, they would open fire. But when they finally arrived within sight of each other, it was to realise that there were no Germans about, just two separate bands of guerrilla fighters – and who should be leading one of them but the future Montenegrin Minister of Transport? And among the other group was his fiancée. They had found each other again. They would have been married at once, had it not been for an order of Tito's forbidding marriage among male and female partisans. Miraculously they had both survived and, the war over, had married and were very happy and very busy, she singing on the radio, running a music school and a children's theatre, and he, as Minister of Transport, trying to mend all those hundreds of broken bridges without sufficient materials to do so.

In Cetinje there was a terrible shortage of everything, and after seeing men pulling and pushing heavy loads of stones, I asked why they didn't use the few mules I had seen about. I was told that there were no blacksmiths, the Germans having exported or killed them all, and no horseshoes either. If you worked the mules they instantly became lame on the rough and sharp stony surface and were of no more use. I said, 'Look, I have seen lots of old bits of scrap iron about, even old horseshoes. If we could get a forge going and make some bellows, I think we could make shoes. I have never actually shod a horse, but I have held a hundred horses and supervised their shoeing. I think I could help.'

The Minister jumped at the idea. Fuel was obtained, a blacksmith's bellows was constructed and one morning a platoon of raggedy soldiers leading a dejected-looking mule arrived at my door to say they were ready to start. The forge worked all right, and a Goliath of a peasant soldier hammered out the red hot iron under my directions. Everybody was delighted except the mule, who came to life and kicked and bit as only a mule can. In the end we had to throw him and lash his legs to a pole held at each end by a group of soldiers. Success rewarded our efforts. A trained smith would have had a heart attack at the sight of the way that mule was shod, but it didn't lame him and he could now be used.

After that I spent all day at the forge as a succession of mules was brought in. The other journalists departed, and Claud wanted to get on to Bulgaria, but there was always some trouble about our exit visas. Everybody was very polite and full of apologies, but they were just never available. Claud got crosser and crosser, and blamed me: 'It's all your fault, you've made yourself so useful to them, shoeing their damned mules, now they won't let us go. You will probably he here shoeing mules for the rest of your natural life.'

He seemed to be right. Next day I said I had taught the soldiers all I knew about shoeing horses and refused to go near the forge any more. In no time our exit visas were delivered. We hung about in Sofia for quite a while as Claud was anxious to interview George Dimitroff, newly returned to his native Bulgaria. Few people today will recognise the name, but in the 1940s he was world famous, and not only among people of the left. This was on account of his courageous stand at the Reichstag Fire trial. He had stood up to Hitler in 1933, and rallied and inspired anti-fascists everywhere.

Having taken on Hitler and survived, he was now apparently taking on Stalin. In his first interview with Claud he spoke enthusiastically about the possibility of a Balkan federation extending from the Adriatic to the Black Sea, composed of Yugoslavia, Bulgaria and Roumania. For Bulgaria's most famous Communist leader to advocate such a plan was political dynamite. Stalin saw it as a manoeuvre by Marshal Tito for his own aggrandisement, directed against the

Kremlin. Though Tito and Stalin were still ostensibly on excellent terms, it was made clear to Claud in subsequent meetings that the federation plan was not for publication.

I was glad of the delay, as I had heard that the Russian army that had defeated Hitler at Stalingrad was arriving at Sofia, and I wanted to see them. Nobody seemed to know when they were coming, and certainly not the interpreter we had been provided with – a very fat man with a squeaky voice called Poppoff.

Poppoff was very far from the trained 'Intourist' guide of today. He told me he was the correspondent of the *Reader's Digest* and was immensely proud of it. I doubt if it was true, but anyway he lived always in a state of utter confusion, and quarrelled ceaselessly with all officials. He told long, rambling stories of these encounters, usually ending with the words, 'You see, he try to put me a leg. But I shall come with my *Reader's Digest* and put him in a mousehole.'

Early one morning, as I was lying in bed, I heard the most wonderful singing. It started faintly, from a far distance, and gradually got louder and louder. I ran to the window, and there, coming up the road, was the victorious Red Army who had defeated Hitler at Stalingrad and, in a sense, won the war.

It was an extraordinary sight. They didn't march, there were no ordered ranks, but surged like a medieval horde, or a slowly moving crowd. Most of the soldiers' uniforms were in tatters, and rags bound their feet instead of boots. These passed, then some smart officers riding fairly sleek-looking horses, then some modern-looking tanks, more soldiers, some farm carts drawn by miserable nags and piled high with cabbages, a couple of shiny black staff cars, more soldiers, tanks, gun carriages. On and on they came, all singing like the Don Cossack choir.

Claud got up and went out to see what was going on, and came back to say that Sofia was full of the Red Army, who would soon be getting very drunk, and that I must not leave my room until he had arranged for a bodyguard.

Some hours later, the bodyguard arrived – a bunch of gloomy and silent soldiers who sat or lay on the passage floor outside my room and followed me everywhere I went like a pack of depressed foxhounds.

One reason for the Red Army's visit to Sofia had been that they wanted to celebrate 'Red Army day' there, and Marshal Koniev invited us to the reception held in the evening. I was told to put on my best dress ('silk if possible'). I shall never quite believe in the reputed inefficiency and disorganisation of the Red Army, despite their appearance on their arrival, because not only did they in the end defeat Hitler, but they put on a celebration in Sofia that can only be compared to King Francis I's 'Feast of the Cloth of Gold' – and this after marching for hundreds of miles over territory that had for years been devastated by war.

The mountains of food were incredible. I remember a sturgeon about seven feet long, propped up on a vast platter, his mouth open and his teeth beautifully gilded. Peacocks, roasted and with their tail feathers carefully replaced, mounds of caviar surrounded by sliced lemon and blini, and to cap it all the entire battle zone of Stalingrad modelled in calves' brains in aspic – even tiny tanks, guns and soldiers were there. It seemed vandalism to eat it.

The feast was attended by all the army officers, most of them extremely young, really boys, the Diplomatic Corps and the Bulgarian government.

We had heard a great deal in London about there being women serving in the Red Army, but I only saw one female officer at the celebration. She was a stout blonde munching away enthusiastically, and she was always surrounded by a group of officers who looked at her, in the words of P. G. Wodehouse, 'like a bear at a bun'.

After the feast and after innumerable toasts had been drunk, there was a performance by the Red Army Ballet, held in a theatre that had been rapidly constructed adjoining the banqueting hall. It was a marvellous performance, and Claud got so overwrought that I had to drag him into his seat, saying 'It's all right to clap. But nobody else is standing up cheering.' However, his enthusiasm was noted by, and delighted, Marshal Koniev, who looked like a North American Indian totem pole carved out of mahogany and was dressed in a peacock blue uniform with a shocking pink order sash. When we came to say goodbye and thank you, the Marshal picked up Claud, who weighed over 12 stone, and tossed him in the air as if he had been a baby.

Next day we went on to Bucharest. There is a saying that 'some countries have organisation, some countries have chaos, only the U.S.A. has both.' Roumania definitely had chaos. When we were there in 1945 nothing worked, neither the oil wells, nor the factories, and above all, not the farms – which was a pity, as much of the land is immensely fertile, and the people were hungry. I had a chance to discuss this problem with the man at the top, Petru Groza, the Prime Minister. We became great friends and I still remember him with amusement and affection.

I met him first at a diplomatic reception given to celebrate some anniversary or other, of which he was the host. We were queueing up on arrival to shake his hand and he was muttering some formal greeting to each ambassador. When it got to my turn what he said, quite loudly, was 'Bravo'. I, taken aback, stammered something. Then he said, 'You are the beautiful Irish wife of Frank Pitcairn [Claud's nom-de-plume], a man who has come to report on me, and probably cause me endless trouble.' Then he began to sing 'The Wearing of the Green'.

It was typical of him, but despite this and numerous other indiscretions, he remained, to my astonishment, the world's greatest survivor.

Way back in the early 1930s Dr Petru Groza was one of the four or five largest landowners in Roumania and a director of between forty and fifty industrial companies. He was also the youngest Cabinet Minister in the government of King Carol. He resigned over what he said was that government's incompetence and corruption, and went back to his huge estate in Transylvania. He was jailed during the war as an anti-Hitlerite and emerged after victory as Prime Minister of Communist Roumania. Despite the well known fact that revolutions eat their own children, he maintained his talent for survival to the end, remaining a powerful figure in Roumanian politics. When he died they named a square in Bucharest after him.

After the diplomatic reception we were asked to stay on for a private dinner, during which he asked us to excuse his English, which was perfectly fluent, as he was a little tired.

'I rose at six, ran round the park, played tennis, and then I had to knock down a man in the foyer of the Athenée Hotel who was trying to assassinate me. And then meetings, always Cabinet meetings, so exhausting. I am not as young as I was. Approaching fifty.'

Checking back on dates, sixty would have been nearer the mark.

He sounded like a naïve child boasting, but in serious conversation, and from his record, it was obvious he certainly was not naïve.

Later, we were invited to stay at his home in Transylvania, which proved to be a large Austrian-type house. We were to fly there in a small plane provided by the Government. But about four days before our departure, we heard a small scratching noise on our bedroom door at four o'clock in the morning. It proved to be our official interpreter, a pale, thin youth, very different from the ebullient Poppoff. He was white and shaking.

'Please, please don't go in that plane. It is a Roumanian plane, it will fall down and if you go in it I will have to go with you. I come here secretly, to warn you.'

Whether he meant that, as nothing worked in Roumania, the plane wouldn't work either, or that he had heard someone was trying to liquidate us, wasn't clear, but in any case there was no sense in taking chances, so Claud told Groza that I hated flying, and in any case if we could go with him by train it would give us an opportunity for undisturbed conversation.

Because of the incessant attempts to assassinate the Prime Minister, we had to board the special train at a remote suburban station, and because it was Roumania, all the food for the long overnight journey over the Carpathians got sent to the wrong station. We did have plenty to drink though, as Groza, used to such mix-ups, had personally brought a case of excellent German wine with him. It wasn't really a train, just two carriages pulled by an ancient engine which huffed and puffed in agony as it slowly dragged us over the mountains.

The train contained ourselves, Groza, his aides, and his large bodyguard, who were dressed in elaborate Ruritanian-style uniforms with cocked hats surmounted by large plumes of feathers. As soon as we started the bodyguard lay down on the floor of the corridor, so completely filling it that, if you wanted to go to the lavatory, you had to walk on top of them.

Groza, on learning that Claud was a classics scholar, insisted on talking Latin all night. I and the aide-de-camp, not being able to understand them, fell asleep in an untidy heap like the bodyguards. I have never seen Claud as exhausted as he was next morning. He said that though he could read and write Latin fairly easily, he had never before tried to hold a long political and philosophical conversation in it, and wondered disconsolately if he had said something disastrous, which would be later held against him. I comforted him by saying that, in any case, Groza had drunk far too much hock to remember what had, or had not, been said.

Coming from an agricultural country, I was shocked to see the state of the countryside. Although it was now winter, many of the crops had not been gathered in, and some of the fields were not cultivated at all and were returning to scrub. No wonder there was famine in the land. When I asked Groza about this, he said that when the great estates were broken up they had had to be divided among landless people, many from the villages and towns, who knew nothing of agriculture, and in any case, often had no farm implements. He said that of course, they, in their turn would have to be evicted, but for the moment it was politically impossible.

From his record, and from the state of the country, it would be easy to write off Groza as a bombastic, time-serving 'Vicar of Bray', interested only in his own survival. But I don't think that would be quite fair. The mess was not of his making: he was entirely pragmatic, though he claimed to be entirely motivated by Marxist philosophy. He did his best to improve matters, and was not happy at finding himself in the position of Sisyphus. It is easy to create devils from a distance, but when you meet them they often turn out to be recognisable, and even touching, human beings. Groza was certainly one. He never failed to make me laugh: he was always making fantasies about himself like a teenage schoolboy. One afternoon we went for a walk, in the course of which he talked about how he was a countryman at heart, how he hated being cooped up in offices, always being surrounded by security men, and ended with a passionate declaration about how happy he had been when he lived here in Transylvania in exile.

'I know every blade of grass and every tree here, they are my friends.'

After that he grew preoccupied and silent and kept looking around him, until I said, 'I'm getting to know the trees round here pretty well myself. Do you know, we have passed that one four times. We're walking in circles. You have lost your way, haven't you, though we can't be more than a mile from the house? We could do with some of those security men right now – maybe they could tell us the way home.'

He laughed, and said, 'You are right, as usual, but you have a terrible way of deflating one. You should cure yourself of it. But all is not lost. If we walk south by the sun we will come to a river, and if we follow its banks we are sure to see the high chimneys of my place above the trees.'

Next week, back in Bucharest, there was an incident denoting the differing national characteristics of various Communist Party leaders. The winter had really closed in, and the large square in the middle of the city was covered with ice. I, who had foolishly put on rubber boots, was walking across this square accompanied by a member of the French Central Committee, a Rumanian ditto, a Russian and Claud. Suddenly my feet shot from me and I fell flat on my back, cracking my head on the hard icy road. I was dazed and incapable of movement and, as in a dream, I heard the Frenchman declaim, as if he was on the stage of the Comédie Française, 'Quelle catastrophe, elle est morte, elle est morte.' The Rumanian started to cry, and Claud, like a typical English husband, said, 'Patricia, don't *do* that.'

The Russian said nothing, picked me up and carried me into the nearest house and called for ice to put on the rapidly swelling lump on the back of my head.

I wasn't seriously hurt, though I had to stay in bed for a few days, which delayed our departure, in the icy hold of an R.A.F. cargo 'plane, to England.

CHAPTER 21

Return to my Homeland

I collected Alexander from my mother. He was pleased to see me, but not pleased at the thought of going back to London. He had had a wonderful time riding a woolly black donkey and scurrying about the garden and in and out of the numerous sheds, stealing fruit.

My mother was enchanted with him, saying he had been as good as gold, the only trouble had been that she could not get him to eat eggs. Having been a 'war baby', he had only known powdered eggs, and when faced with real ones he was disgusted.

The next year and a half I passed in a sort of limbo. I can't really remember much about it. It was like a dream, neither a nightmare nor enjoyable. People came and went, including one, Otto Katz, who passed through London on his way home. He was a well-known Communist who had been a refugee in Mexico during the German occupation of his native Czechoslovakia, to which he was now returning to take up some important post. I paid little attention to him, not realising that later on he would play a certain role in our lives. There were many others in a similar position, but I saw them like figures through a misty glass. Of this period only a few trivial events stand out, without context. I don't know why this should be. Perhaps I had just absorbed too many new impressions, and was now going through a period of mental hibernation.

In 1947 my second son, Andrew, was born and shortly after I put him in a basket and took him and Alexander to Ireland for a brief visit to my mother. Claud had gone to Paris to attend some conference or other. What happened next, I quote from Claud's autobiography, *Crossing the Line*:

> On the evening of our mutual return to London I told Patricia suddenly – I had never even hinted at it before – that I was thinking of dropping everything and starting an entirely new life. I had

expected her to be startled. Instead she coolly remarked that she had noticed for months that for me the savour had gone out of things, that as for her, she had come to the same conclusion, but had not liked to mention it.

Claud suggested we should emigrate to Mexico. I said, 'No, I am not going to bring up my children as strangers in a foreign land, never really belonging anywhere.' I had seen enough of displaced persons to know what psychological problems that produces.

'Well, where then?'

Without a moment's pause my subconscious spoke out.

'I want to go home.'

Suddenly a vision of those early morning rides in the countryside round Youghal swam into my mind. The rising sun shining through the mist and picking up the moisture on the thousand spiders' webs which hung on the gorse bushes, turning them into diamond necklaces, when the world smelled of a new day.

I was overwhelmed with homesickness.

My mother had been right all those years ago, before I married Arthur, when she had warned me against marrying an Englishman.

But what about the second half of her sentence? 'And he won't like it, permanently, Englishmen seldom do. You will slide back into your old ways with your old friends and make him feel an outsider.'

That presented a problem, though not a great one. Claud was not an Englishman. he was a Scotsman – and anyway he had lived so much abroad, in America and Europe, that his culture had become international.

I needn't have worried. Claud took to Ireland like the proverbial duck to water. He really loved the people and the country. He always said that the whole place stood at a slight angle to the universe, which suited him. I don't think he would have been as happy anywhere else, except possibly America.

Claud decided on a total break with his past and, like the Owl and the Pussy Cat in Lear's poem, 'sail away'. Unfortunately, unlike the Pussy Cat and the Owl we didn't have 'plenty of money, wrapped up in a five pound note'. In fact, we had practically none at all. Because of this Claud hovered about for some months without making any final decision. He had not been at all well, and when I finally persuaded him to go to a doctor, it was discovered that he had a fairly bad duodenal ulcer. He was told to go away to the country for a long rest, and to drink at least a gallon of milk a day.

This mitigated the uproar that his defection from the Communist Party would have otherwise engendered. He has explained, if somewhat inadequately, just why he left the Communist Party in *Crossing the Line*, in the chapter called 'Emergency Exit'. When we finally decided to go, we had no difficulty in selling the remaining two years of the lease on our flat.

We had moved some time before from our charming house in Acacia Road, as it had had its back blown off by a flying bomb. Nobody was at home at the time of the explosion, so no one was hurt except my cat, Sally, who was undamaged physically, but had a nervous breakdown as a result of the bomb. She was a grey cat, but after her traumatic experience her fur turned yellow and she developed a hysterical terror of men, feeling, no doubt, that they were responsible for the bomb. She had in the past loved Claud, sitting on his desk and purring as he worked, but after the house had been blown up, she fled from him in panic. She was still affectionate with women, but her distress at the sight or smell of a man was so pathetic that I gave her to an office run by, and staffed exclusively by, girls, where she would not be exposed to any terrifying males.

There was no problem about where we should stay in Ireland. My parents had suggested that Claud and I and the two children should live in Youghal with them at Myrtle Grove until we found a place of our own, and so once again I moved into a large family household.

Besides my parents, there was my brother Bernard, newly retired from the Royal Navy, and his wife Rosemary and their daughter Shirley, my sister Joan, and Teeny's widow Helen. As the house was so large we didn't get in each other's way at all and Claud was given a small cottage in the garden to use as his writing room. A large china bedroom jug, holding over a gallon, was filled with milk and placed on his desk every morning, and my mother checked up each day to see that he drank it to the very last drop. Myrtle Grove was still staffed by five or six servants, the remnants of the thirteen who had originally been employed. They had now reached the status of 'old family retainers', which meant that they lectured one from morning to night on one's behaviour, the upbringing of one's children, and one's general appearance. Danny and Tudgy were still there looking exactly the same.

During World War II Ireland had been almost totally isolated and was forced to try to be self-sufficient. There was plenty to eat, in fact there was such a surplus of meat that the price went down to *6d.* a pound for the cheaper cuts of beef, but there was practically no tea, which was terrible for the tea-swilling Irish, and petrol was restricted to priests and doctors. Some trains were made to run on turf as there was no coal. But it was not satisfactory. There were still plenty of horses and ponies in the country, and these were used for farm work and transport. Everybody who could rode bicycles. Nearly 200,000 people emigrated to England for war work and their wages, high by Irish standards, were sent back home to their families. So Ireland did not do too badly during the war, which was always alluded to as 'the emergency'. In 1944 my mother had driven the 170 miles to Dublin in a pony trap, drawn by my old pony Jimmy, who was only 12 hands high. It took her five days to get there and she stayed with friends along the way. She said it was a delightful trip as the weather was beautiful and stabling easy to find in Dublin. She stayed for a week, then mounted her pony trap and trotted home again.

The social scene in 1947 was very much as it was when I had left Ireland in 1932, except for two new factors. One was the rise of a new educated native Irish Catholic middle class, who had not existed in any great numbers before, and who now staffed the government offices and semi-state bodies, and the other was the fact that, probably due to isolation during the war, everyone seemed to be taking to the pen. From bed-sitters in Dublin to old nursery rooms in Georgian mansions, people sat sucking their pencils and scribbling away. Grudges became novels, and novels were largely autobiographical, a way of getting their own back on those of their families and associates whom they considered to have done them wrong, or frustrated them in any way. These novels were also a way of getting even with people of whom they had always been jealous. Most of these books were written under a pseudonym. Molly Keane, the author of *Good Behaviour*, has said in numerous press interviews that she wrote under the name of M. J. Farrell because to be known as an author would have had a deleterious effect on her social status among the Anglo-Irish hunting set. But I don't think that that is quite fair on these people, uncultured and philistine though most of them were. As I mentioned before, Edith Somerville had always been looked up to with awe, not only because she hunted her own pack of hounds, but because she was a 'famous writer'.

A more usual reason for this universal anonymity was fear of the wrath of those friends obviously caricatured in the novels, and that of their friends and relations.

The would-be Dublin authors often aimed their barbs at the Christian Brothers, who ran the secondary schools. It is true that many of the Brothers were bigoted and violent and earned the undying hatred of their pupils, but without their efforts the rising class of educated Irish would never have existed. As a well-known journalist said to me, 'If it hadn't been for the Brothers, I'd still be snagging turnips.' This was too often forgotten.

Even if they had wanted to, the Irish government at that time simply did not have the money to finance a national education system staffed with lay teachers. If the Church didn't educate the people, nobody would.

It took rather longer for Claud and me to find a home of our own than we had expected. This was due to various reasons, one of them being the political situation in England. When the Labour Party won the 1945 General Election, some of the rich, politically uneducated county families in the shires thought that Red Revolution had come to Britain and saw Mr Attlee, the Prime Minister, as a sort of Lenin – though in reality he was a man of such a pale pink political hue that he was almost off-white. Their commitment to democracy not extending to the idea of accepting the verdict of the people, they fled the country, taking as much of their money with them as they could get past the exchange controls. Many of them came to Ireland and were known locally as the 'Retreat from Moscow'. Once here they purchased dilapidated mansions, mended the roofs, put in central heating and three or four new bathrooms, papered the dining room with striped Regency wallpaper, added a crystal chandelier, and settled down to live what they imagined would be a certainly pre-war, and possibly Edwardian, gentleman's country life. After that they often wrote a book on 'How I found my dream house and restored it to its former glory', which contained many 'Pat and Mick' stories about the local building workers and the Irish in general. The next thing that one heard was that they had sold the whole place at a loss, frequently back to the original owners, and had returned to England.

The effect of all this on us was that it put up house values. We didn't have the capital to buy a house, or to build one – even one made out of whiskey bottles – so we wanted to lease one, and no one wanted to lease a house to us when there was the 'will-o'-the-wisp' possibility of selling it for an inflated price to a rich and foolish Englishman.

Also we had the difficulty of finding a medium-sized house, due to the fact that for so long Ireland had been inhabited only by the very poor and the very rich. Most of the houses we looked at were either too big or too small. The only suitable medium-sized ones we saw had been built for the Protestant clergy in Victorian days and were now vacant because the Protestant population had decreased so much since the Treaty that many parishes had had to be amalgamated. In the nature of things there were not very many of these ex-rectories, and what there were, like all things in short supply, commanded a high price.

Sometimes in despair Claud would say, 'It's no good, we shall just have to go and live in County Leitrim,' which is a beautiful but remote county of Ireland which nobody seems to want to go to, and where we had been offered houses for practically nothing. But, to me, Leitrim was Siberia, and I was determined to stay where my roots and my friends and family were. There wasn't really any particular hurry to get settled; we were very comfortable where we were and my mother liked having us there. Alexander was going to the local Church of Ireland day school and was happy and secure. Claud's health was improving and he was busy writing *Beat the Devil*, his first novel, later to be made into a film starring Humphrey Bogart, Jennifer Jones and Gina Lollobrigida.

I had taken up riding again, mostly on borrowed horses. One day, riding home on a by-road about two miles from Youghal, I saw, through a tangle of brambles and overgrown shrubs, the upper windows of a derelict-looking Georgian house. I knew at once that it was what we had been looking for. Negotiations were started and despite my mother's extreme disapproval, ('You can't live in that dump, it's worse than a ruined Norman keep'), Claud signed a lease of thirty-three years for Brook Lodge and twenty-seven acres of good land at a total annual rent of £120.

CHAPTER 22

Rural Life

The rent was ridiculously low. It really amounted to little more than rent for the land, and our new home was thrown in free – correctly so, as absolutely everything had to be done to make it habitable. There was no water, sewerage or, of course, electricity, but it was worth restoration as it was basically a beautiful structure built by a rich clergyman in the late eighteenth century on the foundations of a much older building, of which one wing remained.

The clergyman, the Revd Drew, had abandoned Brook Lodge at the time of some land agitation, as he regarded it as totally indefensible, as indeed it was, with its great Georgian windows an invitation to attackers to break in. So he built a fake medieval mini-castle a couple of fields away with arrow-slit windows and thick stone walls, and moved in there. But, finding it dark and generally uncomfortable, he added a Georgian wing with one little doorway connecting with the main castle, so that if attacked he could pop in there and shut a strong iron door. This proved to have been a good idea, as the Georgian wing was subsequently burnt down and the clergyman remained unharmed.

When we took Brook Lodge it was inhabited by an old man and his dog and about twenty thousand rats. During the negotiations for the lease the old man died and our eventual landlord was his son, a policeman in California.

To have embarked on such an enormous project of restoration, without adequate money, was an act of audacious folly which horrified my family, who did not have my faith in my Guardian Angel. Claud could be no help – he was no handy-man, and always said material things hated him. He could hardly touch a piece of china without breaking it. So he passed all practical problems over to me.

We could not afford a building contractor so we decided to do the job with previously unemployed workmen, of whom there were plenty in Youghal. I remember the first thing that happened was that when we had replaced the broken panes in the huge drawing room windows, which were at ground level, the rats ate off all the putty during the night and the new glass fell out and broke. So I mixed rat poison with the next lot of putty and after that the panes stayed in. My greatest triumph was the cesspit. We had decided to get a professional firm to do the plumbing, but their estimate was so large that, even in our most optimistic moods, we knew we couldn't possibly pay it. One item was £500 for a cesspit. I went to see the local government Sanitary Inspector in Cork, and asked him, 'How do you make a cesspit?' He was surprised but helpful, and explained its construction very carefully and made some rough drawings.

As a result, we got the two local grave-diggers to make our cesspit at a total cost of £15, and when the Inspector came to see it and give permission for its use, he said it was the finest cess-pit he had ever seen, and took me and the grave-diggers off to the pub and stood us drinks in celebration. Slowly but steadily the house ceased to be a ruin and became a home.

All this time Claud was writing away under about six different names. *Beat the Devil* was published both in England and America, but, as all authors will tell you, you cannot keep a family of four, let alone restore a Georgian mansion, on the proceeds of novels alone, unless you are lucky enough to write a bestseller, which *Beat the Devil* was certainly not to begin with. All authors will also tell you that what you need above all in the literary world is a 'name'. Claud had an internationally known name all right – in fact two. But one was Frank Pitcairn, the sinister agent of the Comintern and foreign editor of the Communist *Daily Worker*, and the other was Claud Cockburn, the extreme left-wing and allegedly scurrilous editor and owner of *The Week*. Publishers and editors of magazines fled in terror from association with such dangerous and subversive characters. At the age of forty, Claud had to start his literary career all over again like an undergraduate just down from university. *Beat the Devil* was published under the name of James Helvick, while Kenneth Drew, Patrick Cork, Hamish Something-or-other and a couple of others wrote articles for magazines. Frank Pitcairn was kept alive to write for some East European papers who paid well, if irregularly.

But despite all his hard work money was very short indeed. So short, in fact, that we soon had bailiffs around the house like other people had mice. There wasn't anything they could seize as the house was rented, all the horses and furniture mine, and the bills Claud's. But they stayed around the place. I soon discovered that the duns were so used to being abused and attacked, that a little kindness and good food astonished and delighted them. They were only too anxious to be helpful and, like Richard Brinsley Sheridan, the eighteenth-century playwright, we soon had them helping in the kitchen, carrying anything heavy, and even cleaning out the stables.

In an effort to help out our dire financial situation I had racked my brains to think how I could earn some money. In the countryside in Ireland it wasn't an easy thing to do. My only experience of gainful employment was writing reports for the Royal Geographical Society and sending out ambulances and fire engines in a city suffering bombing raids. Not very useful occupations in County Cork. I had had no formal education, but my upbringing had taught me something about horses. And it was the chance remark of an English weekend guest that gave me an idea about what to do.

He said that now the war was over, riding schools were being started up all over England but, as during the war nobody had been breeding or importing horses, there was a shortage, and ponies were commanding a high price. In those days, the 'travelling People', or Tinkers, roved the roads of Ireland in their horse-drawn caravans, accompanied by their herds of piebald horses and ponies, who lived by grazing on the wide grass verges during the day and at night were often thrust through a hole in the fence into some unsuspecting farmer's land.

I knew these ponies well – in fact I already owned one, my dear Blackberry, who pulled the 'governess-cart' that took Alexander to school every day. They were, I still believe, a distinct breed, always piebald or skewbald, and often with one, and sometimes two, bright blue eyes. They were usually steady, quiet, strong and intelligent – ideal mounts for beginners. It seemed to me obvious that the thing to do was buy these ponies as three-year-olds from the tinkers, give them some schooling, and sell them to English horse-dealers so that little English girls could learn to ride.

The project was a success from the start. To begin with I had to go about the country looking for the Travelling People, but soon the word got around among them that I was in the business of buying ponies and they came to me. I soon got to know them fairly well, which proved very interesting.

Nobody is really sure of these travellers' origins. They are not gypsies: it is likely that they are the descendants of Irish people evicted from their homes in the distant past, who, having nowhere to go, took to the roads and never settled down again. They have a culture entirely their own and their own dialect. They all have a fear and hostility towards what they call 'the settled people'. This fear and hostility was, and still is, mutual. Most pubs would not serve Tinkers on the grounds that to do so drove away other customers, who feared that the Travellers would certainly get drunk and probably start a fight. In fact, fighting seemed to be part of their culture, but their biggest battles are always among themselves, with one extended Travelling family attacking another.

In those days they were always illiterate – which is still true among the older Travellers – but they were very intelligent and as sharp as a razor, and certainly knew more about horses than any other group of people I have ever met.

To buy anything from them involved bargaining like an oriental merchant. It took hours, sometimes days, and was a game they thoroughly enjoyed. They always employed the Hard Man-Soft Man technique. Two men would appear leading a horse and offer it to me for an outrageous price. If I liked it, I would counter with a very small one. The Hard Man would turn round and start leading the animal away. The Soft Man would race after him, seize the reins, drag the horse back and start arguing with his companion to 'Give the lady a break. Wasn't she always good to the Travelling People and hadn't she been a great customer in the past, and would be again in the future.' The Hard Man would grudgingly bring down the price a little bit and I would edge up my offer. And so we would go on through the long wet afternoon – it always seemed to be raining when they came – with the Soft Man almost seeming to be on my side, calling on the other ceaselessly to be reasonable. It was a question of stamina, and it was two against one. So, to counter this uneven contest, I used to say, 'I'd willingly give you the price, it's a beautiful animal, but my husband, he is a terribly hard man. Himself would never agree.'

Claud, who hated horses, and couldn't tell a thoroughbred from a draught horse, would emerge on cue from the house, sneer at the pony, say it was only fit for pet-food cans, and retreat shouting 'No.' When the price was finally agreed, there was a further session about how much 'Luck Money' they should give me back. This, by tradition, should be about 3 per cent of the price. All transactions were, of course, in cash, and the Luck Money had to be given out of the seller's own pocket, not out of the notes I had just given him – and he would spit on the top note for luck.

Once the deal was concluded it was smiles and blessings all round. I was exhausted after standing there arguing for hours. I couldn't leave them for a minute while they were around, as they would pick up anything that wasn't nailed down with steel nails, such as pitch forks or shovels or even bits of old iron. Once they stole the back gates of the stable yard while my back was turned.

Nevertheless, I liked the Travellers and understood their reaction to a hostile world which had rejected them. Everyone in Ireland is in favour of a new deal for the Travelling Folk who are now motorised and deal mostly in antique junk. You will be told interminably that they should be integrated into the settled community and their children go to school. This is impossible when they are always on the move, but every time a local council allocates them housing there is a riot. Nobody wants Tinkers as neighbours, and, considering their reputation for thieving, untidiness and generally wild behaviour, one can understand why. It is a vicious circle. Travellers will not be welcomed into a local community until they conform with accepted standards, and they will never conform until they are accepted.

We had just really settled in, I was busy with my ponies, my garden and my third son, Patrick, born in 1950, who was just now a toddler, Claud was becoming more accustomed to his new life in the Irish countryside as a sedentary writer, when rather an awkward thing happened. From America Senator Joseph McCarthy issued a list of about 250 of the most dangerous Reds in the world. Claud came about eighty-fourth. This, we thought, would prove embarrassing in Catholic, passionately anti-Communist Ireland, but we underestimated our friends and neighbours. Most of them already disliked and despised McCarthy, and also regarded it as impudence that he should point a finger at one of their own. The vast majority of my old friends and relations remained loyal, and the townspeople of Youghal, who had got to know and like Claud, were merely excited and interested at having such a famous man in their midst. As for my immediate family, they also resented a jumped-up, alcoholic foreigner like McCarthy intruding into their private lives. This was reinforced by the English newspapers, notably the *Daily Express*, who kept telephoning my father from England and asking him for comments on his Red son-in-law, which infuriated him. The remnants of the 'Retreat from Moscow' naturally took fright and squawked with horror, together with some of their Irish hangers-on, but that could hardly distress us.

I think Claud was secretly slightly offended at being put so low down on the list – if he was going to be pilloried as a 'Dangerous Man', his vanity demanded that he should be in the first flight.

Then, not long afterwards, during a purge of suspected dissidents in Czechoslovakia, Claud's old friend, Otto Katz, was arrested. At his trial he made the obligatory confession of being a Western capitalist agent, and added that he had been induced to betray his country and the Communist cause by the wiles of 'Colonel Claud Cockburn' of the British Intelligence Service. That was a bit of a shock.

Personally, I believe that Otto Katz, feeling that he had to name someone, had picked on Claud as being well outside Czechoslovakian jurisdiction, and therefore unlikely to come to any harm. In any case, poor Otto was hanged. I do not know if he has since been posthumously rehabilitated, like Claud's other friend, Mikhail Koltzov.

Of course, among a large number of Irish people, being a British agent was just as unpopular as being a dangerous Red. But, to their credit, the vast majority preferred to back their own judgement that Claud was a 'Decent Man' and a good friend to Youghal, County Cork.

So life continued with the speed that day follows day in rural areas, where nothing much happens and one is always frantically busy. Gradually Claud built up a reputation as a non-political writer. His first autobiography, *In Time of Trouble*, was a Book Society Choice and a great success. He was writing for more and more newspapers and magazines, which was just as well as Alexander was being expensively educated.

I had asked an old friend, Sir George Colethurst, who lived at Blarney Castle and owned the Blarney Stone, about where we should send our eldest son to be educated, as he had now outgrown the little local Church of Ireland school at Youghal. By tradition, kissing the Blarney Stone is supposed to give one the ability to persuade anybody of anything, and Georgie must have kissed it many times, for he certainly persuaded me that the only responsible thing to do was to send Alexander to Heatherdown, a preparatory school near Ascot and one of the most élite and expensive schools in England. Claud had no objection. He held that Alexander would be of more use to the world, and the cause of humanity in general, if he were really well educated. And as to indoctrination, he didn't believe in it. He said that he himself had reacted against his own background of school, home and university and that Alexander would probably do the same. It would be best for the boy to see as many sides to all questions as possible, and then if he had any character, which Claud believed he had, he would make up his own mind. So, thanks to the influence of Sir George, off Alexander went to England.

Despite Claud's hard work and budding success, it was a nightmare trying to pay not only the school fees but also the travel six times a year back and forth from England.

The demand for ponies for English riding schools had tailed off and I had started breeding heavyweight hunters in a small way and also had a flock of purebred Suffolk sheep. But that only really brought in pin-money, so times were hard. Then my guardian angel, that reliable and hard-working character, came to our rescue again. Claud had said, 'We need something to cheer us up. Let's go and stay with Oonagh for the weekend.'

Oonagh, Lady Oranmore, was a Guinness heiress, and a good friend. Luggala, her lovely house in the Wicklow Mountains, was always a centre of gaiety. Arrived there, we found not only Brendan Behan, on the wagon and sober for once, but also John Huston, the film director. Claud had known him slightly in the past, but John had not read any of Claud's books. Snatching up Oonagh's inscribed copy of *Beat the Devil*, Claud thrust it on him. On the Wednesday after our return home, Claud got a long telegram from Huston, saying he adored the book, it had made him laugh so much that he had fallen downstairs while reading it and had twisted his ankle. He was determined to make a film of it. And so he did. It was one of the most successful films ever made. John came and stayed with us for a month while he and Claud worked on the script. Our financial crisis was temporarily eased. Claud settled down to writing again and I to farming and gardening.

To help me in these pursuits I had a number of assistants. One was the beautiful Ann, whom the children called the 'lady horse nurse' and who looked like one's mental image of a Valkyrie: she was in charge of the stables. Not only was she brilliant at her job, but her many admirers were useful as well. Once I came down and found a strange young man energetically mucking out a stable. He turned out to be a rising Cork doctor, who had come on his day off to 'give Ann a hand'. Another swain used to send us five dozen eggs a week for an orphan foal whom we were rearing by hand. A less welcome follower was a neighbouring Master of Hounds who had been unsuccessfully wooing her for some time. One night at 2.00 a.m., after some party he had attended, he had the bad idea that it would be romantic to serenade her. To do this he attempted to climb a drainpipe so she could hear him better. Half way up, the drainpipe, being old and rickety, came away from the wall and he fell sixteen feet into a flower bed, damaging himself and ruining my carefully nurtured flowers. Ann was furious, and so was I. As well as a disturbed night, I had to pay for a new drainpipe, and my plants never recovered.

To look after the sheep and help in the garden there was Paddy McMahon, ancient, tiny and a mine of fascinating information about the past. He was also a living refutation of many modern theories of the importance of a balanced diet. At ninety-eight he was as fit as a fiddle, roaming the fields all night at lambing time in February, and energetically digging in the garden; yet he refused to eat anything but very salty pigs' heads or trotters, and potatoes covered with lots of butter. Nothing else. No vegetables and no fruit. In the morning he put an old tin kettle on the stove with about a quarter of a pound of tea in it and let it bubble away all day, adding more water from time to time. He lived to be 102, retiring from work when he reached his first century.

I spent many evenings talking to him and gradually pieced together his history. He had been born in 1860, on the coast of County Clare, and his family had been shepherds to the same family of landlords for seven generations. They had been good landlords and during the Great Famine, ten years before Paddy's birth, had done their best to feed their people, and demanded no rents. As a result they could not pay the rates, became bankrupt, and were sold up. There was consequently no work for the McMahon family. They scraped a living by fishing and doing any odd jobs they could find, and survived somehow. There was nothing for Paddy when he grew up but emigration, and at eighteen he and two cousins set off for Liverpool to find work. They were all native Irish speakers; Paddy could speak a little English, but the cousins not a word. Their few worldly possessions they carried, like Dick Whittington, in little bundles. Homesick and miserable they travelled in a train to a great city, where their little bundles were instantly stolen. They were not surprised – what could you expect, they thought, in this pagan English place. 'And do you know, Mrs Cockburn, it was six weeks before we discovered that we were not in Liverpool at all, but in Dublin.' They found work, however, in the docks and Paddy eventually got to Liverpool, where he remained unhappily for fourteen years before coming home.

Of course, as he was born ten years after the Great Famine, he had no memory of it, but he had heard many stories of that terrible time from his parents, which he loved to tell. He told us how waves of starving people came to the coast from inland, pathetically hoping to find food by the sea. 'There wasn't a nettle in a churchyard nor a winkle on the rocks left after them, and they died on those rocks,' he would say, with a curious note of triumph in his voice.

It was fascinating to me to find someone who had experienced, even at second-hand, historical events that normally one only reads about. Paddy's stories reminded me of my grandmother, who told me when I was a child that when she was a child she knew an old gentleman – I think named Count Valdeck – who had, as a boy, been a page to Queen Marie-Antoinette before the French Revolution. He had said that all the court pages loved Marie-Antoinette as she was always kind and thoughtful towards them. Grandmama asked him, 'Was she really very pretty?' 'Yes,' he replied, and drew a little portrait of her from memory. Grandmama kept the sketch all her life, and showed it to me. It must be somewhere about Myrtle Grove to this day.

Paddy's inherited knowledge of sheep was phenomenal. Sometimes he would come to me and say, 'Would you cast an eye on that ewe you bought last week, she's looking pale.' How a sheep could look pale defeated me; the ewe seemed perfectly normal, grazing away, but he was always right. Three days later she would be either dead or very sick indeed.

CHAPTER 23

Polio Epidemic

The year 1956 was terrible, the worst in my life, as it was to many others in Cork City and County. For it was the year of the great polio epidemic.

In the late spring we had returned to London and had taken a house in Hampstead for the summer, as Claud was now working regularly for *Punch*. The editor, Malcolm Muggeridge, had asked him to stay in London for three months to help with some project or other. After being Claud's adversary on the Fleet Street branch of the N.U.J. for years, Malcolm had now become a close friend. This was before he had become converted to religion. After that they gradually drifted apart.

Disentangling myself with some difficulty from the house, stables and farm, I and the two younger children, Andrew aged nine and Patrick aged six, decided to accompany him. In July I got letters from home saying that a terrible epidemic of polio had broken out in Cork City. Thousands of children had been affected. Claud and I were worried and talked for hours about the advisability of not returning home at the beginning of August as we had planned. Finally, we decided that it was safe to go back to Brook Lodge. There had been no cases of polio in Youghal, which was thirty miles from Cork, and Brook Lodge was isolated in fields, two miles from Youghal. We decided we would not mix with any other children, and keep the boys around the house.

In September Patrick suddenly complained of a bad headache. The doctor immediately diagnosed polio and within an hour he was on his way by ambulance to the Fever Hospital in Cork. We never knew how he had caught the disease. There were still no other cases in Youghal.

Andrew had just gone to a prep school in Dublin. We telephoned the headmaster, who immediately put him on the train home. When we met him at the station, we saw from the way he was walking that he had contracted polio as well, and he joined Patrick in the Fever Hospital.

Then followed an agonising three weeks. We, of course, were in quarantine, unable to leave the house; and in any case, no visitors were allowed in the Fever Hospital. Twice a day we telephoned, inquiring how the boys were, expecting and dreading to hear that they were dead or dying, and afterwards spending hours mulling over the exact tone of the ward sister's voice, when she said, 'As well as can be expected.' Did she sound hopeful or not?

Naturally I was tortured by guilt at having made the wrong decision to come home. Claud said it was a natural reaction; when a disaster occurs it is human to need to blame somebody or something for it; one can't accept that life can be governed by pure chance, and in this case there was nobody to blame but ourselves.

I think I should have gone mad if it hadn't been for Claud. Misfortune is often said to bring couples together, but my observation is that it usually does the opposite, causing them to lash out at each other as the only available objects to vent their frustrations on. But not in our case. Claud was so patient, so tactful, so determined, despite his own anxiety, to help me weather this storm, that we were welded closer than ever into a single unit.

The boys survived and after three weeks, when the fever and the infectious period was over, they were assessed to see what damage had been done. Andrew was not paralysed, except for his big toe, and was sent home, but I was told to keep him in bed for two months, as in exceptional cases paralysis could set in later if he used his muscles too much. Poor little Patrick's back and legs were badly affected. He could not walk or sit up and he was sent to an orthopaedic hospital for treatment.

The physical side of the treatment at the orthopaedic hospital was good, but the psychological management was appalling. The children were merely regarded as things to be washed, fed and doctored. It was nobody's fault. The epidemic had overwhelmed the health services. The hospital was like something reminiscent of the Crimean War, with beds nearly touching and some children lying on mattresses on the floor. Polio was still raging, and more and more cases were arriving from the fever hospitals every day.

Cork was a dead city: there was a smell of fear everywhere, with no one in the streets. Shops and businesses went bankrupt, as there were few customers brave or foolhardy enough to come into the city to visit them. It is a sad reflection on the selfishness and warped values of some classes of people that I heard that pressure was being put on local papers, by the threat of withdrawal of advertising revenue, to play down the severity of the plague and the risk of infection in order to get more people to come to Cork City and improve business. It is to their credit that the local papers resisted.

The shock of his illness had proved absolutely traumatic to Patrick, who withdrew into himself and refused to speak. The doctors said that perhaps the muscles controlling his vocal chords had been affected, but I was sure that this was not so, and that his silence was mental and not physical. So, against medical advice, I brought him home, taking him up to Cork three times a week for physiotherapy. Once back in his familiar surroundings, he started to chatter away as usual and was wonderfully cheerful.

Gradually he improved, progressing from iron callipers on his legs to crutches, and he had a rigid plastic corset to support his back. He was always a highly intelligent child, full of curiosity, so it was essential to teach him to read as quickly as possible, before boredom set in. I took on the task myself, but I had no teaching experience, and though I did my best, we got nowhere to begin with. Then I noticed that he was highly competitive, and something of a gambler, so I taught him gin-rummy, using letter cards instead of playing cards, and also an adapted form of poker, words taking the place of sequences – a full house was a two- and a three-letter word. After that he learned to read and write in no time. We used Smarties as counters and at the end of the game he ate his winnings, but he was always careful to save his initial stake for his poker session next day.

Claud taught him chess, and he rapidly became extremely good at it and joined an International Chess Club, sending his moves by post. At one time he had seven games going at once with opponents in Russia, U.S.A., Brazil, South Africa, Spain, England and Bulgaria.

Still, it was heartbreaking to see that he had, in a sense, lost his childhood, and that he could never play around with other children.

So as to increase his mobility I got him a tiny, aged Welsh pony called Fluffy. He learned to ride her quite well by balance, and after a bit I didn't have to lead her about. He used to ride her by himself in our fields, sitting on her back, picking blackberries in summer. This gave him some much needed independence. The doctor told me that his condition would probably improve with treatment for two years after his illness, but after that it would become static. A very depressing thought. Fortunately I did not tell Patrick this, and did not really believe it myself, as it proved incorrect. At eight years old he was almost totally incapacitated. After an operation to his feet in London he slowly but steadily improved, was able to go to boarding school with his brother Andrew, and now has been for some years a foreign correspondent for the *Financial Times*, marching, among other places, all over the Middle East, without even needing to carry a stick. Probably because of his very dependent youth, he has always had a 'penchant' for dangerous places. After Oxford – to which, like his two elder brothers, he obtained a scholarship – he did post-graduate work in Belfast before going as a journalist to the Lebanon, where he arrived just in time for the first Lebanese war. He has also worked in Iran and the Yemen and many other disturbed places.

All this time Ireland was changing – its industrial revolution had really got under way. In 1945 the first textile factories were opened in Youghal; in 1956 a local man started Youghal Carpets, which flourished and grew to become a very large concern indeed. No longer were the crumbling houses kept up by the backs of unemployed men leaning up against them. There was a shortage of labour, and factories sent buses round the countryside each morning to pick up workers.

In the 1960s, under the premiership of Sean Lemass, Ireland began to emerge into the twentieth century. The class of native civil servants who had arisen after Independence was augmented by a new class of rich Irish Catholic business people, many of whom bought up the Georgian mansions of the impoverished Anglo-Irish; and gradually social integration between the two cultures became the rule rather than the exception. As a result inter-marriage became common.

When I was a child, all the big estates on the banks of the Blackwater River, that eighteenth-century highway, were in Protestant, Anglo-Irish hands. Now, though in many cases the same families owned them, they had become Catholic, because the children of mixed marriages were still brought up as Catholics.

Those Anglo-Irish, mostly elderly, who maintained their old exclusiveness became more and more isolated, living like a small endangered tribe, ripe to be studied by visiting anthropologists. Books about their way of life began to be published in increasing numbers. Their culture was not to be entirely lost, though, as the new ascendant class of Irish capitalists adopted many of their tastes and prejudices.

Another effect of industrialisation was that farming improved, becoming less labour-intensive as machines replaced workers. The unemployed drifted to the new factories in the cities, as they had in England two hundred years before, and though emigration to the U.S.A. and England continued to be high, there was an air of hopefulness about the country that was entirely new.

Of course, this urbanisation of a previously rural population, and the social upheaval it caused, had a large debit side. Dublin and Cork grew in an unplanned way. They had always had their share of slums, but they were small. Now the new estates built to house the workers and clear the inner cities to make way for office blocks broke up the extended family culture which had always been so vital to Irish people – particularly Irish women who, without the accustomed support of mothers, sisters, aunts and cousins, had no one to turn to and so suffered from loneliness and isolation. The birthrate was, and still is, the highest outside the Third World, and so as there were no crèches and no nearby relations to mind the children, a majority of women could not go out to work.

CHAPTER 24

Dublin

I have always noticed that good and bad fortune seem to go in cycles, supporting the old adage, 'it never rains but it pours'. During periods of bad luck, however, my Guardian Angel, in whom I had such faith, always seemed, like Superman, to come to my rescue at the last minute. The volcano in the Congo had erupted when Arthur and I were climbing it, but the lava had skirted round us and we were unharmed. Once, walking in the bush I unexpectedly came face to face with a lioness; frozen with horror I stood still, and she just gave me a dirty look and walked away. Two of my sons got polio, but they recovered and led useful and happy lives. When we were stony broke we met John Huston, who bought *Beat the Devil* for the films.

During the Asian 'flu epidemic Claud began to run temperatures. Feeling that we were passing through a period of misfortune, I was worried. The doctor at first said it was nothing, but when he failed to recover, sent him to hospital in Cork for a thorough examination. There it was discovered that he had raging T.B. in both lungs.

Because of the prevalence of the disease in Ireland there was a large number of excellent T.B. hospitals available locally, which were free, and to one of these he was sent. He was lucky in that the first of the drugs to combat the disease had just been discovered, but not perfected, as they are today. After ten months he returned home cured, but with part of his lungs severely damaged, and his health never really fully recovered.

From that time on my life became dominated by medical problems. Patrick recovered slowly, but poor Claud developed one devastating illness after another. Altogether he had T.B., cancer, burst duodenal ulcers, emphysema and cataracts in both eyes, for which he had successful operations. Through it all his mind remained perfectly sharp, clear and vigorous, and he never stopped writing. How he could remain so cheerful under these circumstances was a miracle.

When he first went to hospital he asked me to give up hunting. If anything happened to me, who would look after the children? I said that giving up hunting wouldn't help. It was just a question of fate – I could just as easily have a car crash on the way to the hospital to visit him.

I didn't have a car crash, but I did have an accident connected with horses while he was away, but not in the hunting field.

I had a very large and disagreeable mare called Sheelagh, who was the only horse I have ever owned, or indeed heard of, who used to catch and kill rats. If a rat got into her stable she would corner it and, quick as lightning, catch it with her teeth. She was a vicious animal in every way and once killed a pony who had been put by mistake in the same field with her, but she was an excellent brood mare. One of her colts eventually went to Japan with the British team for the three-day event at the Olympic games. One night when I was going to feed the chickens she ambushed me from behind a shed and kicked me with both legs, catching me on the thigh. I was of course thrown over. Knowing her well, and thinking that she would probably come out and finish me off, I leaped up, ran as fast as I could across the field and climbed over the gate.

I was planning to go to London on business next day, and when Ann insisted that I should go to the local doctor, I was reluctant to do so, as I felt he might fuss and say I couldn't go. However, she persuaded me. She drove me to Youghal, and I walked into the doctor's surgery and got up onto his couch, saying, 'It is all right for me to travel tomorrow, isn't it?'

He looked at my leg and said, 'The kick has cut the big muscle of your thigh right through. You aren't going anywhere, except home to bed. You won't be able to walk for six or seven weeks.'

The minute he said that, I couldn't walk. He and Ann had to carry me out to the car. I asked the doctor how I had managed to run across the field, jump over the gate, and get to his house with a severed muscle. He shrugged and said he had known cases like that before; once he had attended a boy who had broken both knees in a motor cycle accident and had got home and walked upstairs to bed before help arrived.

Ann, having got me home, went off to Claud's hospital to tell him what had happened. He was furious, but triumphant. He always said no good would come of those blasted horses.

All during those ten months when he was in the T.B. hospital, Claud continued to write. The doctors didn't like it, but felt correctly that if he were forced to be idle he would only lie there worrying about money. Our financial situation was difficult but not disastrous. My father had died, but had not cut me out of his will as he had threatened. But the income to his estate went to my mother during her lifetime.

The farm didn't make much money, but it paid for itself, and breeding and training horses just enabled me to hunt and ride, which otherwise I couldn't have afforded.

Lots of people came and visited Claud in hospital. I particularly remember a party of old friends who were staying with the Duchess of Devonshire at Lismore Castle. The group included Cyril Connolly, the writer and literary figure, who, while everyone else packed themselves into Claud's small cubicle which had glass walls, was so terrified of infection, despite being told by a doctor there was no danger, that he remained outside, pressing his nose against the glass and shouting through it. Of course he was totally inaudible inside and his huge face, with his mouth opening and shutting silently, made him look like a bloated goldfish deprived of water. Everybody, including Claud, laughed so much at the sight that the Matron turned them all out as she feared that laughing would give Claud a haemorrhage.

Another great friend, who lived near the hospital, was permanently banned from visiting Claud as she couldn't resist telling him incredibly funny stories to cheer him up, and so endangered his life.

As every parent knows, if you live with a child you don't see him growing; visitors arrive and say 'How he has grown', but he looks just the same to you. It was like that with Patrick's and Claud's slow recovery. With Patrick, the only landmarks were his gradual discarding of his various aids – first his iron callipers, then his rigid corset and finally his crutches.

I am quite certain that it was only his iron determination to get well that helped him to achieve this miraculous feat – a case of mind over muscles and nerves.

After Claud's discharge from the T.B. hospital we took a house in Dublin so that Patrick could join Andrew at school as a day-boy.

Eventually he became well enough to become a boarder, and we thankfully returned to Brook Lodge. Neither Claud nor I felt at home in Dublin and were made uneasy by the set we moved in there, who were largely writers and associated intelligentsia. Claud instantly christened them 'Dublects'. Their chief characteristic seemed to be petty jealousy. To be really popular you had to be a failure, and preferably an alcoholic. The minute anyone became successful all his friends, instead of rejoicing, started making snide remarks about his work, behaviour and general character, and comparing his writing unfavourably with that of some unpublished drunk, who could not by the wildest stretch of the imagination be considered a rival.

Of course there were many exceptions to this rule, which, in any case, did not apply to journalists, many of whom we soon met, as it was about this time that Claud started doing a weekly column for the *Irish Times*. This column became immensely popular, and he received a large fan mail, which I could never get him to answer. He hated writing letters, but when he forced himself to write one, it usually went on for pages, leaving him exhausted, and with the determination never to write another letter as long as he lived.

Before we went to Dublin Claud told me that he was looking forward to meeting the author Myles na Gopaleen (alias Flann O'Brien, real name Brian Nolan), as he had always greatly admired his work. Finally this ambition was achieved. Claud went into a pub and there was na Gopaleen talking to another friend. Myles was very drunk, and the minute he saw Claud he started to abuse him violently, calling him 'time server, hypocrite, West Briton' and anything else of a derogatory nature he could think of. Finally he fell down but continued his insults lying on his back on the pub floor. Claud and the friend picked him up, and helped him, still under a stream of abuse, into a taxi and sent him home.

Next day we went to a cocktail party at Lord Killanin's, the then President of the Olympic Games Committee. We planned to leave early as we were going out to dinner, but when we came to say goodbye, Michael Killanin asked us to stay a little longer. 'I have just had a call from Myles na Gopaleen apologising for being late,' he said, 'and when he heard that Claud was here, but just leaving, he implored me to hold on to him. He would come round immediately as Claud was the one person he had always wanted to meet as he had heard Claud was as brilliant a talker as he was a writer.'

I was really sorry that we had to move on and so missed the second meeting of the two fans. I shall never know if this second meeting would have been one of mutual admiration or have gone the same way as the first, of which Myles na Gopaleen obviously had no memory.

During that dreary time in Dublin I used every Saturday afternoon to take Patrick to the Dublin Zoo, and that is how I met the badger. He was a particularly charming badger, who obviously longed for human companionship. He lived by himself in a cage at the end of a long straight path. I became friendly with his keeper, who after a bit of encouragement agreed to let us into the cage to play with the badger and give him some toast, which he loved. Animals have a great sense of time, and the keeper told me that on Saturdays at 3 p.m. exactly the badger would stand up on his hind legs, so that he could see down that long, straight path, and watch for our arrival. When we left Dublin I worried about him – I pictured him standing there watching and waiting for friends who would never come again – so I asked a good-natured friend of mine who lived in Dublin to visit the badger and give him toast on Saturdays.

This she did, and when I next saw her she told me that as soon as she saw him, she recognised the badger; he used to be the pet of friends of hers in County Carlow. They had had him since he was a cub, and he was a great favourite and perfectly house-trained.

As well as the pet badger, these friends owned a large house with a polished wood staircase rising from a front hall with a parquet floor. They also had a stout and pompous butler.

One day the badger was coming downstairs when he slipped and tobogganed down the last flight on his behind, slid across the polished floor and crashed against the butler who was just carrying a tray of glasses and decanters across the hall, striking him just behind the knees. The butler fell down amid a crash of broken glasses and bottles. The badger thought this was the funniest thing that had ever happened to him, and from that day on the wretched butler could not pick up a tray without the badger charging him like a bull from behind, trying to make it all happen again. This went on for a week, and then the butler issued an ultimatum. Either the badger left the house or he did. The family chose the butler, and the poor badger was given to the Dublin Zoo, to be imprisoned for ever.

When I next went to Dublin to pick up the boys from school, I went to the Zoo to see him and heard he was dead. I can only feel it was a happy release.

CHAPTER 25

She Sells Sea Shells

When Claud had finally left Oxford he went on his last day there to say goodbye to his tutor, an erudite but shy man, who felt that, agonising as it might be, he must make some definitive statement to his ex-pupil about the future. He looked at Claud in silence for some time and then said, 'Hitherto, your life has been divided into school terms and school holidays, university terms and vacations. Now that is over, and you have what I can only describe as a straight run to the grave.'

I have never been to school or university, but when Patrick, my youngest child, finally left Oxford, I had a feeling of total disorientation. The straight run to the grave became apparent. For twenty years I had looked forward to the boys' regular return for the holidays, made plans for their entertainment, worried about them, tried to save money with which to give them a good time. Now it was all over, and my job was done. They were on their own, to make what they would or could of their lives. And the same applied to me.

Of course, I was busy looking after Claud, whose health was so precarious, but I deeply felt the need of doing something constructive and above all new. Life seemed flat and depressing, and I began to lose interest in all my previous occupations.

This feeling seems to be universal among women who have spent a great part of their lives dedicated to bringing up a family, and shows the enormous need for the re-training of middle-aged women whose children have grown up and left home. Though they may be aware of the fact, few young people really grasp the implications of the knowledge, that, with luck, half their lives will be lived after the age of forty-five, and so they must prepare to use to the full, and enjoy, this second half of their stay on earth. Too often middle and old age seems to creep up on them unannounced, and they cannot quickly adjust their behaviour and objectives. Many react by trying desperately to hang on to their youth for as long as possible, to the immense financial advantage of the beauty culture industry. They should re-read Hamlet's oration to the skull of Yorick and realise the fruitlessness of that path. What they need is education for a new career, and a determination to develop new interests.

In my case, my new career came to me by chance, but in a sense was based on the days I had spent studying design at art school in my extreme youth.

When I felt depressed I often found peace and contentment by wandering on the beautiful deserted beaches near my home, and had gradually taken to collecting sea shells, idly trying to see how many different species I could find. Soon I became really interested in them, and started haunting libraries for books on molluscs. My collection grew, and I became ambitious, driving long distances to remote areas to find rare specimens. The old nursery was soon filled with plastic bags containing the thousands of shells that I had picked up. In the late autumn I went to Dublin for a brief visit, staying at Leixlip Castle with Desmond Guinness. One night, unable to sleep, I crept down to his library to get a book to read. There, in a folio, I found some prints of eighteenth-century shell pictures. They were quite beautiful, totally unlike the monstrosities that one usually associates with the word 'shell picture'. The sight of them gave me an idea. I had been wondering what on earth I could give Desmond for Christmas. It had to be something really nice, as he had been immensely kind to me, asking me to stay whenever I came to Dublin and being helpful in every possible way. Desmond was the founder and President of the Irish Georgian Society and an avid collector of eighteenth-century art and crafts. There were plenty of charming things in the Dublin shops, but I was quite sure that the sort of small antique that he would appreciate would be far too expensive for me to buy. The sight of those prints decided me to try and make him a shell picture, modelled on one of them, but first I had to discover all about them, and the technique of making them. This proved easier than I thought. Without telling him about my projected Christmas gift, I questioned Desmond about eighteenth-century shell pictures. He didn't know a great deal about them, but said that Mrs Delaney, who lived from 1702 to 1784, had made a great many, and that she had corresponded regularly with her great friend, the Duchess of Portland. In these letters, copies of which he had in the house, she had written a good deal about shell pictures and shells in general, and if I was interested I had better read them.

From these letters, and later from other sources, I built up the story of the great shell craze of the eighteenth century, which happened around the same period as the great tulip craze.

It had its origins in the enormous extension of trade with tropical countries that took place at that time. Sailing ships visiting Far Eastern ports brought back exotic sea shells which had never been seen before in Europe. People went wild about them, and regarded them like jewels. Shell auctions took place, at which the prices rose to great heights. Some enthusiasts mortgaged their estates to buy a single shell, while Frederick the Great paid 5000 gold ducats for a pink Wentletrap shell. At every successive auction shells became more and more expensive, rather in the same way that shares on the American stock exchange were pushed up in the boom of 1929 by gamblers who devoted their time and energy to 'playing the market'.

Prominent artists were commissioned to make shell pictures. Then, at first gradually and then suddenly, the bottom fell out of the sea shell market. The reason was overproduction. It had become worthwhile for ships to bring back very large quantities of shells from the Far East and to go out of their way to places where shells were abundant and colourful and could be bought from the natives for practically nothing. The market was soon glutted – prices fell and many people were ruined. Shells became unfashionable and the pictures and ornaments that were still being made soon deteriorated into the tourist rubbish that one still sees today, sold at seaside holiday resorts.

It is a curious fact that a seashell, one of the most beautiful and fantastic of nature's creations, is capable of being used in such a way as to make it vulgar, ungainly and ugly. The worst crime of all is to paint or cut a shell, and that is constantly done.

Something that has always interested me about molluscs is that they represent the only example I know of beauty for beauty's sake alone. All other living objects, whether animal or vegetable, seem to have a practical purpose for their loveliest attributes. The colour and fragrance of flowers is there to attract insects for the purpose of pollination. The brilliant plumage of tropical birds is usually at its brightest in the breeding season. The stripes of tigers, zebras, and the colourful coats of many animals are a form of camouflage – which is why small far northern creatures turn white in winter. But the wonderful colours of sea shells do not seem to be of any use to the creatures that inhabit them. In fact they are very often found on the inside of the shell, totally hidden until the creatures are dead, and so appear to be nature's gift to man.

I first made two shell pictures, keeping carefully to the eighteenth-century rules I had learned from my researches. They were done on velvet mounted on wood and framed in a couple of antique frames which one could at that time buy quite cheaply. I gave one to Desmond and the second to Norah MacGuinness. This was very bold of me, as Norah was a very distinguished artist indeed, and the president of the 'Living Art' Organisation.

My Christmas gifts were a great success. Desmond and Norah were delighted with them and told me that I absolutely must turn professional and have an exhibition. With their help, that is what I did. My first exhibition was held at Castletown House, the headquarters of the Irish Georgian Society. It was scheduled to be open for a month, but to my delight I had sold all my pictures by the end of the first day, and there was a great deal of press publicity.

From then on I worked very hard, improving my technique and acquiring ever more shells, until by now I must have hundreds of thousands of them. That first exhibition was followed by eleven other one-woman exhibitions in Ireland, England and America, and I have sent pictures all over the world.

In America there is great interest in collecting shells. There are many societies of conchologists and several magazines devoted solely to molluscs. As in the eighteenth century, rare shells command a high price: a 'Cypraea Leucodon' was worth $10,000 a short time ago, though I believe the price has dropped a little recently. There are – or, sadly, were – over twenty thousand different varieties of sea and land shells in the world, but as in so many other areas, man is killing the goose that lays the golden eggs. Scuba divers are bringing back more and more live shells to the surface, without regard to any form of conservation. In some places whole species have been almost wiped out as a result. In some countries, where shell trading is a big industry, they have even dynamited the reefs to get at the shells, destroying the eggs and habitat for ever.

In Ireland, where the waters are supposed to be relatively unpolluted and few people collect any live shells, except winkles, I have noticed that there are many fewer sea shells washed up on the beaches than there used to be, and also that there are many more 'albinos' – shells which are devoid of all pigment. Despite asking many environmentalists and marine biologists, I can get no explanation for this fact.

As well as learning about molluscs and how to make shell pictures, I soon found that if I was to make any worthwhile money I had to learn to pick my way through the labyrinth of the Art business. Like many people who have little experience of trade, I learned the hard way. My first exhibition in New York was held in a very smart gallery on the Upper East Side. I was delighted when I got the contract, and felt my fortune was made, and I signed it without reading the small print. This turned out to include the obligation that I should pay for the transport of the pictures, the catalogue, the drinks for the opening party, and even the wages of the permanently employed gallery workers on the day when they hung the pictures. The gallery was to get 50 per cent of the selling price and the right to decide how much that would be. When I discovered what they were proposing to charge for the pictures I was in despair – as it was so high I felt sure no one would buy them. However, I was wrong there, as about half of them sold. All my friends congratulated me and asked what I was going to do with the money, but after everything was paid all I really got was a free holiday in New York, which was nice enough, as I love the city.

My second experience of American business was more disastrous. The Irish Tourist Board had asked me to decorate the windows of their offices on Fifth Avenue with my pictures for the celebration of the American Bicentennial in 1976. All the national airlines and tourist offices of the different nations on the Avenue vied with each other in exhibiting something both original and typical of their country. Tired of shamrocks, harps and the Blarney Stone, some intelligent executive had thought it a good idea to promote Irish art and also Irish sea shells, and so I got the offer. They paid no fee, but I was to have all my expenses paid, and after a fortnight was to get my thirty-five pictures back.

During that fortnight a director of Abercrombie and Fitch, the huge and famous department store, saw my pictures while walking down Fifth Avenue and came into the office to ask if they were for sale. He was told that for tax reasons the Tourist Board could not sell anything, but that I, the artist, was in New York, and no doubt he could buy them from me when the celebrations were over. He offered a very large sum for the lot – to be paid at the end of the month – and his men duly collected the pictures.

Absolutely delighted, and feeling really rich for once, I went out and bought presents for all my friends and family. Three weeks later Abercrombie and Fitch were declared bankrupt. I was never paid, and I could not get the pictures back. Instead I had the added embitterment of seeing them in the windows of Abercrombie and Fitch in ever-decreasing numbers, as they were sold off before the store finally closed down. After that I got wise, remembering my experiences in trading ponies with the Travelling People, and gave no more credit, not even for a day.

CHAPTER 26

The Last Lap

All this time, when I was busy making and selling shell pictures and gardening (which to those afflicted is an addiction, like smoking and taking drugs) Claud's health was gradually deteriorating. He became weaker and weaker, his body crumbling like an ancient tower, but his mind and spirit remained the same. He was never content to relax as an invalid, but continued working as hard as ever. Nor was he content to stay quietly at home. We travelled to San Francisco for the wedding of our son Andrew – Claud in the wheelchair which all airlines thoughtfully provide – and we several times visited Cape Cod in Massachusetts, where Alexander regularly took a house for the summer. One American airline once provided a new and very superior electric wheel chair. Claud, who was hopeless with anything mechanical, got his finger firmly fixed on the accelerator and shot off at great speed, leaving me desperately running along behind. He circled the airport terminal several times like a whirlwind, scattering the passengers, before he discovered how to stop it.

Shortly before we went to San Francisco a great upset had taken place in our lives. The lease of Brook Lodge ran out. The owner would not sell the house outright, or renew the lease, insisting that he intended to come home from Los Angeles and live as the local squire. We were very upset at being forced to move after having lived at Brook Lodge for thirty-three years. Psychologists say that leaving one's home is one of the most traumatic things that can happen to a person, similar to being divorced.

However I am now convinced that the mind of that Irish-American cop was being influenced by my Guardian Angel, for he never in fact came to live in Ireland but totally abandoned the house, which is now a ruin. With the help of our three sons we bought a lovely house at Ardmore, a fishing village eight miles from Youghal, with a wonderful view over the sea. It is the only example I have seen of a one-storey

Georgian house – ideal for Claud, when his legs finally gave way. We could never have managed to live at Brook Lodge with its miles of corridors and stairs leading to the only bathroom. Rock House is perched on a cliff top, with terraced gardens below it. Rows of sea gulls sit on the roof talking to each other and watching the fishing boats as they come into the harbour, willing them to discard delicious fish offal and other goodies.

The house was built by an old sea captain in about 1810, and tradition has it that he used to sit in the drawing room by the great curved windows, studying the sailing ships passing in the bay through a large brass telescope on a tripod, and sneering delightedly at those that went too near the rocks. Now I watch the water-skiers and the sail-boarders through binoculars and try not to sneer too much when they fall in.

The first of our possessions that arrived at our new home was a lorry-load of earth; I wasn't leaving my compost heap behind. It was followed by another load of plants and shrubs – much needed, as the gardens at Rock House, which had once been beautiful, had been neglected for some years. Brambles, nettles and wild garlic had taken over. I believe it is a proven fact that gardeners have a longer life expectancy than people of any other profession, and I can quite clearly see why. A true gardener is always looking forward to the years ahead, waiting for some rare shrub to flower or some new planting design to fulfil its true potential. He or she only looks back briefly to avoid some mistake made the year before. However old a gardener may be, life is always full of interest and hope for the future. At the age of ninety-four my great-aunt Molly sowed seeds of *Lilium giganteum*. When the seeds germinated in their tray she pointed them out to me in triumph: 'Look Patricia, they are coming up. I can't wait to smell their enormous blooms.' She knew, and she knew that I knew, that they couldn't possibly flower for another seven years at the earliest.

So Claud and I settled down contentedly in Ardmore for what we knew must be the last lap, having circled the course more than once, and so far negotiated all obstacles without mishap.

Then Claud's eyes failed him. This was a great disaster, as it meant that he could neither read nor type. He had to dictate all his work, either to me to take down in long hand, or into a recorder, which involved endless delay in getting it typed out and was also expensive. But again luck saved us. Through a friend we discovered that there was an internationally famous eye surgeon in Waterford, only forty miles away, and Claud had operations on both eyes. When they took the bandages off he found to his delight that he could see better than ever. Sadly, the relief was only temporary, for he was getting weaker and weaker.

We had one last holiday in America in August 1981, staying with our sons. He collapsed on the day we were to leave to come home, and had to be rushed to hospital. When he recovered sufficiently to be allowed to fly home I think that we both knew that he was coming to an end, that even his strong will would not pull him through this time.

Our friends were wonderfully kind and thoughtful in helping me to nurse him. One night a young man who was staying with us, and had been sitting up in Claud's room, came and said in a worried voice: 'He was in good form earlier, but now his mind is wandering, and he is very agitated. He keeps talking about Chinese pirates, and thinks they are besieging the house. He wants me to get Mrs Cockburn to tell something or other to the Number One Boy about firearms.' Claud had gone back in his mind to the legation in Peking, which he had left when he was barely two years old, and of which he had never had a conscious memory. But now the frightening talk of grown-ups, and probably also his Chinese nurse, had come back to haunt him. Obviously the Mrs Cockburn he was talking about was not me but his mother. It just shows how careful one should be in what one says in front of babies.

Shortly after this episode the doctors sent him to the fine new hospital in Cork, where, after seven weeks, he died on Tuesday, 15 December 1981. Even in hospital he continued to work. On Sunday 13 December he dictated to me one of the funniest pieces he ever wrote for the *Irish Times*. They printed it next to his obituary.

I had telephoned to the boys on the Monday morning, telling them to come at once as he was sinking, and miraculously they managed to get here from all over the world in time for a last talk with him. His mind was quite clear until he lapsed into unconsciousness. After seventy-seven years his turbulent and varied life was over.

Although the doctors had told me that he was unlikely to recover,

Claud's death when it actually happened came as a terrible shock to me. To begin with I felt that I was floating alone in space, without contact with anything or anybody, like an astronaut whose safety line to his spacecraft has broken; but I found that the elaborate ritual of the funeral, which I had always thought must be a considerable strain on the bereaved, was in fact a great help. In Ireland funerals are great occasions; every move taken and every word said is laid down by tradition. I knew exactly what I had to say and do next, and that framework kept me together.

Claud's funeral was very moving. The large and beautiful medieval church in Youghal was packed. The Urban District Council, led by the Chairman wearing his chain of office, had asked if, together with our three sons, they might in turn help to carry the coffin. Journalists, including the editor and deputy editor of the *Irish Times*, came down from Dublin, as did many others. It was a great satisfaction to me to see how, though it had seemed unlikely when he first arrived, my nation had taken Claud to their hearts. I remembered the last line in Brendan Behan's play *The Hostage*: 'He died a stranger in a foreign land, and at home he had no one', and thought how little it applied to Claud.

In the weeks that followed I had a fulltime job answering the thousands of letters of condolence that I got from all over the world. That in itself was a good therapy. It kept me busy, with no time to brood, and writing the same thing over and over again had an hypnotic effect, like a Tibetan monk endlessly repeating his prayers.

In the spring, Sean O'Creadain, a kind and thoughtful friend, took me to Oaxaca in Mexico, where he had a house. The interest and excitement of seeing that terrible and beautiful country put me on my feet, and when I returned home I was ready to face life alone.

Shortly after arriving in Ardmore I had joined the *Bantracht na Tuaithe* – The Irish Countrywomen's Association or, as it is usually called, the I.C.A. It says a great deal for the lack of religious discrimination in the Irish Republic, as opposed to Northern Ireland, that I was very shortly elected local president, though I was the only Protestant in the Ardmore and Grange Guild.

The I.C.A. is the largest women's organisation in Ireland and has about 30,000 members. It was formed years ago to bring isolated rural women together to discuss their problems and to promote local crafts.

It owns a large adult education college near Drogheda and has started a college to train girls in horticulture.

I have long given up my horses, but what with making my shell pictures, working in my garden, attending I.C.A. meetings at all levels and visiting my sons and their families abroad, not to speak of my many friends at home, I don't find time heavy on my hands.

Not long ago I celebrated my seventieth birthday, and my biblical 'three score years and ten' were accomplished. The boys came home and gave a splendid birthday party for me with a cake covered in candles. After the celebration was over I lay in bed thinking of the journey I had travelled since that distant St Patrick's Day in 1914.

A middle-aged American once said to me: 'they say life begins at forty. It doesn't; life begins when the children leave home and the dog dies.' That may have been true for him, but it hasn't been so for me. I had found almost every minute of the last seventy years interesting and rewarding, and I hoped life had taught me something. I had learned that all problems in both private and political life are usually more complex than they seem at first. There are few, if any, easy answers. Anyone who thinks there are is a fool or a liar. It is better to travel hopefully than to arrive, and the only true happiness and peace lie in constructive work. All well-known clichés, but true just the same. Like many people of my age I have the sadness that so many of my friends and relatives are dead – Arthur died in 1984, though out of the six Arbuthnot children four still remain: my brother David whom I have not seen for years, in South Africa, my sister, and my brother Terry, now sadly a widower. Bernard has gone and Myrtle Grove has been inherited by my dear niece Shirley, his eldest daughter. She is keeping it up beautifully and restoring the lovely gardens which Bernard, who had no interest in them, neglected.

After all these years I live close to the place where I was born, and in the same kind of house, but my life has been not so much a circle as a figure of eight, and I still look forward to the future. In the last week, like great-aunt Molly, I have planted the seeds of *Lilium giganteum*.